Virginia McGee

DOROTHY RODGERS

MY FAVORITE THINGS

DOROTHY RODGERS

MY FAVORITE THINGS

A PERSONAL GUIDE TO DECORATING & ENTERTAINING

AVENEL BOOKS · NEW YORK

DRAWINGS BY JEREMIAH GOODMAN

PHOTOGRAPHS FROM *McCALL'S* BY NORMAN KARLSON,
TOSH MATSUMOTO AND HANS VAN NES

FRONTISPIECE PORTRAIT BY HOWELL CONANT

I wish to express my appreciation to the many friends
who contributed recipes; to Elna Muinonen, who had
infinite patience in testing and experimenting with
recipes; to Inez Johanson, who arranged most of the
flowers in the photographs; and to Eileen Peterson,
my secretary, who was an invaluable sounding board.

Dorothy Rodgers

517101394

Copyright © MCMLXIV by Dorothy F. Rodgers

Library of Congress Catalog Card Number: 64-22105

AVENEL BOOKS
a division of

Crown Publishers, Inc.
419 Park Avenue South, New York, New York 10016
This edition published by Avenel Books
a division of Crown Publishers, Inc.,
by arrangement with Atheneum Publishers

b   c   d   e   f   g   h

Manufactured in the United States of America

FOR DICK, WITH LOVE FOR LIVING THIS BOOK, AND WITH ME

ACKNOWLEDGMENT

There is no section in this book called *My Favorite People*. If there were, surely very near the top of the list would come Marcia Wallace, whose intelligence, understanding, wit and warmth were invaluable in the organization and editing of this book. It could not have been written without her.

CONTENTS

---

xiii

PART I: THE THINGS THAT GO INTO A HOUSE

1   DECORATING WITH A PERSONAL TOUCH   3
     Beginning with Repairs, Inc.   4
     Style and Personality   9
     Preliminary Decisions   11
       Educating Your Eye   12
       Working within Limitations   13
       Turning Problems to Assets   15
       Creating an Atmosphere   15
     Getting Professional Help   17
       Can You Afford a Decorator?   17
       Choosing a Decorator   18
       Completing Financial Arrangements   20
       Incorporating Personality   21
       The Decorator's Contribution   22
       Your Responsibility   25
     Timing Your Decorating   25

2   ROOMS THAT REALLY WORK   27
     Kitchens   28
     Pantries   31
     Company-Only Rooms   32
     Living Rooms   32
     Dining Rooms   33
     Women's Bedrooms   36
     Men's Bedrooms   37
     Rooms for Two   39
     Dressing Rooms and Bathrooms   41
     Children's Rooms   43

3   GOOD BASIC PLANNING   46
     Innovations in Decorating Materials   46

Contents

Taking Your Time 48

Architectural Alterations 48

    Floor Construction 50

    Wall Treatments 50

Upholstered Furniture 52

Color 54

    Windows 56

    Pattern in Papers and Fabrics 59

    Textures 59

    Floor Coverings 60

Lighting 62

Antiques 63

    Blending Periods 65

    Altering Antiques 67

4 THINGS YOU LOVE 69

Discovering Treasures 70

    Uniquely Personal Touches 71

The Fun of Your Own Creating 71

    Needlework and Related Arts 72

    Starting Steps 73

    Inventing Your Own Projects 74

    Creating without a Needle 76

The Personal Touch with Flowers 78

The Personal Sound of Music 81

The Pleasures of Collecting 81

Living with Collections 86

    The Personal Approach to Collecting Art 87

    The Personal Joy of Discovery 89

    Art Buying on a Budget 90

Auction Buying 90

PART II: ENTERTAINING AT HOME

5 PARTIES LARGE AND SMALL 95

Guest Lists 96

    Special Guests 98

    Guests of Honor 100

    Business Guests 100

    Out-of-Town Guests 101

Setting the Style   102

     Holiday Parties   102

     Formal or Informal   103

     Brunch or Lunch   106

     Evening Parties   107

     Cocktail Parties   108

Invitations and Timing   108

Drinks   109

Dress   110

Making the House Ready   111

Introductions   112

Seating Plans   113

Table Settings   114

     Centerpieces   115

     Crystal, China, Accessories   118

Help Needed   120

     Special Services   123

     Helpful Equipment   123

When Guests Go   124

6   FOODS VARIOUS AND INTERNATIONAL   126

International Cuisine   128

Expanding Your Repertoire   129

Considerate Planning   130

Balancing the Menu   131

     Main Courses   132

     Casseroles   133

     First Courses   133

     Desserts   134

     Wines   135

     Beers   138

     Pasta and Vegetables   138

     Salads   140

     Cheese   140

     Breads   140

Buffets   141

Brunches   142

Canapés   142

7   MENUS WITH A SENSE OF BALANCE (AND RECIPES)   144

Formal Dinners   144

Informal Dinners   151

Lunches   186

Contents

    Brunches   212

    Sunday Suppers   218

    Large Buffets   222

8   PARLOR GAMES AND OTHER DIVERSIONS   226

    Costume Parties   227

    Show-Business Parties   227

        Opening-Night Parties   228

    Special Parties   229

    Surprise Parties   230

    Professional Entertainment   231

    Card Games   232

    Parlor Games   233

        Games for Big Parties   234

        Games for Medium-Sized Groups   238

        Hunting Games   240

        Pencil-and-Paper Games   242

        Prizes   242

    Children's Parties   242

        Children's Prizes and Favors   244

        Children's Refreshments   244

    Teen-Age Parties   245

9   HOUSE GUESTS   247

    The Tempo of Week Ends   249

    Choosing House Guests   249

        Invitations   251

        Clothes   251

        Transportation   251

        Arrivals   252

    Guest Rooms   253

        Maid Service   255

        Guest Closets   255

        Guest Bathrooms   256

        Household Eccentricities   256

    Week-End Plans and Entertainment   257

        Simplifying Meals   259

        Rainy Days   260

    Guests' Responsibilities   261

POSTSCRIPT: THINGS IN THE WORLD OUTSIDE   263

INDEX   275

PHOTOGRAPHIC ILLUSTRATIONS IN COLOR
(Following page 78)

The Joshua Logans' living room

The Otto Premingers' living room

The Rodgers' New York dining room

       Degas bronze (DANCER)

       Judy Brown steel (STEEPLES)

       Bambara wood (ANTELOPE HEAD)

       Giacometti bronze (TALL FIGURE)

Another View of the dining room

       Pre-Columbian (TOTOLNACAN) *figure*

       Soulages oil

       Rodin bronze mask

Dorothy Rodgers' New York bedroom

       Renoir water color (SMALL)

       Magritte oil

Dorothy Hammerstein's bedroom

The Rodgers' New York library

       Picasso oil

       Gauguin water color

       DeStaël oil

       Amlash terra cotta zebu

       Krinjabo terra cotta head

Dorothy Rodgers' Rockmeadow bedroom

The Rodgers' New York living room

       Corot oil (PORTRAIT OF DAUMIER)

       Reg Butler bronze

       Amlash terra cotta figure

Richard Rodgers' New York bedroom

       Eilshemius oil

Picasso drawing

Small African and American Indian sculptures

F. E. McWilliam bronze

Dorothy Rodgers' memorabilia

The Rodgers' Rockmeadow entrance hall

Some of Dorothy Rodgers' favorite things

An epergne flower arrangement

A flower and painting grouping

Toulouse-Lautrec gouache

Another grouping of art and flowers

Bonnard oil

Degas bronze

The Rodgers' New York entrance hall

Pollock oil

Marini bronze bull

Renoir watercolor

The Rockmeadow terrace

The Rockmeadow living room

Doris Lee oil

The Rockmeadow dining room

Introduction

I A M a domestic creature, and this is a personal book about the things I love. For although I get great pleasure from travel and theatre and art, my husband and my family are the center of my life. My house and the things that go into it—the way it looks, its atmosphere, the parties we give and the food we serve—these are a way of expressing my feelings about the people I love.

My education in homemaking has been anything but organized. When I should have been learning cooking and sewing, I was being propelled through museums and chateaux during summers abroad with my parents. Although I did my best not to get any of the culture on me (I would rather have been at home with my friends), some of it did rub off—enough to inspire me to study sculpture, first in New York and later in Paris.

As a young girl, I never paid attention to the business of making a home, and I took for granted the things that made it run smoothly. Then suddenly, at the age of twenty, I found myself married and living in London, where Dick and Larry Hart were writing the score for *Evergreen*, in charge of a big house and a staff of six servants. Their functions were highly specialized, and it took me weeks to sort out who did what. There was also the language barrier. While I spoke American, they spoke English: they said "sweet" instead of "dessert" (which in England means simply fruit), "tin" instead of "can," "biscuit" for "cracker" and "bun" for "roll." Food, I discovered, was kept in a cold, windowless little room called "the larder." There was an electric refrigerator, but it was considered too expensive to run. Because of British tradition and also because our friends were all a good deal older than we were, entertaining was, both figuratively and literally, full dress. And so my domestic education began, postgraduate course first.

After London came a brief stay in California while Dick composed his first movie score. Then back to New York, where our daughter Mary and the show *America's Sweetheart* were born almost simultaneously. Needing more space, we moved from Dick's three-room flat to the first apartment we chose together. Here I had my first experience in decorating a house of my own. I worked with leftovers (I did discard a terrifying *moderne* "den set" from Dick's bachelor apartment), some furniture of mine, and a few pieces that my parents could spare, as well as some new things we bought ourselves. We didn't have a decorator. (The relatively few professionals practicing at the time were, for the most part, very grand: they specialized in creating "cultured" museumlike backgrounds for clients with lots of money.) Uncoached, we made mistakes; but many of the things we bought then we still have and love.

No sooner was everything finished than movie work—*Love Me Tonight* with Maurice Chevalier and Jeannette MacDonald—took us back to California, and we had to sublet our apartment. Three years and three furnished houses later, we returned to find the apartment a wreck. Chewing gum, teething puppies and a staggering lack of concern on the part of the tenants had done their jobs well. Shocked and distressed, I dreamed of a genie to whom I could say, "Put things to rights; make everything just as it was." But since there was no magical creature, and because Dick was busy with *On Your Toes* and *Jumbo*, I went to work. And a whole new phase of my education began. What I learned in the restoration process resulted in the formation of Repairs, Inc., just after our second daughter, Linda, was born. (Repairs, Inc., was the first business of its kind, and when it expanded to include interior decorating, I was finally able to put to practical use the knowledge gained from courses in furniture design I took just before we were married.)

During the war we found ourselves living in Connecticut. Zoë, the daughter of English friends, had been sent to us for the war years. I had given up my business and was devoting my time to taking care of a house and three children. The few extra hours I had went to the Red Cross.

When we had been married for thirteen years, we moved back to the city, and the upside-down timetable of my education took over once more. Although I knew nothing about its preparation, good food had always been important to me. Suddenly I felt frustrated at not being able to work out the recipe for a *mousse* served by a friend or for a special restaurant entrée. So I enrolled in a cooking school. And there I was, stirring up sauces in New York the night *Oklahoma!* opened in New Haven. (In those days Dick always wanted me to wait until his shows had played a few performances on the road before I saw them. No sauce could keep me away today, and *Oklahoma!* was the last out-of-town opening I missed!)

I had always loved crocheting, knitting and needlepoint, but until I took the six lessons that came with my new sewing machine (we'd been married twenty years then), I never knew how to sew. Nowadays one of the things I enjoy most in the world is making things for the children, the house, my friends and myself—even sports shirts for Dick.

What pleases me most of all is learning new things. I am addicted to lessons the way other people are to sports cars, gin rummy and eating chocolates in bed. In the last few years I've gone to the Berlitz School for Italian lessons. I've spent some time trying to learn embroidery at the Royal School of Needlework in London, and on our next trip, I'm hoping to try some advanced needlepoint. With the possible exceptions of skin diving, and coconut farming, there is almost nothing I wouldn't take lessons in. And judging by the signs, my education will go right on as it started— in any and many directions.

I know no single title that adequately describes all the things a woman does; but whether she calls herself housewife or homemaker, there is no disagreement about the importance of her job. If she does it well, it is a source of both inner satisfaction and visible rewards: a happier marriage, happier children and warm friendships.

Certainly I've been lucky. Over the years I've always been helped by talented servants, and I don't want in any way to minimize their importance. But as in most successful cooperative efforts, both parties must not only like one another but also understand and respect the skills involved. I have known the same cook in two vastly different households; in one, the food she produced was indifferent, in the other, superb. The people who have worked for us have been superb, and their willingness to explore the new ideas I am always anxious to try have made them invaluable to me.

This book has taken a long time to write because I had to live it first. It is not a blueprint or a textbook—no two houses could or should be exactly alike. It is concerned with the senses that go into the making of a home: the pleasures of textures to feel, sounds to hear, foods to taste, everything to see. And it is about that other sense too—sensitivity to others, to their needs and their comforts, the sense that brings the house alive. In

(xv)

Introduction

this book I hope to share with you some of the great joys I have found. Even more, through its pages I hope you will discover fresh pleasures in your own home.

Dorothy Rodgers

PART ONE

THE THINGS
THAT GO INTO
A HOUSE

1

Decorating with a Personal Touch

I C A M E to decorating through the back door, and a pretty unglamorous back door at that. My training began in a properly ladylike fashion. My mother loved lovely things, and on summer trips abroad I can remember trudging along when she went to buy laces and linens in Venice or to look at antiques in Paris or London or Rome. Mother favored Jacobean, Italian and Spanish antiques, the dark-red velvets and tapestries that to me have always seemed heavy and gloomy. Still, although her tastes were quite different from mine, her interest in art and her affection for all beautiful things were contagious.

Though I had no formal courses in interior design, I studied sculpture, and I went to sketching classes at the Grande Chaumière in Paris. In New York I attended Alexander Archipenko's school, and I took a course with Paul Frankl, who was in those days one of the best and best-known designers of furniture.

My early decorating experience was purely personal. The first room I ever did was my own bedroom; it happened when I was seventeen, and I felt terribly grand and sophisticated because I was allowed to choose the furniture in Paris. I planned a bed-sitting room with pieces that were basically Louis XV, upholstered in beautiful silk velvets and embroidered fabrics. (I wouldn't dream of having such elaborate fabrics today; they would seem too formal and too grand.) Although I hadn't chosen the furniture from that point of view, most of these pieces turned out to be long-term possessions; reupholstered, they are still in use at Rockmeadow, our place in Connecticut.

Beginning with Repairs, Inc.

Repairs, Inc., which was never meant to be more than a business dedicated to mending things people needed or restoring things they loved, was my back door to professional decorating. Actually, the firm was born of spontaneous combustion. After a stay in Hollywood, Dick, our daughter Mary and I returned to the New York apartment we had left, only to find an incredible shambles. Clearly, it was a disaster area. First I exploded. Then my mood changed to deep gloom at the thought of all the time and work it would take to put things right again.

"Oh," I moaned to Dick as I waved a tragic arm at the mess all around, "I wish there were some magic place I could call and say, 'There it is—you fix it,' and have everything back together again."

"Why don't you start one?" he countered quite reasonably.

So, using our own restoration as a take-off point, that is what I did. I began by making a long list of all the different kinds of craftsmen I'd need to help me. I lined up all the obvious ones: I found experts at china and glass and silver; I located several different kinds of cabinetmakers—one who knew all about finishes, one who did carving and one who did ordinary repairing; I unearthed really skilled weavers and carpet people and people who worked with lace and needlepoint and Aubusson; there were clock makers and piano tuners; I even found a man whose sole mission in life was restoring tortoise shell, ivory and mother-of-pearl.

It was no simple task. I followed up all sorts of leads from friends, from directories and from suggestions I got from the first craftsmen I found. Knowing that most large museums have their own expert restoration staffs, I went to the Metropolitan for help. They did not, of course, take on my work for me. But in some cases they could supply names of men who had worked for them and then started in business for themselves.

In the fall of 1935, having assembled what seemed to me a very extensive list, I rented an office on East Fifty-seventh Street, sent out hundreds of announcements aimed at making a clever yet tasteful impression and waited for my first clients. They came, and with them, the realization that my most complete list was only a start. There were, it seemed, states of disrepair I had never imagined. We tackled simple projects (like making two sets of curtains do for three windows) and intricate ones (like reactivating miniature waterfalls and songbirds in a mad, marvelous Victorian clock that belonged to Helen Hayes). We repaired liners in silver salt dishes and slashes in a huge mural at the Waldorf. Once we even rejuvenated a "singing" poodle, a devoted family pet stuffed some seventy-five years earlier. Suddenly, faced with that dusty animal, I realized there was no stuffed-dog man on my roster—let alone one who understood how to replace roses between said poodle's front paws.

I had never planned to handle mechanical upkeep on radios and phonographs and such, but I should have remembered music boxes; I had no one who could cope with the really complicated models. My piano tuner came highly recommended, but I didn't know a soul who could cure an asthmatic melodeon. Our most complicated problems taught me how lucky I was in the people I had found. For through them I discovered that often the more skilled the man, the more he loved the challenge of a really difficult job.

As time went on and work settled into a pattern, a number of interesting assignments came our way. A museum in Pittsburgh sent us the shards of a tiny Phoenician vase because they had no local people who could put it back together and maintain its peculiar iridescence. Mrs. Theodore Roosevelt, Jr., sent us an incredibly beautiful Aubusson rug—an incident that was only amusing because she herself was such an extremely talented needlewoman that she could probably have restored it more skillfully than any experts I knew; yet, like most of us, she preferred her own projects to mending—no matter how valuable the article that needed repairs.

Often through work I made friends with people we've been close to ever since. I met Howard and Peggy Cullman through Repairs, Inc.—or rather, through their dog, who was actually responsible for sending us many jobs. He was a highly resourceful creature who spent all his waking hours chewing up table legs, bowling over lamps and restyling carpets— all of which we were hired to put right. I was so grateful for his help that at Christmastime I picked out a delicious chocolate bone at Abercrombie & Fitch and sent it to him with a card that read, "From your good friends and grateful admirers at Repairs, Inc. Keep up the good work."

It was through Edna Ferber that we became involved in insurance-company work. At a dinner party one night a guest burned a hole in one of Edna's rugs. When she reported the damage to the insurance people, she asked that they give us the reweaving job. The insurance men were delighted; they had been afraid that no one could repair this particular piece to its owner's satisfaction. They said if we were successful they would like to send us some of their other business. We discovered insurance work to be very pleasant; things good enough to insure were usually worth the effort and care of restoring. And because the companies were only concerned with making things whole again, there were no over-all instructions to cut costs here or to economize there. We were always to do the most perfect job possible. As time went on we made a point of soliciting such business. At one point, to demonstrate our versatility, I planned a cocktail party built around displays showing various kinds of jobs before, during and after completion. It was such a success that Dick, who had dropped by to pick me up, has always said he was really rather proud when one of the insurance men asked him what kind of repairs he specialized in.

Things were perking along nicely enough to warrant moving from my first small quarters to larger offices. To the marvelously efficient secretary I had I added a bookkeeper, a packing-delivery boy and a woman to handle arrangements for insurance-company work. Damage done by temporary tenants—the same calamity that had inspired me to found Repairs, Inc.— continued to be a major source of business. We did so much of this work that when legal complications arose, my word was accepted as "expert testimony" on the not-very-fine line that distinguishes "ordinary wear and tear" from "wilful damage and neglect."

–As time went on, I became more and more aware of the fact that it was impossible to divorce repairs from decorating. We would start out with carpets that needed to be refitted or dyed or stripped or with old draperies that didn't fit or were too skimpy to cover new windows; inevitably we were asked to help in finding floor coverings or in choosing paint and wall-papers that went with what our customers already owned. Imagi-nation and experience often made it possible for us to make use of the old and to add a minimum of new things. The work was much appreciated, but it was time-consuming and not very profitable. However, when clients were happy with the results, they would let us start from scratch to do new rooms, and eventually many of them called on us to help with all their decorating problems.

Then one day a tremendous commission came our way. A friend returned to town to find his triplex apartment utterly demolished—again, by subtenants. The damage was incredible: chairs with their legs snapped off had simply been tossed into closets; the Venetian blinds were hanging on the floor. My assignment was to restore the apartment to its original beauty. At this point I realized what I needed most in the world was the help of someone with a good background in decorating. And fortunately it was then I met Frederick von Auw, the gifted young man who became my assistant and worked with me for years.

Many of our clients were young married couples who were either moving into their first homes or going from a first apartment into a larger place. I became intrigued with the factors involved: the hand-me-downs, the budgeting, the challenge of creating a maximum of atmosphere for the least possible money. I got to be expert at cutting corners where draperies and carpets were concerned, so that the money saved could be invested in the upholstered pieces and furniture that would eventually move with a couple and work for them through the years. The fact that many of these people are still enjoying the objects I helped them choose twenty-five years ago makes me feel quite proud.

In my Repairs, Inc., scrapbook there are photographs of one young couple's apartment I remember especially well. It had no dining area, and as we worked along, it became apparent that the only place to put one was just inside the entrance, where a single table for six would effectively block all comings and goings. We ended by building an L-shaped banquette on each side of the door and by having two small pedestal tables for four made to fit in front of them. After guests arrived, the tables could be pushed together to seat six quite comfortably. Separated they could seat as many as eight. The nicest part of the story is that a few years later when the couple moved, they took along the two tables, joined beneath a new top, to use as a single two-pedestal table in their new dining room.

Occasional glamorous jobs were, of course, pure delight. One of the happiest associations I've ever known began when a charming French woman referred by another client came into my office expecting to buy a dining-room table. I told her that although I kept no stock of antiques, I would be happy to help her find what she wanted, and we started shop-

ping that very afternoon. She could not have been more pleasant about it, but nothing I showed her was quite fine enough or important enough. Finally I took her to a dealer whose vast stock included many real treasures. She not only found her table there, but also fell in love with all kinds of other things. And after a few more shopping expeditions, she asked me to do her whole apartment.

Her decorating scheme was built around some very beautiful pieces she had had shipped from her house in Rome. To these were added exquisite pieces we found through New York dealers. Our most daring stroke was to pave the entrance hall with great diamonds of gold and silver Chinese paper. Eight or ten coats of varnish made the floor so practical it could not only be walked on but could literally be scrubbed, and the whole effect was extravagantly beautiful.

This one was a dream job, and she was a dream client, a woman of great knowledge and taste who was open-minded about suggestions yet knew exactly what she wanted and had the means to buy what she liked. Such commissions were as rare for us as for any other decorating firm. Our everyday work was pleasant but less exotic. And in it, one basic truth was proved again and again: there is no one way to decorate a house. Everything depends on the people living in it.

I love coming home to Rockmeadow, our house in Connecticut. After fifteen years, I'm still aware of a fresh excitement each time I walk in the door. Standing in the front hall, walking into the living room, seeing the flowers through the windows of the sunroom, I feel a very special sense of pleasure.

Rockmeadow is anything but elaborate. It is not filled with priceless antiques. We're very fond of the paintings on its walls, but you'd never call them "important." The sunny look of the yellows and pinks and greens in the living room, the way the sunroom's white and green bring in the outdoors please me—but not because the color schemes are new; they have been that way since the beginning. The hall wallpaper, for instance, has been the same for fifteen years. In fact, the only new furniture we bought expressly for the house was a small secretary, a curved sofa to fit the bay window in the living room and a few pieces for the sunroom. So it is not Rockmeadow's novelty I love. What pleases me is the sense of ease and well-being Dick and I feel when we're there. To me, one of the greatest pleasures and satisfactions a woman can know is creating in her house the atmosphere that exactly suits her family.

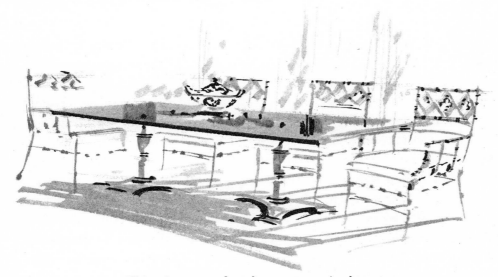

Here the two pedestals support a single top

To visit both the Josh Logans and the Otto Premingers is to learn how marvelously successful two intensely personal and disparate homes can be. In the Logans' Manhattan living room, overlooking the East River, patterns and colors force themselves on your attention in a mad kind of jigsaw puzzle where everything fits in its place exactly, like a painting by Vuillard. Glowing impressionist pictures hang against red walls. There is an irresistible collection of antique mechanical toys. Masses of flowers and plants seem to be growing right in the room. The carpet is Brussels—brilliant flowers on

Style and Personality

(9)

a black background—and the chairs and sofas are fat, tufted and Victorian. It is wild, exuberant, flamboyant—and utterly captivating because it is so right for Josh and Nedda.

The Premingers' town house is completely different—a great example of simple elegance in the contemporary manner. It is a high-fashion house, entirely in black and white: walls, upholstery, carpets throughout all the rooms and the halls. The ash trays are heavy crystal, the lighting is dimmed or brightened by rheostats and the only color anywhere comes dramatically from the exciting collection of modern paintings. I especially remember one evening we spent there. Hope Preminger looked beautiful; her black hair is prematurely frosted, and she was dressed in white. Otto wore a black suit. We were served caviar and sour cream. I really felt I might spoil the decor if I asked for a piece of lemon.

Each of these houses is very sophisticated, each is very consciously decorated, yet no two places could possibly be more different. Switching the occupants would be unthinkable. And it is just that which makes each, in its own way, perfect.

I don't think any two houses should be exactly alike. Trying to make a home look like anyone else's would be, for me, like stepping into another person's skin or trying to live someone else's life. It is simply inconceivable. Genes make our eyes blue or brown, our hair straight or curly. Family backgrounds give each of us a make-up that is sentimental, practical, economical, generous, studious, gay—in varying degrees. No one starts out just the way anyone else does; nor are the results the same. The variants are different for each family. And all this individuality determines the style reflected in our houses.

If you are lucky enough to be able to build your own house, you will, of course, turn to expert professional help. The best architect for you is not only one whose work you like, but also one with whom you sense a sympathetic bond. If you haven't already bought land, his experience may guide your decision on the property you choose. Every site presents its particular problems, and it is well to know before you buy just what limitations the land will impose on the house you have in mind. An architect's advice is especially pertinent if the acreage involved is hilly or rocky or perched on a bluff, where topography might make building prohibitively expensive, if not impossible. If you are considering a secluded country spot, it is important to investigate roads, water and sewage systems, electricity and gas mains—all the utilities you might take for granted in a city or a suburb. Installation of any missing service links could add tremendously to the cost of your property.

Location will also, to some extent, dictate the style of a house. A beach house in Southern California may be rambling, open and airy with lots of wide-view windows; on the other hand, a house on the coast of Maine, while built with the seascape in mind, should be cozy and protected. I've seen houses on New England hilltops that look like nothing so much as stranded aircraft carriers; they seem completely out of harmony with their surroundings.

Neighbors are important, too; so you should consider both the character of the land and the people who live nearby when you are planning your house.

One suggestion: chances are you know a great deal more about the working end of your home than even the best architect. Don't be afraid to let him know what you need to suit your family's living habits.

Obviously, these comments underscore only a few very basic factors in a very complex process. Although we have never built a home of our own, I still dream of doing it some day. Meanwhile, I keep experimenting with my own amateur plans and trying to conquer my only difficulty: the fact that, as Dick very accurately points out, what I really want is "a small house with large rooms and a great many of them."

A house tells a great deal about the woman who lives in it, certainly more than her dresses do. Clothes, after all, are not a permanent commitment. Homes *should* have a feeling of permanence—which is why, when it comes to a house, chic is almost always a failure. The very words "high-fashion decor" sound wrong to me. They imply that the look of a room goes out of style the way a hemline might. They suggest periodic change for change's sake rather than the kind of peaceful evolution that results in a room that is wonderful to live in. Decorating is too expensive a proposition to take lightly. An exotic hair-do washes away in the morning. An exotic chair may well become a permanent horror. Where a home is concerned, it's not fad, but feeling, that matters. For this reason I've always been a bit fearful of the chic decorators who change "their style" every year. The only style that is important is your style, your particular way of putting things together.

Essentially, the house you live in has to please you and your husband. You hope your friends will like it, too, but that isn't the point; you are doing this for yourselves. Even your children aren't primarily concerned. When they are young and growing up, I don't think they really care—except perhaps about their own rooms. By the time decoration does make an impression on them, they are within minutes of moving out and establishing homes of their own.

Preliminary Decisions

(*11*)

The process of reflecting two people's likes and dislikes in one house may sound complicated. It is, but it is not impossible. And pleasing both yourself and your husband is at least as much fun as it is work. After all, liking the same things probably helped bring you together.

Before you start making definite plans for decorating, it's important that both of you together look at as many things as possible: rooms in houses you both know, department-store displays, museums, set designs, shop windows and magazines. Look at furniture, fabrics, wallpapers, floors and colors—not all at once (few men have the time or the patience to digest long taste-probing sessions), but as opportunities present themselves. Take a few minutes' time when a magazine arrives in the mail, when you've had dinner at a house you both like or when there's time for a brief Saturday afternoon expedition to an antiques show or an art gallery. All this groundwork serves two purposes: it gives a man some idea of costs; it also helps you to discover, specifically, the things both of you like and—possibly even more important—the things you don't like.

Both Dick and I, for example, love beiges and yellows and blues. Dick likes a room to look "a little messed up"—by which he means, not too precise or cold; it's a term akin to what I mean by "livable." On these points and on furniture, we're in harmony; this accord, however, doesn't always prevail. Dick loathes shiny fabrics, brocades and damasks; I think they can be lovely in some rooms. I would be bolder than he in choosing accessories. And, while we both love paintings, we don't always like the same ones.

After all these years, we agree on an enormous number of points. There are some about which one of us is more passionate than the other (Dick doesn't much care what I do to the kitchen). But anything either of us genuinely dislikes is automatically eliminated from our scheme. This is the only sensible rule. You may find that your passion for porcelain ash trays doesn't mean much to your husband one way or the other; he says, "Just so they're big enough," and you can buy all you like. But if he really hates green, he'll always be miserable in a green room, and you'd be foolish to insist on having one.

Educating Your Eye Taste is made, not born. There is no mystique about it; it is not an occult science, and it doesn't spring full-blown like Venus. It is a matter of educating your eye, and it is really no different from developing any other sense to its full power. You have to do a great deal of concentrated listening to train your ear to music. It takes a lot of tasting to develop the sensitivity of a gourmet palate, but given enough interest and exposure, anyone can do it.

Developing an eye for furniture and color and fabric—for any of the beautiful things you learn to love—is a continuing process. There aren't any short cuts. But it can be fun from the start. You sharpen your awareness by looking and looking and looking again. Most antique dealers are happy to have you come in and browse; they are also willing and eager to answer any questions you may have. Gallery and museum people are just as delighted to give you information; they love the objects they work with and like to talk about them. Simply by asking, I've discovered so many things I'd never have known about otherwise.

Selection starts without your actually knowing. You find yourself returning to two or three places because pieces they have seem to please you most. At first you are tempted to swallow periods whole. You fall in love with Empire or Regency or Eighteenth-Century English. Still, you can probably count on expense to stop you short of doing your living room over as a mirror-for-mirror reproduction of the great hall at Versailles—or a whole room from any other period, for that matter.

At first, sticking to one period or country seems safest. But gradually you'll find you have strong feelings about the things of different eras and places. What's more, you can begin to see them all living pleasingly together. In our dining room in the city we have an Eighteenth-Century English lacquer chest; on its top are a green bronze Rodin mask and a pre-Colombian figure that dates back to about 500 A.D.; on the wall above it hangs a painting by Soulages done in 1958. They are wonderful together—yet they cover a time span of 1400 years. Whether two objects were made within twenty or five thousand years of each other couldn't matter less. If you think both are beautiful and enjoy seeing them next to each other, that is how they belong.

In addition to the conditions your tastes set, you begin with other given limitations. No artist can work without them. No painter can paint on a canvas that has no end; nor can you decorate a room with no walls, no floors, no problems. Oddly enough, it was a "dream job" that showed me this most clearly. Knowing that both Dorothy Hammerstein and I had done professional decorating, the editor of a well-known magazine for women offered us what sounded like a magnificent proposition: he wanted us to collaborate on doing a house—a new sort of Rodgers and Hammerstein composition. We were to have absolute *carte blanche*. And he meant it. Where was the house? Anywhere we wanted. He would rent it, buy it, restore it, remodel it, anything we liked. What mythical family would live in it? That was up to us. Probably a married couple would be best, but whether they had one child or six or no children at all was for us to decide. Servants, cars, hobbies, backgrounds—all these were left to us to fill in. The sky was the limit in all directions. That was the trouble: we were

Working within Limitations

suspended in air, with not one solid fact to anchor to. Weird as I'm sure it sounds, that kind and thoughtful editor had handed us an utterly impossible assignment. In the end we were forced to decline and the R & H dream house went undecorated.

Everyone begins with a budget; no house—or hardly any house—starts naked, unfurnished except for a checkbook with a balance that goes on forever. Then there is physical space. The chances are that even a house you build for yourself will be a little disappointing. There may simply be no way of incorporating all the closets you'd like or of putting the utility room just where it would make most sense (near the bedrooms, not in the basement), or you may underestimate the number of electric outlets you need.

There's another kind of physical limitation: you may adore fragile things but have only one living room and several small children. Much as you'd like to decorate with French antiques and fine crystal, it just isn't practical. So you find a way—with color, with fabric, with special effects and specially chosen accessories—to create an impression of delicacy while eliminating things that would be perishable.

Finally you are limited by what you already own. When we moved into our first New York apartment, we were owned by a solemn Flemish tapestry, a William and Mary love seat covered in tapestry and a gloomy portrait of an old Dutch burgher—not a famous painting, but a fine one. It and the furniture had belonged to my family. All these things were of very good quality and quite depressing. We were young, and none of them was right for us. Still, we lived with all of them until we found, and could afford, replacements we really liked.

In addition to hand-me-downs, you often have to live with your own early mistakes. Not long after we were married, I invested a good deal of money in a Sarouk rug and red damask draperies for the dining room, only to discover after living with them for a while that I hated them cordially. What's more, I became increasingly aware that I wasn't terribly fond of our walnut Queen Anne chairs, either.

It took quite a while to rectify my errors. I began by having the color stripped out of the draperies; to my delight, they came out a lovely pinky beige. Eventually I managed to sell the rug and replace it with a pinky beige carpet. Painted beige to match the carpet, the chairs took on an interesting Venetian air. And when the walls were painted a dark bright blue, suddenly the room was handsome. I loved it more because of its ugly beginnings—and the fact that I'd been able to solve its problems.

So often the solutions you are forced to find for mistakes, hand-me-

(*14*)

downs, space quirks and budget limitations turn out to be blessings. The results are so much your own that they create an atmosphere that is uniquely yours. Elsie de Wolfe, one of the first recognized professional interior designers, once had a place in California. The house was exquisite, but its tiny garden distressed her until she hit on the idea of covering the wall that marked the end of her property with mirrors; suddenly, miraculously, you felt you had a whole park to wander through, right there in the middle of Beverly Hills. It was typical of her brilliantly imaginative style.

Turning
Problems
to Assets

I remember, too, when Eero and Aline Saarinen bought their New Haven house. From the outside, it was one of those ungainly no-period places. Inside, the windows and the radiators below them were uncompromisingly hideous. Since the view of the street was no particular asset, the Saarinens stretched translucent white fabric on big rectangular frames and suspended these so that they hung from about a foot below the ceiling to the floor and about two feet out from each window. In the daytime, sunlight filtered in through the shades; lit from behind at night, they added a pleasant glow. The result was a problem solved and an intensification of clear-cut, modern atmosphere just right for the Saarinens.

Needing more room and loving their river view, the Richard Hallidays (Mary Martin) glassed in the terrace off Mary's bedroom to make a year-around room that's so pleasant to be in they now spend most of their time there. Another of our friends, Sue Cott, loves to paint and also had living-room walls to decorate. So she hung her own copies of Picassos and Rouaults. She's changed the canvas sizes and made no attempt to fool people; the effect is great fun, entirely her own. It is another example of the sort of problem-turned-into-asset that makes a home pleasing, not only to its family, but also to everyone who sees it.

The expense or elaborateness involved in a decorating scheme is never the measure of its success or its failure. Given the same number of dollars and left to their own devices, women will react quite differently. One will end with a series of rooms that are all carefully, safely dull. Another woman will operate on another "safety" formula: she will assemble only things that are unmistakably expensive. A third will end with a room or a home really marvelous for her because it exactly suits her life and because its rightness is born of combining the colors and fabrics and furniture she and her family like best; no single detail will clamor for attention, for a genuine affection for all a room's elements will produce an over-all effect that is "like her" without being self-consciously clever.

Far more important than money is the kind of atmosphere you want your house to have. Does a certain formality please you, or would you much

Creating an
Atmosphere

(*15*)

The Saarinens' window treatment

rather create a casual sort of feeling throughout the house? Would you like your house to be the kind of place where guests feel free to sit on the floor, or does that make you uncomfortable? How old are your children, and how much room do they need? Do you have only one room that is literally a living room, where family and guests relax and live and have fun? Or can you keep one room for special entertaining and have a family room for informal everyday goings-on? How do you relax? Is it important to you to have several chairs with good reading lights? Should the television set be in the center of things? How much do you care about hi-fi or built-in stereo? Ask yourself every large and small question you can think of. Though you may feel a little silly at first, keep track of the answers on paper. When it comes to the actual planning, having these ideas in writing will help give your decisions your special kind of focus and your finished rooms an atmosphere that is particularly yours.

Getting Professional Help

This kind of analyzing could and will go on forever. But once you have settled the major questions, how and where do you start the real decorating? How do you know which comes first, the ceiling or the rug? Certainly you could manage by yourself. Starting from Ground Zero, you could learn all about floor coverings, fabrics, wallpapers, colors. You could catch up with the latest in plastics and synthetic fibers. You could locate antique dealers, upholsterers and painters whose work you like. And, if you've a great deal of time and love and patience to invest, you may want to do just that. Otherwise, I think the surest way is to start with a decorator —a man or woman whose intensive training qualifies him as an expert in all these matters.

Having worked as a professional decorator, I know that people fear decorators the way they do headwaiters and teachers. Some women who are never self-conscious about asking their lawyers and doctors all sorts of questions feel that asking advice from a decorator shows shameful ignorance. They forget that a decorator is a professional too. And no one without his years of experience could possibly be expected to have his very specialized kind of knowledge.

Can You Afford a Decorator?

The question is not really whether you can afford a decorator, but whether you can afford the things you want to do, and your preliminary research should give you the answer to that. The more limited your budget, the more you need a decorator's help. You may have set aside a sum of money to invest in two or three important pieces of furniture. On the other hand, that amount may have to do a whole room. The larger the area to be covered, the less you can afford expensive mistakes. And the smaller the budget, the harder the job—both for you and for the decorator, who works harder for a smaller profit. But no matter how little money is involved, a good decorator tries to do his best with every assignment he takes. It is his most effective way of advertising. Hopefully, even the smallest job will lead to more business later.

It costs you no more to do your decorating with a designer's help. There are several kinds of financial arrangements. All a decorator's resources—stores, antique dealers, fabric houses—give discounts on his purchases. And as a rule the decorator makes his profit from buying at wholesale and charging the retail price for furniture and materials he provides. Other decorators charge a flat fee for the whole job and pass discount savings on to you. Still others charge so much per hour for their services; in these cases, they, too, charge discount prices for what they buy for you. And a fourth group operates on a cost-plus-percentage basis; in other words, the profit derives from an agreed percentage added to the wholesale price of purchases made for your job. If yours is a fairly small project, it is just as well to let the decorator make his profit by charging you retail prices for what he buys; but if you are spending vast sums, it will probably be to your advantage to agree on a set fee before work starts.

Choosing　　　　There are a number of ways of finding a decorator. Decorating de
a Decorator　partments of most large department stores actually perform two functions: they offer customers free advice on individual and specific problems, such as the kind of lamp that might go well in a particular study or the color of carpet that might work best beneath an eggplant-colored sofa; for this sort of one-shot help, they make no charge. For more extensive projects the store will have one of its designers do a full-scale work-up, complete with swatches and sketches. The designer may actually be a member of the store's permanent staff or he may belong to a roster of independent professionals. He is at perfect liberty to go outside the store to locate accessories, antiques and individual pieces you and he think would best suit your needs; but obviously he will rely heavily on the store's merchandise, and you will merely pay the store for everything you buy. At the start you will be charged a token fee—say fifty dollars—which is later credited against merchandise you actually purchase. Should you, for any reason, decide against going through with the plan, the sketches are yours to keep, the money is the store's. Otherwise there is no charge for the service.

But suppose after inspecting room settings and merchandise at several stores, you haven't found any one place that particularly strikes your fancy or suppose that from the start you've wanted to find an independent decorator. Then you begin by asking questions—of people whose homes you like, of furniture and antique dealers whose merchandise you find consistently interesting and whose taste you have come to trust. You watch newspapers and magazines for pictures of rooms that appeal to you particularly; often the captions give credit to the decorator involved. In New York there is the Design Center for Interiors, where model rooms by many designers are on display; like those in similar centers across the country, the rooms are redecorated frequently and may give you some idea of the designer's range, what colors and periods and lines he is happiest with. But it will not tell you half as much about him as will seeing a room or an apartment or a house he has done for real people.

Professional organizations can also help you. In the decorating field there are two. The first is the AID which is the American Institute of Interior Designers. ("Decorators," the word that comes easiest to me, is, it seems, as old-hat as another of my favorites—"icebox.") The NSID, or National Society of Interior Designers, is a newer but similar group. Members of both must meet high educational and ethical standards. If you call the local chapter of either with some idea of your needs, the names of three or four members who specialize in the sort of interior design that seems best for your job will be supplied to you. It is then up to you to get in touch with the likely candidates, explain what you hope to accomplish and settle on the one you think you'd most like to work with.

Making a final choice is a very important and very personal matter because as the work progresses, you will find your decorator becoming more and more like a member of the family. Somewhat like your doctor and your lawyer, he will come to know many intimate details of your life. Obviously, the first question is whether you really like him. If he has three eyes and two heads and you can't stand three-eyed, two-headed men—let him go. More important, if you sense a coming struggle, if you feel, for whatever reason, that it will always be a question of his taste against yours, or if he makes you feel you ought to apologize for your grandmother's portrait or the children's spaniel, now is the time to sidestep the conflict and look further.

You must completely trust the decorator's taste and his understanding of your taste. A major part of any decorator's job is the intensive research and leg work he invests before you see even so much as a swatch. (It's an essential but anonymous kind of labor, and something for which I think clients are inclined to give far too little credit.) He does not show you every chair, every sideboard, every fabric. Before you make your first choice, he has made his selections from hundreds. While he will, of course, try to be objective in covering the market for you, he owes his skill and his professional reputation to his eye, his unique sort of selectivity. And the things he picks to show you will, to some extent, reflect his own sense of style as well as his feeling of what is right for you.

Most decorators work out of offices. A few have elaborate showrooms stocked with quantities of merchandise. On the whole, I think I approve of the office type more than of the showroom sort. A decorator who does not have substantial sums of money tied up in goods he must sell is more likely to shop for you with your particular needs in mind.

Before you make a final decision on hiring any designer, you should see some of his work. Display rooms give a flat picture at best. Because no family lives in them, they are impersonal. Many decorators have photographs of various rooms they've worked on. And most of them can arrange to take you to see the houses themselves; such visits not only give you a three-dimensional look, but also show you how well the room has worn after being lived in for a while.

Completing Financial Arrangements　　Once you're fairly certain you've found the man or the woman for you, get the money question settled. You owe it to the decorator and to yourself to be frank and as accurate as possible about the total amount you have to spend. Settle on whether he is to be paid a fee or by a retail-price arrangement, how often you will be billed and what the terms of payment will be. Ask about sketches; independent designers often charge for them. And also find out for certain whether, once paid for, the sketch is yours or whether, because the fee you pay is for the mechanical work of the drawing rather than for the original conception it illustrates, it remains the decorator's property.

Money inspires strange emotions and some rather curious legends. One of the mystic beliefs decorators have to combat is the notion that their chief delight is in settling on a price and then tricking clients into spending more and more and more. For very sound business reasons, a good decorator simply doesn't work that way. Still, in the very nature of the work, he is going to make suggestions that he hopes a client will find appealing and will want to go along with. Suddenly the client finds herself wanting to do this *and* that rather than this *or* that. The result is higher cost. But if extravagance is involved, it can honestly be traced to the client more often than to the decorator. Holding to the agreed budget is a joint responsibility, and it is one in which you, as the customer, must be prepared to share.

It is the decorator's job to remind you when changes and additions threaten to send the budget soaring. You may fall in love with a far more expensive piece than the one you had originally planned to use in a specific spot; and you may want it so much that you are willing to cut corners elsewhere. But before a final decision is made, there should be a realistic reappraisal, so that you will know without any doubt just what you are giving up for what you are getting.

Changes always cost money—even the simple ones. A five-dollar difference between the price of one doorknob and another sounds too small to bother with; but, multiplied by the five doorknobs you need, it may be worth thinking about. It is easy to say to a workman, "Oh, put a drain there while you're at it," or, "You may as well repaint this along with the rest." In most cases, he'll do what you say without a murmur. But the price difference will, most assuredly, show up on your final bill.

It is best to make a firm rule that all orders to contractors, painters, upholsterers—all the people who work on your project—must be given by the decorator. I learned this somewhat painfully when I was working on an extensive remodeling job for some friends. The house was in town, and it was therefore easy for them to drop in to see how things were going. Quite understandably, seeing the work in progress gave them all sorts of new ideas. On almost every visit they'd ask the contractor to do this or that instead of, or in addition to, the work already ordered. Each time I went to the house to check, I'd find surprises, and I'd try to warn my friend-clients about the rising cost. But after a while I had to give up; they were, after all, friends and, I knew, fairly well off. I hated to sound like a scold. The denouement was unhappy for all of us. The time for accounting came, and they were horrified and blamed me, not for trying to deceive them, but for letting the contractor put something over on me. In the end a substantial share of the difference came out of my pocket, and they—probably uncomfortably embarrassed—went to someone else for their next decorating job.

Strange as it may seem, a decorator does not dream of being turned loose in an empty house with a purse full of money and blithe instructions from a client to "go ahead, do it *your* way." Without the client's help, the finished job, no matter how much it costs, will have all the personality of an expensive hotel suite.

Not knowing his client's feelings can make a decorator's work almost impossible. In my own decorating days, I once agreed to do an apartment for a girl in one of Dick's shows who had never had a home of her own and who didn't really know at all what she liked or needed. She wanted "a pretty place" but could give me no hint about her favorite colors or styles or atmosphere. I got the same sort of noncommittal reply to every question I asked. Desperately searching for just one decisive answer, I said, "Well, at any rate, I can estimate how much furniture you'll need to put books in. Do you have many of them?" "No," she answered, "but I'm going to get some.

*Incorporating
Personality*

How many do you think I'll need?" Though the apartment was small, it was one of the most difficult jobs I ever tackled.

By comparison, Ben Hecht's exotic bathroom—in which he used to do a great deal of work—was a cinch. He knew exactly what he wanted: flocked velvet walls, a marble washstand, a mural by Henry Varnum Poor, an Aubusson rug cut down to upholster a baroque Italian stool and a mercury-backed French mirror lit by two oil lamps. All this he insisted upon. For practical reasons (he couldn't see to shave), he later allowed me to substitute a modern clear-faced mirror and electric lights. There were problems involved, but compared to building a room around a personality that doesn't exist, furnishing Ben's bath was childishly easy.

Evidence of a distinctive personality is always more interesting than careful conformity. It is wrong to choose even the smallest accessory just because you feel it is "safe"; choosing something simply because it is different is just as bad—the result is a house that clamors for attention rather than one that allows people the pleasure of discovering it gradually and enjoying its details one at a time. Consciously bright witty houses, like some bright witty people, are often exhausting to be with for any length of time. The only successful decorating scheme for you is one that reflects your personality truly and unself-consciously. And such a scheme can be achieved only by choosing objects because you really love them.

The Decorator's Contribution

Decorating is a kind of client-decorator collaboration at which neither can be as successful alone as both are together. There are necessary jobs to be done by each. The client needs the designer's help to solve the problems her house presents and which she herself cannot solve. For while she may know quite clearly the feeling she wants a certain room to have, she often does not know how to achieve the effect she hopes for. For his part, the decorator needs both the client and her problems. The measure of his success is the degree of pleasure the owners feel as they live in their homes. The rooms should bear the stamp of the client's personality rather than that of the decorator.

What should a decorator do for you? He should handle basic design and supervise minor architectural changes and building arrangements—new doors, bookcases, closets, built-in hi-fi equipment, lighting and so on. He should take charge of such practical matters as electrical outlets and rewiring where they are needed. He can guide you in searching out the air-conditioning and heating systems best for your home. He is invaluable in overseeing details that most people take for granted—cornices, moldings, doorknobs, hardware, the finishing touches that can make the difference between perfection and a near-miss.

On the more exciting side, he will help you settle on color schemes, wallpapers, floor coverings, draperies and basic furniture (the big pieces) and ways of arranging it. He should guide you on such important accessories as mirrors and lamps and lighting fixtures.

Top interior designers influence the styling of fabrics, floor coverings and color ranges. Most new colors, new fibers, new developments in every division of interior design reach professionals long before they are available to the public. In this sense decorators do educate, raise sights and enlarge their clients' horizons. But a good decorator will never lay down the law to a client. He is, wherever it is at all practical, more than willing to go along with what you like, what you need and what you can afford. He knows when general rules can successfully be broken to gain just the effect you want.

While preserving the basic personality that is yours, a decorator can suggest the most effective ways of giving continuity to the elements of a room or a house. He can strengthen the total impression and make it more pleasing. One of his greatest assets is his ability—gained from experience and training—to help crystallize your ideas, to sift them and to show you not only which ones are unworkable, but also, through use of materials you may not even know about, how ideas you thought impossible can be included in your plans.

The elevator hall in our New York apartment

But a decorator should not make all the decisions. You should not want him to. You must be prepared to care enough about some things, things that are within your power to acquire, to incorporate them in your schemes without regard to what is considered safe or correct or what magazines say or what the people next door think. The touches, often small in scale, that give the room your distinctive personality are your responsibility. Such things as the way you frame pictures and group them on a wall, the kind of vases you like to use for flowers, cigarette boxes, ash trays and ornaments, all should reflect only the tastes of the people who live in the house. The pleasure of the thinking, browsing and discovering that goes into the selection of such small but important pieces as a table for a certain chair, a corner piece for the living room, just the right chest for the wall between the windows should be yours.

Your Responsibility

Once you've started on a project, the work proceeds according to an approximate schedule. But it should be one based on enough time for each part of the job rather than one that strains to meet a deadline. In an over-all sense, decorating cannot, should not, be hurried.

Timing Your Decorating

It may be months or even years before you know what you really want to do with a room. Recently I redid the entrance hall of our apartment. I hadn't been completely happy with it for a year or so. But on the other hand, I hadn't known exactly what I wanted to do about it. It had pale beige walls, a black-and-white terrazzo floor, a mahogany spinet with a Chippendale mirror painted black hanging above it; a pair of regal gilt Empire chairs upholstered in red stood on either side of the doors to the dining room. Actually it was handsome, but I had come to feel I wanted a change to something lighter, not quite so staid in feeling.

I didn't know, specifically, what changes I wanted to make until I discovered a pair of Louis XV chairs painted a charming blue and upholstered in off-white damask with a delicate blue pattern. At first sight I loved them, and suddenly I knew just what was needed to complete the picture. I covered every source in the city. It took weeks of intensive hunting to unearth a marvelously graceful Regency console to replace the spinet. (As a matter of fact, the console turned up at an antique dealer's six-floor establishment, where I'd searched minutely and unsuccessfully for one just the week before; a woman who had had it out on approval had returned it the morning I found it.) The walls are now white; the floor is the same as it was. And although I have hung a gilt-framed Louis XVI mirror above the console, it is not exactly right, and the dealer whose shop it comes from has promised I may trade it in when we find the perfect one.

The point is this: everything does *not* have to be completed at once.

(25)

Good decorating takes time. It takes time to know what you'd like to do, and to make a general plan, time to find the right furniture and—most important of all—time to add the finishing touches that turn a good scheme into a real room that is perfection or near it.

I think rushing out and filling a room with "just anything" because it is all you can find or afford at the moment is a tremendous mistake. Cleverly used, color and pattern can disguise empty spaces and temporary solutions. A room where one or two beautiful pieces stand on their own is infinitely more interesting than one that is crammed with furniture nobody loves. The sight of a treasured chair or chest or table is somehow a promise of more handsome things to come.

It may be months or even years before you find the perfect console. Especially if it is an antique, what you need may not be available in July. But it could be in August. Meanwhile you have all the fun of browsing and looking and learning. In the process you'll discover more beautiful things than you ever knew existed. And finding them is one of the things that turns decorating into a continuing pleasure.

CHAPTER
2

Rooms That Really Work

I N all decorating jobs, certain rooms present more difficulties than others. An informal family room, for example, is comparatively easy because it is so very closely related to a family's life and interests. A man's den is generally successful because it is designed to be used. Oscar Hammerstein's workrooms in town and in the country were wonderful for that reason.

They were intensely personal, from the photographs on the walls to the high, old-fashioned bookkeeper's desks (he always wrote standing up) and the chessboards he liked to have set up within reach wherever he was. There were always masses of books—every reference work you could think of—and a number of the lightweight kidney-shaped tables he especially liked to move around and put papers on. Almost everything in the room was used, and the more use a room is put to, the better its chance of success.

Kitchens   Because it is her workroom, a woman usually has very definite ideas about the design of her kitchen. She spends enough time in it to know what equipment works well for her, how she wants things placed and where she needs storage space, as well as the kind of atmosphere she enjoys working in.

My own ideas about kitchens are more those of a wife who likes to cook than those of a decorator. I admire restaurant kitchens—with their big work tables and racks of hanging pots—because they are so clearly designed to produce good food efficiently. And to me, a kitchen's beauty lies in the way it works.

Before it is pretty to look at, a kitchen should be as smoothly functional as time and thought can make it. It is, after the bathroom, the most practical room in the house, and everything about it should be designed to facilitate fixing meals and cleaning up afterward. I like kitchens big enough to move around in, but not so huge that they add extra steps to the job. I like plenty of air and light. There should always be an exhaust system adequate to carry off strong lingering odors. Blue-toned fluorescent lighting should be avoided because it makes food look embalmed, but there are a number of excellent new fixtures on the market that cast almost shadowless light that is bright without glare.

I'd be lost without a good big marble-topped center table—one I can get at from all sides when I'm rolling pastry or making a chocolate roll— and I think every kitchen should have a butcher's block or built-in wood counter on which to do pounding and chopping. I love lots of clear counter space with a handy supply of electrical outlets and enough room to store utensils where they can be reached readily. In our city apartment the back staircase starts in the kitchen itself, and we have utilized what would otherwise be waste space under the stairs for Formica-lined shelves that are stacked with pots and pans. Their placement in plain sight saves burrowing in dark cupboards. Not only is the arrangement an awfully convenient one; I also love being able to see the pans, because my hammered-aluminum pots are like old friends; my mother brought them from France before Dick and I were married.

Major appliances—dishwashers, freezers, refrigerators and modern stoves—are so temptingly automatic and easy to clean these days that it seems to me manufacturers have really done more than their part. It's up to you to decide not only which ones will do most for you, but also where, in terms of placement, they will work best in your kitchen. A dishwasher, for example, should have a place near the sink; both refrigerators and stove tops need clear counter space around them.

I think colored appliances are risky. Once delivered, they are yours and you are theirs for a long time, and if one piece of equipment breaks down before the rest, you may be unable to match the color. Besides, combined with color and pattern on floors and walls and in curtains—any or all of which can be changed several times in the lifespan of one machine— white appliances needn't look at all cold or antiseptic.

To me, kitchens that are not at least partially screened off from the rest of the living area are unrealistic. A friend of ours in Connecticut has one standing, wide open, in the middle of his living room. I have never seen dinner cooked in it, and I doubt that I ever will. Having food actually prepared in it would not be very pleasant for guests because there is absolutely no way to mask any of the mess: the parings and stalks and empty containers, the greasy pans and strong smells.

Another friend of ours has a kitchen that looks like a magazine page— all pink and pretty and full of potted flowers and herbs and every sort of gadget. But it is hard to say how it works; the family always eats out. I suspect too many things would have to be moved before you could get down to any serious cooking there. And too many of them are pure decoration. Decoration for decoration's sake interferes with one of a modern kitchen's greatest assets: the ease with which you can clean it. Nonfunctioning copper molds that have to be polished, empty antique jars that have to be dusted or wiped off are a nuisance. I am appalled when I see a magazine photograph of a kitchen in which an oil painting hangs. It isn't that the juxtaposition of food and art offends me; but my mind boggles at the thought of all the damage a few months of exposure to a kitchen's grease-laden atmosphere can do. Any print or painting, sketch or cartoon that is part of a kitchen's decor should be protected by glass if you care for it at all.

Of course, when a kitchen serves as dining or living room, too, it should look less businesslike. Alice Knopf's kitchen in Westport is divided into three areas. There is a big brick fireplace with love seats and a low table before it—awfully pleasant for cocktails and talk. The working part of the kitchen is built into the opposite wall and bounded by ceiling-to-floor bookcases that not only act as a divider, but also partially hide from view the strictly functional areas. Dinner is always served buffet style, and the dining table is so placed that although it does not dominate the room, it is easy for guests to serve themselves and move to their places. Remembering the room, I am aware of the warmth and beauty of the wood in the paneling, the cork floors and the books rather than of any particular period style. It's not only a very pleasant room—it also works.

　　While I am against too-big kitchens, I'm all for big pantries. If you entertain at all frequently, it is a tremendous help to have not only an area for storing glasses and china, but also a place where you can wash and replace them on their shelves without involving your cooking room. At Rockmeadow, we made the present pantry by doing away with the old breakfast

Pantries

room and adding the space to the original pantry, which was little more than a passageway. In terms of square footage, the pantry is now larger than the kitchen. It has its own refrigerator, dishwasher and sink, in addition to the ones in the kitchen, and it also has a hamper for soiled table linen, a plate warmer, sliding tray shelves for linens and cupboards for china and glass. There is also a great deal of counter space, which is an enormous help, not only in serving company meals, but also when it comes to everyday flower arranging or setting up breakfast trays or Thermoses and fruit for the bedrooms at night.

Company-Only Rooms   Whereas clients almost always have strong, clear thoughts about kitchens, they are very apt to be vague about other rooms. Experience taught us that a woman spends more time planning a company living room than she does any other area of her house—and it is there she is also likely to make the most mistakes. The reason isn't hard to understand. In spite of its name, the family actually does very little living in it. In practice it is a room reserved for special occasions, and the English are much more accurate about naming it than we are; they call it the "drawing room"—short for "withdrawing room," a place to which ladies retreat after the dinner part of a party. (The men usually stay in the dining room over their cigars and port.) Being rarely used otherwise, this kind of living room is apt to look rather chilly and stiff, its colors a bit too careful, chairs a shade too precisely placed, cushions a little too plump—the whole on the barren side. The most effective cure for its ills seems to be a bit of clutter—family photographs, personal bibelots, flowers, all sorts of things that are loved and lovingly placed.

Living Rooms   Such well-loved things automatically find their way into a room that is really lived in. Leonora and Arthur Hornblow's living room is a wonderful example. The first impression it gives is of red and white, of warm, gay style and of books. (Both Hornblows are writers and avid readers.) Books reach from floor to ceiling on one inside wall; around the others—from which there are magnificent East River views—counter-high shelves hold more books and built-in television and hi-fi; on top stand photographs, small paintings, bits of porcelain, pieces of sculpture. The furniture is consciously overscaled, comfortable; the effect is easy, informal.

Different in almost every possible way, yet with its own tremendous charm, is Frances and Harold Brooks' living room. I always think of it at night, full of crystal, candles and beautifully dressed people, with the women looking their loveliest, thanks to the superb lighting. The creamy beige color scheme gives the impression of almost an absence of color and plays up contrasting textures. The furniture is small in scale, delicate-

looking, antique, but arranged in groups that actually seem to invite people to sit down and talk to each other. It is a formal room, but enormously livable because it so perfectly suits the kind of entertaining—dinner followed with music by a new young singer or pianist—that the Brookses enjoy so much and do so often.

Dining rooms, too, are dull if they are little-used one-purpose rooms. They seem to gain charm through serving more than one function. The Dore Scharys' dining room owes a great deal of its warmth and color to its having started life as Dore's study; the walls are still lined with hundreds of books. Harold Rome works at home, and his office equipment is concealed in the dining room. As a matter of fact, the combination of his work and their parties, which are almost always buffets, inspired the design of a marvelously functional piece of furniture Florence Rome has had built into the dining room. It is a long cherry wood storage wall. The white Formica top, fitted with electric outlets and lighting slots, provides plenty of space to set out the most extensive array of dishes. The space beneath is divided into efficiently proportioned storage sections: narrow drawers for

Dining Rooms

(*33*)

linens and silver, deep drawers for files and doors behind which stationery and a typewriter are stored. When there is no party in progress, plants are set out on top. And when guests are expected, whatever the size of the group, Florence not only has the essentials at hand to set her table beautifully (as she always does) but also has an ideally equipped serving space.

Time and time again, dining rooms are decorated according to a tradition that has little or no connection with the way their owners actually entertain. If your favorite parties are buffet dinners for ten to twenty people, it scarcely makes sense to settle for a standard rectangular table with eight massive chairs and a sideboard to match. Dining rooms, I think, are particularly susceptible to good contemporary furniture. For one thing, it is often terribly difficult to find in any but the most expensive antiques the quality a sideboard or dining-room table must have. No matter how lovely the lines, rickety period pieces will not work. Dining-room chairs especially, must be in good condition, standing firmly on all their legs. For this reason, the dining room is one place where I like to use good reproductions.

The Romes' cabinets are only one example of contemporary furniture designed to do exactly the job that is needed. Partly because I'm partial to round dining tables, but also because this particular one is so ingenious, I've always loved the table Leopold Godowsky designed. It is a beauty to begin with, made of marvelously grained wood. A round center section, flush with the rest of the table, revolves like an old-fashioned lazy susan. But the most wonderful aspect is the way this table expands: not from round to oval as most round tables do, but from round to large round to larger round, thanks to leaves that are sections of a circle rather than long narrow boards. Admittedly, tailor-made pieces cost a good deal, but when they are so perfect for the place and the use they are put to, they are often well worth the price. (What's more, with a century's aging, they may become treasured antiques.) After all, although people seldom remember them as such, Messrs. Chippendale *et al.* in their own day were designers of contemporary furniture to fit specific needs and places.

Our friend Grover Loening had a table wonderful in quite a different

way: it had "retractable landing gear," so that it could be wheeled in all set for dinner, stand firmly—gear down—during the meal and be wheeled away into the kitchen to be cleared. Roll-away tables have always seemed an ideal solution for an apartment in which there is enough kitchen or pantry space to set the table properly in advance and where the living room must be the dining room too.

Where wheeling in and out is impractical, a dining-area table may either sit uncluttered and ready for service in the living room itself or be disguised with a floor-length skirt of velveteen, brocade, felt or any fabric that looks right in the room. But since uncovering, setting, clearing and recovering before and after every meal can be such a nuisance, many people we know seem to prefer using fold-away tables that can be simply cleared and stored in a closet when not in use. If your living room is your dining room too, it is helpful to have a decorative screen to mask the table area before and after the meal. There should also be storage space nearby for linens and silver. (At Repairs, Inc., we used to make a screen that had shelves in back where glasses could be stored: it was most useful for very cramped apartments.)

Women's Bedrooms   Unlike formal company rooms, bedrooms are so personal they stand little chance of being dull. Though it might seem strange in an apartment as big as ours, I spend a great deal of time in my own bedroom. The walls have always been the soft blue I love best. The plum-brown painted Venetian secretary not only has graceful lines but also has a reasonable working surface on which I do all my paying of bills and paper work and letter writing. Big bottom drawers hold stationery and such; the top doors hide a television set properly placed for the rare times I watch a program from bed. (Unlike most modern TV consoles which are designed with knee-high screens, this set—and the one in the living room at Rockmeadow —is placed high, where furniture and passing people do not obstruct the view.) The room has a white faïence mantel as well as a big tufted scarlet velvet sofa where I like to sit, where visitors can be comfortable and where, when they were small, the children used to spread out their homework. The table tops are full of framed family pictures and a very eclectic and sentimental collection of small objects—boxes, bits of Battersea enamel, small porcelain pieces, a gold coin from Siam, a tiny balancing statue that twirls on its toe when you touch it and a particularly fine toothpick construction hand-wrought by my grandson Tod. The room has looked the same for years and so many things I dearly love are there that it is the most comfortable and comforting place I know.

Dorothy Hammerstein's bedroom is beautiful—one of many she has designed through the years and exactly right for her. In a lovely New York town house, hers is a perfectly proportioned room—almost square with very high ceilings. Both in scale and color it has always been dramatic. Not so many years ago it was glowing yellow and white; now the walls are white, the ceiling is a pale blue, and the floor is covered in bright Bristol blue. The bed is a magnificent Eighteenth-Century four-poster, dressed from canopy to carpet in a bold black-and-white *chinoiserie* cotton print. The chaise, a large sofa and a big upholstered chair by the white marble fireplace are all covered in the same fabric. Electrified five-branch wall candelabra take the place of bedside lamps. Bristol blue is repeated in lampshades at each end of the sofa, a pair of Minton birds, Meissen candlesticks and an opaline box on the mantel. There are blue pillows, a blue beadwork footstool and two chairs (one a miniature) done in a small gray, black and white silk plaid. An important gilt-framed Chippendale mirror hangs above the fireplace; a big painted armoire stands in one corner and a mahogany *bombé* secretary in the other. The walls are hung with family portraits and groups of small paintings. It is a handsome, exciting room—as perfect a background for Dorothy as it would be wrong for me.

A man's bedroom has a different look—more substantial than a woman's and with greater depth of color. The fabrics are usually sturdier and have stronger textures. Whether the furniture is contemporary or antique, it should have a feeling of good solid weight about it. There ought to be a

Men's Bedrooms

comfortable chair with a good reading light and a table by it, a place that is right for hanging or laying out clothes and, of course, a mirror hung at tie-tying height.

Both at Rockmeadow and in the city, Dick's bedrooms are furnished with antiques. His big empire sleigh bed at the apartment is one he discovered himself in an antique dealer's one Saturday. Made of mahogany ornamented with bronze *doré*, it has an inclined headboard that gives wonderful back support for reading in bed. I've made needlepoint panels for the headboard and footboard to match the yellow bedspread. To give his otherwise dark room an illusion of sunlight, the carpet is pale-lemon yellow; so is the flocked wallpaper that gives the room a slight feeling of pattern without detracting from the pictures on the walls.

In the country Dick's long and relatively narrow room with its sweeping view serves as both bedroom and study. Once upon a time it actually was two rooms. Now that it is one room, it is completely carpeted in warm pale-beige cotton. To detract from its length, we've built floor-to-ceiling bookcases two feet wide at right angles to the long walls at the place where the old wall used to cut the room in two. In the sleeping end, painted a deep yellow green, there is a bed, a big comfortable chair, a floor lamp and a low

round Biedermeier table with plenty of surface space for a lamp and a bowl of flowers and the stacks of books Dick is always reading. The other section of the room is painted beige, and standing free in it is a French provincial fruitwood table that serves as a desk. In Dick's city study there is a similar one, with a big working space, room for a blotter, pens, pencils, lamp, dictionary and phones. The least personal things in any of these rooms are the television sets Dick needs to help him keep up with show people and productions—especially important when it comes to casting a show. The most personal things are the mementos—medallions, awards, an Oscar and the original designs for sets in his shows which hang on the walls of the study in the New York apartment. The pictures in his apartment bedroom include not only a striking Soulages and watercolors by Henry Moore, Sam Francis and Dubuffet that are special favorites, but also old photographs of his parents, primitive-style portraits of Rockmeadow in summer and winter, pictures of the children and a small informal portrait of me that stands on his chest of drawers.

Rooms for Two

A room designed for one person gains from its individuality. But a couple's bedroom should never be blatantly all "his" or all "hers." Doing it all in oak and deep-red tie silks would be just as wrong as are those frilly candy-box rooms you occasionally discover, where a man would be in torment without a blindfold. The fact that American men often defer to their wives when it comes to decoration should never lead to a man's being condemned to live tangled in ruffles or to teeter on a frail gilt chair every time he pulls on his socks. Pink is not the only pretty pale color, upholstered chairs need not be covered in satin, and a print that is both bright and pleasing need not be fussy in feeling.

Especially when growing children tend to appropriate the rest of the house for themselves, a couple's bedroom should be a haven to which they can retreat, not a cell to which they feel exiled. It should combine comfort and privacy in as near-perfect proportions as you can possibly manage. It begins, of course, with a good bed, or beds, equipped with properly focused reading lights and flanked by night tables big enough to hold all the books and clocks and radios and tissues and other miscellany you'd like to have within reach. If you are sensitive to daylight, make sure window shades are meticulously fitted and opaque. And if you're lucky enough to have an alcove for the bed, paint the walls a dark, light-absorbing color.

More than just a sleeping area, your bedroom should be the place where you feel most at home in the world. It is a place for your best-loved photographs and trinkets, a place not only for the books you're currently reading, but also for particular favorites you love to leaf through every month or year or so. It should have easy chairs for reading, talking, sitting. And if you like to do paper work and write letters in your bedroom as I do (for some reason I can't imagine doing them in the library downstairs), there should also be a desk in good working order.

We have friends in California whose idea of heaven is a chance to go to bed early and watch television; so they've installed electrically controlled beds which can be adjusted to the absolutely perfect viewing angle. Other bedroom TV-watchers, not quite so dedicated, keep sets disguised when not in use. Mine, as I've said, is installed behind doors in the top of the secretary; Mrs. Moss Hart (Kitty Carlisle) keeps hers, hidden by a floor-length skirt, on the bottom shelf of a small table.

I can't think of a place where a touch of luxury is more soothing or justified than in a bedroom. If you love hi-fi or stereophonic music, a record player should be a part of your scheme. One couple we know is addicted to elaborate bedtime snacks; so, to save trekking down to the kitchen every midnight, they've installed a miniature kitchen—complete with tiny refrigerator, hot plate, bar and space to store plates and glasses—in a big painted cabinet in their bedroom. A sewing table for you, a desk for your husband—whatever you want is right, as long as it contributes to making this a room where you both can go and, happily, shut out the rest of the world.

Dressing rooms are nice if you can afford the space. But rather than two cramped rooms, one for dressing and one for bathing, I prefer a single good big working-model bathroom. I have never seen a bathroom that was too big. In addition to floor space for the essential plumbing fixtures (which, to my way of thinking, include a bidet), there should be a place to store such bulky items as extra towels, cleansing tissue, toilet paper, plus the collection of seldom-used items for which there's no room in the medicine cabinet; often you can create such space by building cupboards beneath or around a washstand or over a bathtub or by adding a small chest of drawers. There should also be some out-of-the-way arrangement for hanging hand laundry. To me, a bathroom is the perfect place for a dressing table, chiefly because it can be well lit (no blue-toned fluorescent or pink bulbs) and spills present no great problem. There are so many marvelous washable floorings now—vinyl tile, mosaic tile, even polished marble or terrazzo if you're feeling terribly extravagant—that I deplore the trend toward wall-to-wall bathroom carpeting. Even when the material is theoretically washable, spot cleaning is almost impossible, and you simply can't take the whole business up and rush it off to the laundry immediately after every spill or splash. Give me a floor that can be wiped up whenever it needs it and cotton rugs small enough to be tossed into a washing machine and returned to the floor brand clean the same day.

Where fixtures are concerned, I am a confirmed conservative. I think sunken bathtubs are lovely to look at, but they're the devil to clean. And handsome as distinctively colored ceramic and porcelain can be, they are also terribly permanent. So I think it makes better long-range sense to keep tile walls and washstands white or a pale neutral tone and let wallpaper and towels provide the color. Moisture-proof paper and cloth are now available in hundreds of different patterns; and on a painted wall, appliquéd fabric or paper flowers used to garland a mirror or frame a door can be wonderfully effective. A switch in towel color or style is one of the most striking, least expensive ways of redecoration known to modern woman. What's more, the latest floral and geometric designs are so handsome in their own right that they do away with the need for fancy monogramming.

In a shared bathroom, I'm all for following the European plan of adding an extra wash basin and closeting off the toilet. The scheme—inspired, I'm sure, by a scarcity of bathrooms abroad—makes the same space useful to more than one person at a time and, adopted here, could considerably shorten the waiting time at American family bathroom doors.

Many people feel that beautiful things and small children cannot co-exist peacefully. I do not agree. I think it is a shame to deprive the adults in a family of things they love for no better reason than fear that a child will smash them. With reasonable caution and training, it is almost always possible to work out a live-and-let-live arrangement. I have seen it done successfully with both our children and our grandchildren. It is a matter of establishing mutual respect: yours for their belongings—their toys, their rooms—and theirs for yours. Accidents will happen, of course, but they happen with adults, too.

I do think it is important for a young child to have some place of his own where he can feel free to do anything within reason—even write on the walls, if they are sufficiently scrubbable. Walls paneled in blackboard, perforated board (with hooks for displaying treasures and trophies) and acoustical tile or bulletin board on which to tack up original art also work awfully well. When he was three, our grandson Peter "helped" an artist friend of his parents to paint murals in his room. Our daughter Linda and her husband, Danny, consider the fact that Peter is still allowed great latitude within his own four walls a kind of insurance policy for grown-up accessories and furniture in the rest of the apartment.

Pastel myths to the contrary, most children show a preference for bright, gay colors the minute they are old enough to reach for blocks and rattles. The happiest rooms I've ever seen or designed for children have been strong on color. Mary's first room was not baby pink but a flag-waving red, white and blue. And I remember a circus play room—beige walls with real Barnum & Bailey poster cut-outs and lots of kelly green for the upholstery, the felt draperies and the valance that circled the room at cornice height. I designed it for Daniel and Anna Massey many years ago, when they were not the successful young actors they have both grown up to be but simply the young children of our friends, Raymond Massey and Adrianne Allen. I particularly remember the floor of that room because it was covered with cork, an especially fine idea not only because it muffled sound, but also because it was not chilly to the touch of small children who loved to sit and play on it. Cork is also kind to both people and things that fall on it.

In grown-up rooms a certain amount of clutter adds atmosphere and charm. In a child's room it is cheery to see dolls and stuffed animals and books on open shelves, where they can be reached and read. But I think the general conglomeration of playthings most children accumulate is best confined behind closed cupboard doors when they are not being played with. The more extensive and concealing the storage space, the wider and

freer the play area, the better. Furniture should be arranged to allow as much open floor space as possible. Trains and trucks and doll houses need plenty of setting-up room and very little carpeting; push toys, pull toys and toys that go by themselves move more easily over smooth surfaces than they do across deep-piled rugs.

As far as furniture design is concerned, rounded corners and edges cut down on bruises and collision injuries. I like legless beds and chests that sit squarely on the floor because crayons and jacks cannot possibly roll away out of reach under them. Ceiling and wall lamps seem best for

(*44*)

children's rooms, not only because they shed a nice even light, but also because they have no exposed cords. For safety's sake, table lamps should be extremely steady and should be used only where it is possible to keep outlets and wires out of the way behind immobile pieces of furniture.

No matter how many kinds of rooms a house contains, it should have a sense of flow about it. Each room should be considered in relation to the others that open into it. It is nice to be surprised when you turn a corner; it is unpleasant to be shocked. While this flow does depend to a great extent upon color, painting everything apartment-house cream is not the answer. Light, texture and pattern are important, too. And good basic planning—in which each of these plays its full role—makes a house an inviting whole, not just a collection of rooms.

CHAPTER

3

Good Basic Planning

THE BASIC problems involved in decorating a living room, a bedroom, a kitchen or any of the rooms we have been discussing have not changed since the days of Repairs, Inc., but the ways of solving them have. Our success was built around and totally dependent on the work of a group of extraordinarily skilled craftsmen, men who were expert wood carvers or glass cutters or cabinetmakers because their fathers and grandfathers had been before them. Skills were a family tradition; the father of one of my cabinetmakers was a staff cabinetmaker at Buckingham Palace. There are few such artisans left. And, while the tooling techniques and design of much mass-produced furniture may have improved immensely in the last few years, they will never completely fill the gap left by the disappearance of things made by people who, from design to finish, were responsible for and took a personal pride in every completed piece.

On the other hand, the question of durability no longer inhibits the choice of decorating fabrics and colors as it once did. Great new finishes have made hundreds of materials that once faded or shredded or frayed strong as iron without looking it. Thanks to synthetics and improved cleaning methods, a light-colored carpet can now be as practical as it is good-looking—provided you keep a reasonable distance between it and any mud-bearing feet that enter through outside doors. There are imitation moirés and taffetas in butter yellows, powder blues, any color you please and—far from being their old perishable selves—any one of them is a perfectly sensible choice for walls, since all of them are made of vinyl and can be scrubbed clean with a brush. Delicately colored cottons and silks can be treated before they are used to make them soil-resistant and easier to clean. And some present-day wallpapers shed everything from crayon marks to fingerprints and ink.

In decorating as in any field, there are certain unchanging truths.

*Taking Your
Time*

Perhaps the most basic is that hurry never helps. The decision you rush for the sake of being able to check off one more item on a list of things to be done almost always leads to disappointment. Time spent investigating all the possibilities, "just looking" at fabrics, colors, wallpapers, magazine pictures, model rooms (always keeping in mind that the latter often put style before such real-life considerations as livable color schemes and practical traffic patterns) is always time well invested.

Our New York dining room illustrates this theory perfectly. Originally it was two rooms, and, although we knew we wanted to make one dining room of them, we did not act on the decision for more than four years. The combined area was just what we wanted, but in the beginning, I had no idea of how to cope with the problems that came with it: the great length of the room, the unconventional L-shape, the existing doors that would be made useless and the doors we needed that didn't exist. I didn't try to hurry things. I just kept looking and thinking until, one by one, all the difficulties were worked out in my mind, then on paper. When I finally set out to buy the furniture my plans called for, I knew so exactly what I wanted that not one piece sent on approval had to be returned. What is more, I developed space for two big new closets—one in the hall for coats, another off the dining room where Dick keeps his tapes, records and a collection of bound scores. We also built in wall-storage space for silver, linens, china and glasses. The result is a room as right for the paintings we love as for the dinner parties that are our favorite way of entertaining.

*Architectural
Alterations*

Any necessary architectural changes must, of course, be made before surface decorating starts. Such major alterations obviously require expert advice, not only because most people are not aware of the structural principles involved, but also because an experienced designer knows an infinite variety of ways to solve the architectural problems a room presents. He has dealt with them before. From the aesthetic point of view, he knows how to disguise bad features, how to mask jogging beams, how to give a room graceful proportions by changing the shape of a door or lowering a ceiling. He knows when two rooms can be joined to advantage. Practically speaking, he knows where putting in a new door or closing an existing one will solve a traffic problem. Possibly most important of all, he can often find or create storage space you never dreamed of having. He might accomplish such miracles by simply closing in space beneath a staircase or framing a window or door in a wall of built-in cupboards and shelves or paring a foot off the end of a room to make a storage wall.

In our first apartment I stole a full fifteen inches from the width of a twenty-eight-foot gallery to deal with what seemed to be an insurmountable storage crisis. The cupboards and closets made by this new "wall" held an incredibly miscellaneous collection of bridge tables, games, cameras, table linens, Dick's steel filing cabinets, records and a concealed bar stocked with bottles and glasses—all beautifully organized. The doors worked on spring locks, with no visible hardware, and looked like solid wall panels when they were closed. I have to admit I worried to death while this brain child was being installed; I even had a nightmare in which the gallery became so narrow you couldn't get in or out. But I don't think I have ever invented anything that solved so many problems at one time.

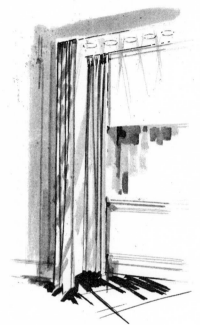

Placement of lights   *Draperies in place*

It is most important to consider electrical wiring, built-in lighting and telephone placement at the same time you make plans for architectural changes. Such electrical adjustments are easy to make while construction is going on, but are delaying, annoying and very expensive later on, when baseboards are finished and walls are plastered. Be sure your power supply and wiring will be equal to the job of running, not only the appliances you now own, but also those you plan to buy in the foreseeable future. And make certain every room—especially the kitchen—has all the strategically placed outlets it needs. Consider built-in lighting for rooms that get no sun, rooms you use mostly at night and wherever you've hung paintings, prints or other objects you love. The kind of built-in lighting we like best comes from a bank or row of individual reflector bulbs which can be concealed in any number of ways. They may be hidden behind a fake cornice, installed

(*49*)

above a false ceiling, sunk in a real one or built into a window frame. Wherever we have used them in the apartment—in the living room, the dining room and the halls—the light they shed bathes the wall evenly; we think this shows paintings to best advantage. Rheostatic controls make it possible to dim or increase light to exactly the degree of intensity we want at any given time.

As I have said before, I think blue fluorescent light is unpleasant. But my least favorite built-in fixtures are those tiny pin-point ceiling spotlights. They give paintings an eerie look the artist certainly never saw or intended. What is more, once installed, they are permanently set and difficult to refocus; this not only means you may not rearrange pictures without tearing up the ceiling, but that you must also keep constant check on hanging wires to make sure they haven't stretched half an inch, leaving pictures partially in the dark and brilliantly illuminating part of the frame.

Floor Construction

Floors may also enter into your construction plans. If yours are already beautiful or if you plan on carpeting or painting everywhere, your basic considerations are not structural but decorative and may be left till later. Otherwise, there are all sorts of possibilities. I am especially fond of fine parquet floors that have been stained almost black and waxed until they gleam. Vinyl and rubber tiles offer any number of good-looking choices because they can be patterned and inlaid in so many different ways. Marble is extravagantly elegant. Terrazzo is messy and expensive to install, but it can add a distinctive look of substance, particularly in an entrance hall. My favorite floor material of this kind is travertine, the lovely porous Roman marble that has a far less formal look than highly polished stone. The Averell Harrimans have used it wonderfully in their Florida house at Hobe Sound, where their living room is informal, gay, almost casually beautiful. Windows face the Atlantic on one side and on the other, the gardens. When I last saw the house, the living-room draperies were Gauguin pink, the walls pale blue, and long sofas in front of the windows faced each other across the room; there were long coffee tables and comfortable chairs. French porcelains and pieces of pink opaline were scattered around, and a marvelous Walt Kuhn still life of green apples hung above the fireplace. Except for a white bearskin rug in front of the hearth, the floor was bare travertine; because of its wonderful texture, it added just the right cool touch for that site and climate without seeming formal.

Wall Treatments

The only remaining major consideration from a structural point of view is wall area. Here, being utterly realistic can make an enormous difference in your future satisfaction. Especially with plaster walls, there is a tremendous temptation to overlook imperfections or to treat them superficially. A complete replastering is troublesome, costly, and something no-body notices unless it is done badly. On the other hand, if you try to deal with basic wall problems by spotty patching and spackling, you can count on the reappearance of cracks and other defects to spoil the looks of new paint or paper within a few months' time. Paper, of course, does a better camouflage job than paint, but my own favorite cure for aging walls is a covering of unbleached canvas. I have used it both in the apartment and at Rockmeadow. And although it is initially expensive, it provides the kind of life-time base for paint that seems to me a thoroughly worthwhile invest-ment for any permanent home.

When it comes to wood wall treatments, the variations are endless. Choices range from pedigreed antique paneling to modern veneers, from near-black to pale blond or painted tones. There are moldings, dadoes and chair rails as well as full floor-to-ceiling coverage. Some of the new vinyl "woods" are extraordinarily effective and can be used in many ways. Only an expert can guide you through all the possibilities, but patience devoted to thoroughgoing research can be rewarded with walls of great permanent beauty.

Once all these structural matters are taken care of, the truly aesthetic aspects of decorating begin. It is this work with fabrics and colors and furniture that is most fun. But when you are suddenly faced with a house full of bare rooms, it can also seem overwhelming. The solution to any job that seems impossibly large is to cut it down to size by listing the rooms to be dealt with in order of difficulty, then tackling the easiest (the ones about which you have the most definite thoughts) first, always keeping in mind the relationship of one room to another in terms of color, design and scale.

Because spatial relations are so important in any decorating scheme, my planning always starts with a pad of graph paper. On it, I make a scale outline of the room I'm working on. Then I measure all the existing furni-ture and cut out a scaled circle or rectangle to represent each piece. (I understand that you can now buy planning kits like this, but they are so easy to make that I have always assembled my own.) By moving the paper shapes around my graph-paper floor plan, I work out the furniture's final placement. It is great fun, and the only way I have ever been able to move a piano all by myself.

The graph-paper plan serves as a kind of insurance. It points out clearly that a grand piano and a sofa at one end of a room cannot be bal-anced by small chairs and tables at the other. Then, too, when existing pieces have been put in positions that allow for proper function and passing traffic, my graph pad shows me where new pieces are needed. When I come to blocking out color and placing upholstery fabrics, it helps me distribute patterns and textures and keeps me from overloading one part of the room with prints and the other with solid colors.

*Upholstered
Furniture*

In almost any redecorating plan, three kinds of furniture are involved: the things you have, the things you will buy immediately and the things you will look for in the future. In all these categories, upholstered furniture represents the most important investment. Sitting or sleeping, people depend on it for comfort; and a lumpy couch can literally cut short a conversation or destroy the mood of a party. On the other hand, a well-built sofa or chair will be a comfort for life. It is therefore wise to allot as much of your budget as possible to such pieces and to take time to investigate sizes and shapes with great care. Two chairs that look the same to the naked eye may be as different as can be way down deep in their frames where it counts; and in any reliable store, the more expensive of two similar pieces will almost always give years' more service. This theory has proved true in our own upholstered furniture; almost all of the pieces we have are over twenty years old, and some of them go back to the days before we were married.

Choosing upholstered furniture involves several material considerations. There is the upholstery itself, which may be either down or foam rubber, plain or tufted or cushioned. For frequently used pieces, uncushioned styles that require no fussy plumping obviously save time and care. Tufting is not only trouble-saving, but it also reduces the bulky look of a really big chair or sofa. When it comes to cushions, I know of nothing that equals down for comfort or appearance. Foam rubber can be very comfortable, but it does have a stiff, unyielding look about it. A clever upholsterer can give you the best of both worlds by combining down with layers of foam rubber in chair or sofa cushions. But loose pillows which are intended only as touches of beauty and luxury should always, I think, be down-filled.

Basically, you shop for shape and size. The ideal sofa or upholstered chair is neither exotically *moderne* nor Victorian; in fact, the simpler the lines, the more useful the piece and the longer it will live compatibly with either contemporary or period furniture. One essential requirement is that each new piece be right in scale for the room and the things you already own. Too small is as bad as too big. What seems like a very slight difference in measurements can have a tremendous effect on appearance and practicality. Two inches here and three there can make the difference between a passable and an impassable space between two living-room chairs. So this is another place where a floor plan, accurately kept, can save you expensive and time-consuming mistakes.

Variety is also important. When Dick does a show, he tries to make each song different in pace and mood. Rooms need change of pace, too. There are all sorts of different styles in upholstered furniture: there are solid, boxy sofas and chairs upholstered right down to the floor; there are open-armed chairs with a lighter look. Some pieces have short legs; others, cabriole legs or no legs. No room should contain only one sort. A pedestal table breaks the monotony in a group of four-legged pieces; so does a Louis XV chair in a collection of modern furniture that sits squarely on the ground. By the same token, braid or fringe or a guimpe may be smart on a pair of love seats, but used everywhere in a room, it becomes exhausting.

Thanks to newly durable fabrics, upholstery coverings are seldom any problem. It is now common practice at most stores to show customers floor samples of furniture they can have made up in any color, print and texture. If you are using a light-colored fabric, you may want to consider ordering an all-upholstered piece in muslin and having it slip-covered. We have done this with chairs in our Rockmeadow living room to minimize cleaning problems. Slip-covering has undergone drastic changes since the days when I was a girl and an unbroken law said slip covers had to be cotton twill or dowdy cretonne and ugly. Before any family went off to the shore in the summer, everything—including Aunt Hannah's portrait and the piano— had to have its dust cover. On everything except paintings these summer dusters hung to the floor (paintings and mirrors were covered with tarletan); it was all very baggy and dreary, especially for the poor man who joined his family for week ends but was forced to live with these frumpy ghosts in between. Slip-cover salvation began with the first woman who decided to pay attention to fit and use a fresh attractive chintz instead of the traditionally dun-colored cotton. Since then there has been a continuous change for the better-looking.

Now that air-conditioners keep rooms clean as well as cool, slip covers are valued as much for their decorative as for their protective qualities. In my New York bedroom, for example, I cover the wing chairs and red velvet sofa in summer, not to shield them, but because, combined with crisp white curtains at the windows and on the bed, the change to blue fabric gives the room an entirely new and cool look. If storage and money are no problem, it is fun to invent two entirely different color schemes for a room that is neutral in color and to have two complete sets of slip covers, cases for little pillows and small rugs that can literally change the atmosphere of the room in minutes. In contrast to English ladies who apply the same casual tailoring to brocade slip covers that they do to their own country tweeds, I think slip covers should be trimly fitted and look as much like built-on upholstery as possible. Wrinkled and loose, they give the whole room a sloppy look.

Color   When you know a room's shape and its basic furniture, then fabrics, paint and papers can begin to work for you. Color alone does marvelous things. It is, I think, the single most important factor in any decorating scheme. Take a ceiling, for instance: a dark color or pattern lowers it to improve the proportions of an abyss-like room; painting a cornice to match the ceiling also has a lowering effect, while painting cornice and walls the same shade will make the ceiling seem higher. In a long room, painting the end walls a deep tone makes them seem closer, gives the whole room a slightly more square appearance; on the other hand, painting them a light shade makes them seem further away. Wisely used, color can lend coziness to houses in Wisconsin and Vermont or cool comfort to Florida and California homes.

Many of our friends have color tastes so distinct that they have become trademarks. White always reminds me of Mary Lasker's beautiful town house alight with crystal, mirrors and her fabulous collection of impressionist paintings. Red belongs to the Logans. Warm beiges and pale lemon yellows that create the illusion of light are my own particular favorites, and I love almost all shades of blue.

Mary and Dick Halliday are drawn to beige and "the natural color of anything." Dick recalls that the day Mrs. Charles Dana Gibson came to visit them in their first New York apartment, she stopped at the door of the living room and exclaimed, "Oh, you darling children—you are going through the bleached-wood period!"

"She was quite right," he admits, "except that we started with bleached wood and still have bleached wood. We always seem anxious to get down to the natural wood of a piece of furniture, to see what it really looks like, to discover its original beauties."

Colors are so personal and mean such different things to different people that I hate giving them more than the most primary names. Dick Halliday told a story not long ago that may help explain what I mean. A friend of theirs, a nun, had been walking in a pine forest when suddenly she saw a baby fawn sound asleep in a brilliant spot of sun. She sat on a rock and watched as he slept for almost two hours, and in that quiet time she counted forty shades of green in the woods around her.

"I'm sure if we asked her to name her favorite color," Dick concluded, "she'd say 'The forty greens that I saw in a pine forest once—they are all my favorite color.'"

The only firm color rule I know is this: once you have found the colors you like, use them generously. Be it somber, gay, striking, dramatic, subdued, warm or cold, nothing does more to set the mood of a room than color unstintingly applied. And nothing deprives a room more than skimping on color in any area.

Fortunately, color wears no price tag. When I was working on strictly budgeted Repairs, Inc., projects, I remember going again and again for drapery fabrics to a theatrical supply house that had a vast stock of inexpensive fabrics in a marvelously wide range of shades. There was monk's cloth, burlap, velveteen—all of them so inexpensive they could be used without counting the yard cost. Where draperies are concerned, freedom to be lavish with fabric makes a tremendous difference in the impression a room gives. Better an unpretentious fabric richly used than a too-small bit of the world's most beautiful silk. The depth of the red or the blue or the gold tone that covers the wall makes much more difference than whether the material is brocade or burlap. Whether the curtains are silk or cotton sheeting, if they are billowing and full and a pretty pale yellow, they will still look like sunlight blowing in the window.

Walls are the largest color area in any room. In finishing as in construction, there are any number of different ways to treat them. Ready-mix paints now come in hundreds of minutely differentiated shades. Fabrics in solid colors, tone-on-tone patterns and prints are increasingly popular. And wallpapers, in a tremendous variety, work wonders. Thanks to pattern and marvelous new washable vinyl finishes, wallpapers help hide imperfections and often stay fresh-looking longer than paint. There are papers that make a point of texture, like grass papers which, incidentally, can be painted over, not once, but several times. In a small room where you plan to hang few pictures, patterned paper adds a cozy atmosphere.

My own preference in patterns is for designs that are sprawly and free rather than for formal, frequently and geometrically repeated patterns. To me, strong geometrics and polka dots have a disturbing way of turning active and overpowering when applied to the walls of real rooms. Because it is so difficult to visualize how paper on a dealer's display panel will look on four walls at home, and because there are so many styles to pick from, I think this is one place where a decorator's years of experience can be of immeasurable help to an amateur.

Windows   Wall treatment almost always involves windows. If yours are perfectly proportioned, perfectly placed and command a perfect view, you are enviably free to do with them as you wish. You may treat them entirely separately or link them as a single spatial unit by bracketing them beneath one long valance or hanging a continuous series of curtains that covers not only the windows themselves but also the wall space in between.

But windows are seldom perfect. Frequently they are unbalanced: they are off-center in a wall; or one is small and one is large; or one has a radiator beneath it while the others do not. Decorators have a hundred different camouflaging ways of dealing with such inequalities. Although I have always disliked elaborate valances, when they are simply designed, they can be of enormous architectural help. They mask unattractive hardware; extended from the window top to the ceiling, they add a look of height; drawn out, they can make a single window look wider or connect two or three in a row. The technique of treating several windows as one is so often successful that it has almost become a decorating cliché, but it is still tremendously effective. In some rooms draperies hung along a wall from one corner to the other have a soft, luxurious look, especially at night. In my New York bedroom, where the two windows are close together but not centered in the wall, I have draperies at the outside edge of each window and a permanently fixed matching panel of fabric between them. At night the two outer draperies are pulled inward until they meet the middle panel. Joined this way— and with one of my very favorite paintings, a night scene by the Belgian surrealist René Magritte, hung against the center panel—they become a single graceful unit instead of what they really are: two rather badly placed windows.

Many people feel reluctant to curtain a beautiful view. Yet no view is enchanting 365 twenty-four-hour days a year. Even when the outlook is spectacular, rain and snow and black of night can have their chilling effects, and there should be some way to shut them out. Sheer curtains that can be pulled across cold glass after dark or in bad weather have a pleasantly warming, even cozy, effect on a room with a great expanse of window.

If your windows command a reasonably dull brick wall or a downright ugly city back yard, you may hang opaque curtains and keep them permanently shut. You might even reverse tradition, as we have in our dining room, where the opaque draperies hang about twelve inches *behind* the glass curtains; because both are pale yellow lit by banks of lights above, the effect is of depth and sunlight, particularly inviting at night. Or you might borrow an idea from our friend Sue Cott, who has done such a beautiful job of faking with her "blind" windows that it is hard to imagine a real view with greater appeal. Her windows are slightly recessed, and she has framed them with molding that goes to the floor. Inside the molding she has hung tall narrow doors with grillwork tops to mask the windows themselves. Behind the metal grille she has used pale green curtains shirred on rods, and on the window sills inside she has set pots of imitation greenery. The filtered light and the sight of the "growing" things through the doors which stand ajar make it seem as though there is a whole lovely garden beyond.

Whether your windows are large or small, unbalanced or perfectly matched, in contemporary homes the treatment that achieves the smoothest over-all effect is usually the most appropriate. I like drapery fabrics that match or blend closely with the color of the wall upon which they are hung and styles that are simple but generous with special attention given to color and texture.

No sooner have I said this than I realize that I also like draperies that contrast with the walls, or patterned fabrics against a plain wall, or plain fabrics against a patterned wall. And I have seen handsome effects created by covering a wall and draping the windows on it with the same fabric or using wallpaper and fabric with matching patterns. The point is that there are so many possibilities that you can never afford to be rigid. Every rule can be broken at the right moment; the trick is in knowing when that moment has come.

Your whole color scheme may evolve from the pattern of a fabric or a paper you fall in love with. Two or three appealing prints may suggest two or three entirely different color schemes. Or you might begin at the other end, with the mental image of a particular color range, and search until you find a pattern you like within it.

The size of the room and the furniture shape your final choice. Scale and mood are almost as important as color. The chintz that is just right for a contemporary love seat is all wrong for a delicate French antique. Great bold prints that might overpower an average-sized library may make strikingly beautiful draperies in a large living room. You can't get into nearly as much trouble going for patterns that are too small; but the effect will be extremely dull. For scale's sake especially, you should, before you make final selections, see sample lengths, not microscopic swatches, in the room and on the furniture it will be used to cover. Often when you have narrowed the field to two or three alternative color schemes (never face a man with a wider choice than that if you want a concise reaction), spreading them out "on location" this way makes your decisions seem almost obvious. You won't place orders until you know exactly where you will use each fabric and have checked your floor plan to make sure no one part of the room is overloaded with print; it is also essential to check your sample against the current available dye lot of the cloth to make sure that the color you have in mind is the one that will be delivered.

Patterns may either disguise or emphasize a point in a room. While curtains of a printed fabric that matches the wallpaper play down the fact that windows may be uneven or strangely proportioned, the same print may be used on a small chair seen against a solid-color background to call attention to the chair's particularly pleasing shape. There is no established formula for mixing patterns, stripes and plain colors. For me, too many prints give a room a restless feeling, but I know a number of people who disagree. Some decorators like mixing five or six patterns in one place. Others believe in repeating the same print again and again for walls, draperies and upholstery. Still others follow a rule of thumb that calls for combining one pattern with one stripe, one plaid or check with a number of different textured solids.

Variety of texture makes a tremendous difference in the total effect of a decorating scheme. Though you may not immediately be conscious of the reason, your eye will register boredom at the sight of a room in which there is only one kind of surface, whether that surface is all silk, all gold leaf or all gingham. The look of wood or stone or metal can provide striking contrast with fabric-covered areas. In a room with a great many paintings, one wall at least cries out for a beautiful tall piece of furniture made of wood.

The effect of texture is subtle. The satiny finish of a beautifully grained piece of wood, the gleam of silk, the nubbly feel of tweed—each contributes its particular sort of dimension to a room. Without demanding too close attention, the surface of velvet adds a depth of color and softness to a decorating plan; a tone-on-tone wallpaper whose pattern becomes clear through a contrast in texture rather than color offers a good background for paintings; a tweedy bedspread has a masculine air.

Basically all fabrics fall into one of two texture categories: formal or informal. Formal fabrics have a silken, fragile look; satins, damasks, brocades, taffetas, moirés, velvets and their near relatives all come under this heading. Informal fabrics have a sturdier look and generally a rougher "hand": coarse cottons, linens and wools are all good examples. By combining several variations of texture from one group or the other in a room, you achieve harmony as well as variety. A couple of cut-velvet pillows on a chaise and a needlepoint footstool work a subtle change in the finished look of a room that is otherwise all Thai silks. The smallest touch—a side chair, a small rug—can make all the difference between appeal and dullness.

Floor
Coverings
The only major color area remaining to be considered is floors. And in spite of all the beauty polished surfaces offer, floors as a rule mean rugs or carpets. In the days of Repairs, Inc., variety in floor coverings was so limited that room plans often began with available carpeting and went on from there. Colors ranged from gray to mud to eggplant and back again. The only available patterns were oriental or the kind of floral swirls that grace hotel corridors. Nowadays there is such great variety that decorating plans need no longer be earth-bound. With the advent of one-of-a-kind designer rugs, there are probably more exciting things going on in carpeting than in any other phase of interior decoration. You can buy looped or shagged or sculptured carpets or rugs in patterns and solids from white or blush pink (Heaven forbid) to ebony. Rugs are even shaped like free-form pools and fruits and flowers—though I feel that the last two categories are best reserved for children's rooms.

Important as floors are, I have always felt it foolish to spend huge sums on rugs for a house or apartment you plan to live in only a year or two. Carpeting never seems to move well from one place to another. And money saved by concentrating on color and effect instead of pluperfect quality pays longer-lasting dividends when it is invested in a really fine piece of furniture. It follows that I am partial to cotton rugs, not only because they come in wonderful colors, launder admirably and wear well, but because they are relatively inexpensive. When it comes time to invest in carpet for a permanent home, I like wool because it takes such glorious dyes and wears so very well. The new synthetic fibers are almost unbelievably easy to clean, but they also soil quickly; and while spots and dirt are easily taken care of, burns are almost always disastrous.

I have always preferred the look of a border of floor framing a rug to wall-to-wall carpeting, but I have not always been able to have my own way on this score. In one case I have had to defer to the piano which is, of course, the single most important piece of furniture in our household. It is an enormous concert grand, and its tone is so beautiful and so lively that we found the living room rug we had, which left part of the floor uncovered, allowed the sound to be too brilliant. So we have had to replace the rug with a wall-to-wall carpet for the acoustics' sake.

Patterned carpet lends a room a warmth it might not otherwise have. Imported rugs now offer a world of intriguing designs to pick from; the Spanish ones seem to me especially fresh and interesting. Oriental rugs are regaining popularity, and though new versions tend to be overly bright, colors in the old ones are wonderfully warm and rich.

Given all these magnificent possibilities, figured rugs must still be chosen with great patience and care. I once set my heart on a glorious full-sized needlepoint rug, only to find when I got it home from England that it fought with the living room paintings and was the wrong size for the dining room. There was nothing to do but sell it and resign myself to the fact that, having hung the paintings we loved so, we would probably have to give up the thought of patterns on the floor. It was not until very recently that I finally got my figured rug, a handsome muted beige-on-beige one for the library, where its design seems to live happily with fabrics that are textured rather than patterned and where the paintings are small in scale, with a quite personal sort of feeling.

While large expanses of pattern may be too much, subtly patterned area rugs can add pleasant color and emphasis to a room without causing conflict or throwing the budget off balance. We have used a number both in New York and in the country, and I honestly think I'd love them even if they weren't my own needlepoint. Before a hearth, in front of a sofa or beneath a coffee table they add a warmth and focus. But once you have them where you want them, it is a good idea to stitch them to the carpet to prevent their "walking" or wrinkling.

In small areas where rugs would be too skittery, I have found paint very successful. I have seen photographs of carpetlike stencil treatments and *trompe l'oeil* effects that were great fun (I'd like to try painting a "rug" on the floor complete with fringe and one corner turned up), but the system that has worked wonderfully for me is spatter painting. You pick a basic color and dot it with any other two or three shades you choose. It's an old New England trick that not only stands up well under traffic, but also goes a long way toward making a poor floor presentable.

Lighting   Next to color, lighting does more than any other single element to create atmosphere. Badly lit, the most exquisitely decorated salon is lost on its audience; the most hospitably designed room can look garish and uninviting. Never was this brought home to me quite so strongly as when we redid the hallway of our apartment not long ago. I had shopped for and assembled all the pieces, including a console and a pair of Louis XV chairs I dearly loved. The only thing left was the painting and a bit of trimming and papering in the elevator hall. That was to be taken care of while we were in Europe. The color change was not drastic; but walls that had been a very pale beige were to be white when we returned. Six weeks later, when we stepped off the elevator, we were almost blinded. When we opened the door, we found the entrance hall as socially appealing as a surgeon's scrub-up room. Yet all the graceful furniture was there and properly placed. The paintings had been rehung just as we'd asked. There was, as a matter of fact, only one thing that hadn't been taken care of: the halls were still lit for beige walls. I couldn't wait; that evening I cut the hallway wattage to less than a third of its former brilliance. (Good rule: when light seems wrong, try changing bulbs before you decide you need a whole new deal in lamps.) I turned off the chandeliers (though they are decorative, the light isn't needed), removed one of three bulbs from the lamp on the console and replaced the remaining forty-watt models with a pair of fifteen-watt bulbs. It was as simple as that: I subdued the light—nothing more—and the glaring canyon became the hall I'd dreamed of.

If it were not so impractical and so wildly expensive, I would probably consider using candles as illumination for every social room in the house; they provide the pleasantest, prettiest, most flattering light I know. This being out of the question, I limit myself to candles on the dining-room table and here and there throughout the house at parties; otherwise I try to make electricity imitate their glow. This means adding lamps to the banks of built-in lights I've already described. Chandeliers are lovely in certain rooms and hallways, but as serious sources of light, they are inefficient and harsh. Many people seem to feel that the bigger the room, the more lamps it needs; I emphatically disagree. I remember once seeing a drawing room lit from sixteen different spots: eight table lamps and eight picture lights; it was like sitting in a lamp store. Too many small lights are distracting; I've seldom seen a room so large that it couldn't be pleasingly lit with four or five good-sized lamps. These may be of various heights, but the light they cast should come from approximately the same level, and the pools of light around them should overlap, not leave corners and edges of darkness all over the room. Spotty light is not only a strain on the eyes; it gives a whole room an eerie, unwelcoming look.

Shades determine the quality of light—whether it will be hard or soft, glowing or glaring. I don't like opaque shades that shed cylinders of light. Nor do I care much for light bounced off ceilings or dimly diffused through glass reflectors; too often it casts hard unbecoming shadows. And although I think ruffled cotton is occasionally pretty in bedrooms, I hate fancy shades. The shades that I think do the pleasantest job of lighting a room are tailored white or pale beige silk with an interesting texture and silk interlinings of very pale beige. On the strictly practical side, since these are sewn rather than glued, they are very easy to wash. But most important is the fact that without colored bulbs that do strange things to a room's colors, this combination produces the kind of candlelike downglow and soft over-all effect that is most inviting in rooms whose function is purely social.

Card tables and reading chairs need good strong well-directed lights beside them. In a shared bedroom, the adjective well-directed is especially important where it concerns bedside lights. They should be strong enough to read by, yet not disturb one person's sleep for the sake of another's novel. One very neat solution to this problem is the miniature spotlights—like the ones used on planes—our friends Barbara and Ted Low have had built into their bedroom.

It is boring to have every intriguing object in a room lit with the same kind and intensity of light, whether it is a picture or a piece of sculpture, large or small, bold or delicate. I think paintings look their best bathed in an even light from below, and this can often be arranged by concealing a fixture behind a small framed photograph or sketch or a flower container that sits on a table or desk. When this is impossible, we use standard picture lights made as inconspicuous as possible by having their reflectors painted to match the walls. Some things should be, in the theatrical phrase, "thrown away"; perhaps a little painting on a stand, a piece of beautiful porcelain, a Battersea box, should be allowed to sit, inviting, not demanding, a closer look. This kind of allowance for discovery makes a room more enjoyable both for you and for your guests.

Antiques

I have left antiques, like dessert, for last, not only because I love them, but also because acquiring them cannot be kept to any kind of schedule. You may start with a well-loved piece or two, find another while you are working out your decorating plans and years later discover something else so perfect for the room that you will wonder how you ever lived without it. The government defines an antique as anything made before 1830; my definition is not so narrow. For me, antiques are any aged pieces that owe part of their beauty to use and loving care. Such pieces give a room its personality, for there is a warmth and charm about them that brand-new, lean-lined modern furniture simply does not have.

A fixture concealed behind the small drawing lights the painting

Many times contemporary furniture does a wonderful job. It is at its very best when built to fit a specific space and serve a particular purpose. Much antique furniture, having been in its own time contemporary, gives clear evidence of the kind of functional design that we are inclined to consider so modern. Armoires were invented to conceal clothes in the days before there were built-in closets. Sideboards were specifically designed to store flatware, hollow silver and linens. Draped beds were built into alcoves for protection from drafts in houses heated by hearth fires. And one of my own favorites, a marvelous table, was made for Louis XV's personal apartment; it would drop through the floor to the kitchen below and reappear laden with food. Its practical purpose was, of course, to protect the privacy of the king and his guest of the moment.

Then as now, craftsmen were commissioned to make any piece of furniture needed for a particular use; since all furniture, standard or specialized, was bought and sold this way, the extra expense involved in a specially designed piece was negligible. Today commissioning special pieces is costly for two reasons. First, there are so few self-employed craftsmen; most skilled designers work, not for themselves, but for mass-producers. Second, a piece designed specifically for a certain job and space rarely fits anywhere else, and this, taken in the light of today's highly mobile life, can turn an otherwise reasonably priced custom piece into an extravagance.

But to me, the greatest extravagance of all is money spent on modern reproductions of antique furniture. Occasionally a reproduction is essential to fill out a set of chairs that must be sturdy and practical. But even when a new table is hand-finished, and when old woods have been used in its construction, it cannot have the glow that comes with years of polishing. It is still a new table, and, as such, it becomes a second-hand table the minute you have bought it. When you sell it, you will never get your money back.

Old copies are quite a different matter; their value increases with age, but not nearly so fast as authentic period furniture actually made in the time when its style was in fashion (these are known as pieces "of the period"). Few people can afford a house full of such rare museum pieces, and even fewer can recognize them. Often a dealer calls a chest or desk "of a certain age," by which he means he is entirely *un*certain how old it is. The only authenticated signed pieces we own—the pair of Louis XV chairs and our dining table—look less antique than much else that is in the house. So it has always seemed to me that, unless you are one of those rare souls who are shopping for museum pieces, it is a waste of time to worry too much about period authenticity. The mere fact of age lends a patina no factory can reproduce. A desk executed after a Chippendale design may be a very fine desk although it only dates back to the early nineteenth century. An Eighteenth-Century chest, though it is actually only a copy of a Seventeenth-Century piece, will still have the beauty that aging can bring.

Blending Periods

When people first became conscious of, and self-conscious about, interior decoration, there was a wild scramble to re-create—chair for chair, tapestry for tapestry, candle snuffer for candle snuffer—a room from another period. A client would direct his decorator to produce a Queen Anne room or a Napoleonic room. The inevitable result was an atmosphere as cheery and warm as a roped-off museum display. No other feeling was possible since, though commissioned by twentieth-century people, the room was designed for the life of another era. Today we have rediscovered the good sense of our ancestors who brought together in their homes not only things

from another country or year, but also anything that made life more comfortable and attractive.

In other words, they blended periods and styles, as we have relearned to do in the past twenty years. The more you look at antiques of all places and periods, the more you recognize a kinship that crosses geographical borders and century marks. Close bonds exist between pieces made in different countries at roughly the same time in history. The furniture of Regency England, Biedermeier Germany and Empire France have an obvious relation to one another. Fine early-American furniture is clearly linked to Georgian English. There is a kinship of levels, too, as witness the similarities between provincial furniture from Sweden and France and Switzerland made during the same periods. All these and many others can live happily in the same house, the same room.

The secret of successful blending is a sort of unself-consciousness that comes with browsing and looking and shopping around until you genuinely know how you feel about this sort of chair, this table, that kind of chest. Only when you really like, even love, a particular piece should you consider

buying it. Then there is only one more caution: keep a wary eye on scale. Handsome though a particular secretary may be, don't let yourself become so enchanted with it that you forget all about the place in which it is to be used. Emotion thus spent can throw a whole room off balance. Fortunately most dealers are happy to let you try out prospective purchases in your home before you buy. This is especially true of major investments. For not only does he, the dealer, usually have an affection for the things he sells and feel some interest in seeing them properly placed, but he also wants to keep you as a contented customer.

    In the course of your browsing and searching, you may come upon a piece that appeals to you very strongly and that is almost, but not quite, right. What can or should you do about it? For a while you should go on

Altering Antiques

(67)

looking; just what you want may be waiting in the shop next door. If, however, you can't forget your first love after a decent interval or if it seems an irresistibly good buy, consider having it altered to fit your purpose. No one would suggest you saw a signed Chippendale table in half to make it into matching consoles; but if the piece is old without being authentic period, you can take liberties. Dealers often do. If a breakfront is too tall, they may cut off a shelf. If the lines of a piece are good but the surface is too poor to be restored, they paint (exactly what we did with the secretary in my bedroom).

Be it known here and now, I do not think coffee grinders make good-looking lamps or planters, and I heartily disapprove of cobbler's-bench coffee tables. Still, since the coffee table is a modern invention, if it is to have any antique charm it must be made or altered to your order. A big table cut down or a handsome old tray with legs added may serve the purpose nicely. I think the lines of Chinese tables have a great elegance and simplicity that go well with both contemporary and classic design. Two of our coffee tables are Chinese and antique. One is a tea table that hasn't been changed; the second, which was too high, I had cut down. (I gave the bottom halves of the legs to a cousin, who added a new top to make her own new coffee table.) Two others, including the long coffee table in front of the library sofa, I designed and had made; both are Chinese in feeling and turned out to be wise investments. They not only fit the places for which they were planned, but, being new and very solidly constructed, are also strong enough to serve as extra seating space when needed.

Two antique Korean chests in our living room began life with bases too ornate for my taste; so I had new, simple ones made and sold the old ones to a decorator, who mounted glass tops on them and sold them for coffee tables. You may find an antique washstand that, with the mirror removed, would work beautifully as a bar. The only way you can train yourself to see all the possibilities is to look and look, ask questions and look some more. At first the process is bewildering. As in a museum, when you look at too much, you find you see nothing. But it is astonishing how quickly you will acquire a feeling that a piece is right by its line, its look. Nobody can rely entirely on his own judgment; even museum curators have been fooled by clever fakes. But you won't be fooled by bad examples. With practice, your eye will learn to reject pieces that don't fit your needs, and you will also begin to catch faint signals from pieces almost hidden in dusty corners. Sooner or later the perfect piece will come to light. Meanwhile you will enjoy the ever-increasing fascination of getting to know a world of beautiful things.

CHAPTER

4

Things You Love

N O home is ever finally, completely, finished. The building may be done and the furniture bought, the color schemes set and the draperies hung, but all this is actually background. The things you search for, discover and collect as long as you live give a home its heart and its feeling.

The pleasure you find in the objects you care for lends them a special quality others sense and share. Since people remember houses in terms of details and touches as well as by general impressions, an heirloom chest, a porcelain box, a big bowl of peonies—though not artistically remarkable or expensive—are infinitely more effective in creating atmosphere than an acre of costly neutral carpet. The latter is there of necessity, because the floor must be covered; the chest, the porcelain, the flowers are there because you love them.

Loved things become a sort of personal signature. The Howard Lindsays have a marvelous chandelier—one of the most beautiful pieces of Venetian glass I have ever seen—that I picture whenever I think of their house in town. White freesia or stephanotis or blue Bristol glass always remind me of Dorothy Fields' apartment; Dr. Wall Worcester porcelain makes me think of our friends Elly and Leonard Bernheim's home. And the mention of the Hallidays' living room conjures up visions not only of clasped hands (they collect them in pictures and sculpture, in china and bronze and even in an Eskimo carving on an ivory tusk), but also of two wonderfully sentimental souvenirs: a needlepoint rug made by Mary that tells the story of Mary and Dick's life together and, resting against an antique music stand, a graceful old violin that belonged to Mary's mother back in Texas.

When John Hay Whitney was our ambassador to Great Britain, I saw the power of personal treasures demonstrated on an enormous scale. The Residence of the United States Ambassador in London is a formidable house, where it would be no trick at all to lose five hundred people. One huge room opens into the next, ad infinitum, and no amount of furniture could. make the place look cluttered, let alone cozy. But with the aid of a number of Jock Whitney's beautiful impressionist paintings, his wife Betsy proceeded to work miracles. The touches she added were personal; in addition to the paintings, she used pieces of her exquisite porcelain, intimate photographs of the family and their friends, small needlepoint rugs here and there and flowers absolutely everywhere. (I remember one great Sèvres vase holding a marvelous arrangement.) True, the paintings were fabulous, and the weekly flower bill was probably one that only Jock could have afforded to pay, but the chill was killed not just by spending vast amounts of money. What really mattered was that Betsy picked the things she added with such care and love that you could feel the warmth even in those mammoth rooms.

On an utterly different scale, a few personal things can make a stiffly conventional hotel room seem easier, more homelike. When, for example, Dick has had to spend five weeks in Boston and a hotel has been home for all that time, I have learned that a few small photographs make us feel we have friends with us; oddly enough, even your own clock, which you need anyway, does a great deal for a room. Your own blanket covers are always an improvement over hotel bedspreads. And even in ten-cent-store brandy glasses, fresh flowers make a world of difference.

Discovering Treasures

It is not size or price but the fact that you care that matters. A great oak highboy, a painting worth thousands of dollars and a shell washed in by the sea may all be among the things you particularly love. A tortoise-shell box you are especially fond of may have been a present from you to you or a birthday gift from a friend. Personal treasures are never acquired all at once.

The furniture in our entrance hall at Rockmeadow illustrates my point. The French provincial chest came from Third Avenue years ago; the carved and gilded French mirror turned up in a Connecticut shop a few years later. Dorothy Hammerstein was with me when, on a pre-Broadway stay in Boston, I discovered the white Meissen clock; she and Oscar gave it to us as an anniversary present the following spring. The hooked rug is one George

Wells made for us (its pattern matches the wallpaper), and the Eighteenth-Century tea caddy we keep full of flowers has been mine for so long I can't remember where on earth it came from.

The most truly personal touches in any house are the things you your-self have made or that friends have made for you. There is a very personal quality about the painting hanging in Madeline Sherwood's dining room—a marvelous reclining man-faced lion that Bob painted for a charity auction. One of the most memorable things about the Rouben Mamoulians' sensational contemporary home in Hollywood is the *trompe l'oeil* Pompeian wall Azadia has painted for the living room; Rouben's delightful contribution is a group of fascinating portraits of Azadia made from shells, from pressed flowers, from semi-precious stones; there is even a *découpage* one that incorporates luggage stickers and post cards from a South American trip they once took. In the Richard Lewine's summer house in Connecticut, the walls are covered with the family's paintings: still lifes by Mary, an enchanting impression of a dog by their daughter Kimmy and a number of the meticulous portraits of houses Dick Lewine loves to paint.

Among our precious possessions are works by, in a sense, "amateur" artists. A tiny squared-off white Lewine house hangs at Rockmeadow. In Dick's New York study there is a pillow with a needlepoint portrait of his hands that Mary Martin made from a photograph. A small bit of needle-work Phyllis Cerf did for Dick in honor of *Flower Drum Song* decorates the Rockmeadow sun room. On my desk I have a stone paperweight Orry-Kelly embellished with *trompe l'oeil* fruit, and my copy of *Mrs. Beeton's*, the English housekeeper's Bible, wears a damask dust cover Dorothy Hammerstein tailored for it.

I especially love the Christmas ornaments friends have made for us. These are self-renewing presents; you have the fun of "receiving" them again each year when you take them out. Georgann Prager does beautiful things with Styrene balls—covering them with bands of glistening ribbon and fancy pins. My niece Margot hung bits of colored glass from a piece of white coral to make a glamorous Christmas decoration. And we have a de-lightful set of blown-out eggshell decorations done by her sister Judy Crichton and her children. Peggy and Howard Cullman once gave us a miniature Christmas tree decorated with special "toys"—a tiny piano, record discs, a Repairs, Inc. ledger, even a little Jonny Mop—and finished with small birds and flowers and ten-cent-store "jewels." Make-believe presents (sugar lumps wrapped in fancy paper) were stacked underneath; a "diamond" hatpin made a star on top; the whole was sprayed with glitter and covered with a glass bell. It was—and still is—absolutely enchanting.

(71)

I have a rather special affection for the needlepoint hearth rug at Rockmeadow because it is the first one I ever made. Having heard the jokes about "loving hands at home," many women shy away from handwork because they are afraid they won't be any good at it. They forget that for ages men and women who have made hobbies of arts frequently produced results that outshone the professionals'. Consider Thomas Jefferson as an architect, Da Vinci as an engineer, Rousseau as a Sunday painter—not to mention all the part-time inventors who, while their creations lack the all-around importance of the wheel, have made more money than the wheel's inventor ever knew existed. Martha Washington was a skilled cook, and Mary Queen of Scots was a needlepoint expert. Though they accomplished wonders, none of these "amateurs" took up his or her hobby for the sake of showing up the professionals. Quite the contrary. They did what they did, as the word "amateur" implies, for the love of it. The work of art, the stroke of genius was an incidental by-product. The important thing was, and is, the pleasure of doing.

Needlework and Related Arts

For many people like me, manual activity eases tension. Once the rhythm is established, needlepoint, knitting or crocheting requires so little conscious thought that I can make all sorts of progress while watching television or talking to a friend. There are other times when sewing provides a welcome chance to be by myself; after an hour or so, problems that have been troubling me often seem to have solved themselves, and I actually feel rested. I know lots of theatre people who find this true. Betty Furness, for example, loves to sew, and she has performed some remarkable feats like ripping apart two dresses to copy the worn-out one she loved by using the fabric from the other. When a busy schedule cut down her sewing time, she switched to knitting (once upon a Fourth of July she did a set of three socks for Frank Sinatra: one red, one white, one blue); she does needlepoint, too, and is wonderfully skilled at both. Celeste Holm once made all her own clothes and still loves to design them, but her all-time pet project is a great hooked rug she has been working on for years. A few Decembers back I went to the Lunts' gem of a house for lunch, and Lynn told me one of Alfred's Christmas presents to her was one of those marvelous sewing machines that does everything but talk; you never have seen a woman more delighted. At the Boston opening of Noel Coward's *Sail Away* a few months later, she was wearing a full-length warp-print taffeta dress and coat she had made herself. The best amateur dressmaker I know is my sister-in-law Wilhelmina, who not only sews beautifully, but also has a sense of style and color that make her clothes marvelous.

The pleasure you take in the final product makes an enormous difference. Even the very first thing you set out to create should be something that you will enjoy having when the sewing or stitching or knitting is over. Carrots may be a foolproof crop, but what's the fun of raising them if they give you hives? By the same token, potholders are a snap to crochet, but unrewarding to own; knowing this, I skipped them and, after a bit of concentrated practice, confined my crocheting to bedspreads. The popcorn-stitch hexagons, of which the finished covers are made, are not that much more complicated to do, and I still feel pleasantly proud every time I see those spreads on two of the beds at Rockmeadow.

When making clothes, it is important to use the best materials. Sleazy fabrics are a great waste of money because they look just as sleazy made up as they do in the bolt. Not only do good fabrics help distract attention from minor errors you may have made, but, in addition to being handsomer, they are usually easier to work with.

There are limits, of course. Tackling a silk-chiffon evening dress or a tailored suit as your first venture in sewing could be a disaster. But there are any number of things that are as simple to make as they are nice to have or to give. A blanket cover of flower-sprigged cotton is both pretty and uncomplicated. And a tablecloth or a breakfast-tray set done in bright patterned linen instead of a solid color has custom-made style in spite of the fact that it is no trick at all to make.

Starting Steps

There are beginners' steps in any kind of handwork. If you have never sewed before, for example, those six lessons that are included in the price of a new sewing machine can be invaluable not only in terms of money saved over trial-and-error starts, but also in the satisfaction that comes from just taming the machine. Although it has been fourteen years since my own free lessons, I can still remember how thrilled I was the day I mastered the threading process. After the sixth session, I not only knew enough to control the machine, but could also adjust patterns so that dresses came close to fitting me.

Since then I have studied the ways in which good clothes are made, the techniques of facing and lining and finishing seams. I have watched fitters pinning alterations in ready-made clothes, and I have asked hundreds of questions. Doctors, artists, lawyers, theatre people—every one loves to talk about his work, and dressmakers are no exception. Flattered by genuine interest, they are helpful, even eager to share tricks of their trade.

Inventing Your Own Projects

Each thing you make teaches you something new. I have discovered that the most satisfying projects for me involve making things I want but am unable to find in stores. I must have made Dick a dozen sports shirts because the ones he likes best to work in are raw silk—impossible to buy ready-made and terribly expensive to order custom tailored. (On one of them I absent-mindedly put the buttonholes on the wrong side, but he wore it in spite of the struggle it was to button.) For myself and for friends, I have made several handbags from a flat foldable design I invented that saves a great deal of packing space and weight, making them ideal for travel. Another sort of invention—this one for people who, like me, read newspapers in bed—is a small washable throw to protect sheets and blanket covers from newsprint smears.

To many people, needlepoint means only chair seats, but it also makes handsome picture frames, book covers and beautiful handbags. Inadvertently I seem to have concentrated my efforts on rugs, but I have also had fun making men's slippers, cases for glasses and compacts and any number of projects smaller in scale. Though their servant-summoning days are all but gone, bell pulls can be more interesting to start out on than cushions; and they make handsome trimming for chair aprons or valances for tester beds. Even pillows have their range of variations; in addition to all-over stitching, I have done them with center medallions and borders of needlework.

To practice the basic background needlepoint stitch, most people begin with a "canvas" (actually it is a stiffened mesh) on which the central fruit or flower design has already been worked. All needlework stores sell such pieces. Once you have the knack, you can try all manner of wonderful things on painted but unstitched canvases with colors and shadings you work out yourself. Or you can design your own pieces, which some stores will then paint to your order. They will do the same with original patterns for other handwork forms, too.

　　If I were a devotee of hooking rugs, I am sure I would avoid those fleets of dreary clipper ships as well as all the variations on the welcome-mat theme. Instead, I might copy motifs from a piece of porcelain or adapt the pattern of a favorite wallpaper. As it happens, I gave up the art almost before I started for two reasons. First, hooked rugs are bulky to carry around (you can do needlepoint rugs in sections and sew them together later). Second, and much more important, the squeak of that immense needle punching through the heavy cloth almost drove Dick wild.

　　On the other hand, since the click of knitting needles has never caused him anguish, I have executed all the classic projects: throws and socks and sweaters and things for the children. For me, knitting dresses is utter folly. It is not just the risk that by the time I have purled my last purl, a hem-line change has probably made the whole project obsolete. Nor is it only the fact that machine-knits are so handsome and so reasonably priced these days. It is purely and simply that by the time I finished the one suit I ever tried, I was so sick of looking at that yarn and those stitches that I could only force myself to wear it once or twice. And the boredom was so acute that, except for an occasional baby blanket, I haven't taken up the needles since.

This brings me to a point which, though it sounds small, is major: don't let yourself fall or be forced into a rut. While you have a big project— a rug, for example—in the works, keep a couple of less ambitious things going, too, for change of pace's sake. When you feel like trying something new, do. If in mid-needlepoint, you have a sudden desire—as I had a few months ago—to try your hand at crewel embroidery, I think you should. Don't let yourself be side-tracked by a backlog of requests for coverlets or carpet slippers. It is fun to comply with such wishes because they represent sincere compliments. On the other hand, a hobby is only worthwhile as long as you enjoy it.

The very thought of sewing or embroidery or needlepoint makes some women so nervous that they turn to other hobbies. Suzanne Taylor doesn't sew, but she has become an expert at refinishing furniture and has, for instance, done a masterful job of decorating a provincial cupboard that is the focal point of the Taylors' dining room in Maine. My sister-in-law Ethel has painted many pieces with the skill of a professional. Most often, what you like to do, you do well. Edna Ferber's gardening skill once coaxed *fraises des bois* out of a penthouse plot in Manhattan; she later made jam of them—labeled "From Ferber's Farm"—while I, with my gangrene thumb, looked on in envy.

Some women take up sculpture; others, music. Whatever the medium, perhaps the greatest pleasure in a hobby comes from the chance to feel your imagination grow. To me, it is exciting just to be among all those bins of different colored wools in a needlework shop. I find myself wandering around the room matching and blending, sorting out families that would be fun to work with and ending, of course, with many more intriguing color schemes than I have projects to use them in.

Creating without a Needle

But you don't have to sew or knit to enjoy this kind of fun. A quick eye, some paste-and-paper skill and practice can add up to a kind of creating that is a tremendous pleasure: the ingenious art of combining. A ten-cent store is a wonderful place to flex your imagination. Walking through one, I know what it would be like if someone turned me loose in a gold mine and told me to stuff my pockets. Everywhere there are plain, basic shapes— jars and baskets, boxes and brandy glasses—and all the trimmings: papers, ribbons, sequins, jewels, fake flowers, spray paints and glitter. One of the first group plus one or two of the second can add up to something very pretty and special, the nicest kind of gift.

The list of things you can put together without resorting to needle and thread is almost endless. Ten-cen-store apothecary jars—small ones for candy, middle-sized for cotton or powder puffs, the big fellows for soaps or a lifetime supply of bath salts—look terribly elegant trimmed with embossed gold paper cut-outs (cherubs, ferns and flowers and borders come in strips and stamped sheets; card shops and stationery stores have them). You can make a useful gift decanter by simply painting the word "Martini" on the front of a big fancy jar. Hatboxes, shoe boxes, glove boxes, any-purpose boxes look wonderful covered with colored or patterned paper, sometimes with leftover pieces of wallpaper (or fabric if you are ambitious) and finished with fringe or braid or a bunch of fake flowers. Given a topping of fake jewels or tiny sea shells, small plastic or lacquered wooden boxes become real works of art. Match boxes and desk accessories can be covered with printed papers; match books, with embroidered ribbon. And brandy glasses, sprayed with paint inside, become custom-colored flower containers.

One Christmas, Danny Kaye's wife, Sylvia, gave me a set of small china flowers so pretty that I hated to lose sight of them. Though they were designed for occasional use to dress up the bottoms of finger bowls, I cemented them like a frame around the edge of a small make-up mirror on my dressing table. The effect was so successful that, using the same technique, I did a big mirror for the guest room with larger porcelain flowers I found on Third Avenue.

Though ten-cent stores are magnificent, they are not the only place to unearth materials. In an antique shop or a card shop you may come across Victorian valentines and sentimental cards; stationery stores are stocked with tapes and ribbons and rickrack-edged notary seals in scarlet, blue and gold. Old magazines, garden catalogues and greeting cards sup-ply the wherewithal for *découpage*. If there is no beach handy, you can find shells in hobby stores. Notion shops and upholstery fabric departments offer braids and fringes and bindings. A hardware store carries paints and jars and glasses; frequently you will find hurricane chimneys there too. A very talented woman, Mrs. Torelli, made two of my favorite lamp bases by lining two giant chimneys with bits of *découpage* I chose from her great stock; when all the cut-outs had been pasted in place, she sprayed the inside of the chimney with white paint to form a background that looks almost like porcelain.

I hoard all sorts of materials for such projects. I save wallpaper sam-ples and bits of fabric from sewing. Wherever, whenever I find them, I buy especially pretty ribbons, papers, bindings, miniature birds, fake flowers and fruit, little toys, bits of porcelain—anything that might con-ceivably be used to make or wrap a gift. (Decorating gift packages is almost as much fun as making the gifts, I think, and Rodgers' Rules of Wrapping state that the slighter the gift, the prettier its cover should be.) All these treasures are stored in clear plastic boxes in the cupboards of my workroom, where they are handy whenever I feel inspired or when a gift-giving day comes along.

The Personal Touch with Flowers
In a sense, flower arranging is also a combining art—one I have always loved. And flowers are, of course, still another way in which to add your personal touch to a room. For you are reflected as much in the kind of

The warmth of the Logans' living room reflects its owners' personalities more than any room I know.

The black and white of the Premingers' living room intensifies the beauty of their paintings.

Our dining room in New York is contemporary in feeling, yet the furniture is antique.

Objects spanning fifteen centuries live happily together in our dining room.

My bedroom in New York is the room in which I feel most at home.

Dorothy Hammerstein's bedroom has tremendous style and elegance.

*The beige tones we love make an excellent background
for the paintings and sculpture in our New York library.*

At Rockmeadow, as in New York, my bedroom has to be blue; it has not changed for twenty-three years.

e height and beautiful woods of this secretary in our New York living room contrast effectively with its surroundings.

The colors and textures in Dick's bedroom in New York make it right for a man.

The personal clutter in my New York bedroom: photographs, flowers, porcelain and little boxes.

The entrance hall at Rockmeadow suggests the feeling of the whole house.

A few of my favorite things: a small flower arrangement, the Henry Moore sculpture, some of my needlepoint and the pitcher Larry Hart gave me for my twenty-first birthday.

A graceful epergne almost guarantees a lovely and lasting flower arrangement.

I like to use flowers that pick up the colors in a painting.

These flowers and the sculpture create a dramatic harmony.

Flowers welcome guests in our New York entrance hall.

Lunch on our terrace at Rockmeadow is one of the pleasures of summer.

The curve of the sofa in the living room at Rockmeadow not only fits the bay window but makes conversation easy. The petit point on the round pillows was done by me.

This painted Swiss cupboard in the dining room suits the informality of our lives at Rockmeadow.

flower you like to have around you as you are in your clothes or furniture or the pictures on your walls. Far too many people feel that flowers are too expensive except for special occasions. As a matter of fact, flowers are only wildly costly when you think in terms of large arrangements or dozens of long-stemmed roses. To me, little bouquets just big enough to catch your eye as you pass a table or desk are most appealing. And these often take only three or four blooms, not a dozen. You can make delightful arrangements by using part of large blossoms. On one week end a few summers back, our house guests became intrigued with some little bisque baskets filled with unfamiliar blue flowers. Actually these "strange" little flowers were not exotic new hybrids but the tips of delphinium from our own garden.

Small flowers are my favorites, but I love lush ones, too. I think rhododendron are glorious, and from English friends I have learned the trick of bringing them indoors beautifully. We wait to do our spring pruning until just before the buds are ready to burst and we use the cuttings to fill big bowls; the flowers then bloom in the house. This system, which seems not to harm our shrubs, gives us magnificent arrangements that last a week or more.

There are flowers—some daisies and Oriental poppies, for instance —meant to live out their lives in gardens. On the other hand, several varieties that are not thought of for cutting give a great lift to indoor arrangements. I have had marvelous luck with hyacinths and geraniums, to take just two examples.

I treasure peonies, lilacs and lilies of the valley, not only for their fragrance, but also because, whatever other miracles botanists have brought to pass, they still have not managed to extend these flowers' season beyond a small part of each year. Some plants—lemon and rose geraniums, for example—we grow for the sake of their wonderfully fragrant leaves, which are particularly nice in small arrangements. I adore ranunculus because they look like chiffon, anemones for their color, freesias for their perfume, carnations and double white stock for their shape and spicy smell. And I don't know of anything lovelier than a bowl of mixed garden roses—especially if there are yellow buds and cabbage roses among them.

I love sharp coral-colored pinks, but we don't grow any truly orange-colored flowers because they do not go well in any of our rooms. As a matter of fact, though I am very fond of any number of flowers, I cannot honestly say I adore everything that blooms. It may be heresy, but I find gladiolas, birds of paradise, poinsettias and anthurium stiff, unyielding and impossible to work with (besides, they are ugly). And if I never see another football-stadium chrysanthemum, I will not feel the least bit deprived.

As far as flower containers are concerned, I like many kinds—porcelain *cache pots*, earthenware bowls, old copper pots—as long as they are opaque enough to hide stems. (Stems are really not pretty, and I have never been able to understand why florists place a premium on long ones.) Whether they are made of metal or glass, I am especially fond of epergnes because their form almost guarantees a graceful arrangement. I also find oval containers congenial, and I like to see cut flowers arranged in masses, not straggling or whisping off in all directions.

Massed plants can also be tremendously effective. The living room at Rockmeadow has a deep bay window that gets good direct morning sun, and instead of upholstering it to use as a window seat, we keep it filled with potted gloxinia, cineraria or begonias, depending on which are fullest and handsomest at the moment. Dick has designed night lighting so that even in the evening the corner lends life and color to the room. Because we are lucky enough to have a greenhouse, we have been able to make a sort of indoor garden of potted plants set along the baseboards of the front hall in our apartment. Our gardener, Paul Heetman, has the greenest thumb I've ever known, and it is thanks to him that we have had such beautiful flowers and plants over the years. In summer when most of our time is spent at Rockmeadow, I substitute fake geraniums—or as Linda calls them, "stuffed flowers"—for the real ones. Although as a general rule I am opposed to imitation flowers, I confess I also use them as an expense- and labor-saving summer replacement for the big bouquet on the living room piano in New York.

The piano, incidentally, is a plain black one (the only finish we like), a concert grand with its graceful curves and satiny surface. It is the only obviously musical part of our decorating scheme. When you consider how big a part music plays in our lives, this may seem surprising. However, there is nothing intrinsically beautiful about the look of a record player, no matter how glorious its tone; for the library I therefore designed a rosewood Regency-style cabinet with grillework doors to hold the hi-fi components. (The expert who installed the set-up assured me the fireplace was the ideal spot for the speakers and was obviously put out when we assured *him* we felt the fireplace was the ideal spot for fires and he would have to work out something else.) To real buffs, our sound system probably seems primitive. Though the sound is stereophonic, we have outlets in only one room. I can only say that, for us, this system is right. Because we are conditioned to concentrate on music, we need only one comfortable, adequately equipped listening place; music that followed Dick casually from room to room would be pure torture to him. For the many people who really feel and hear the difference, elaborate sound systems are certainly worth every bit of the money that is lavished on their installation; for them, the placement of speakers should take precedence over furniture or fireplaces. Our ears are just not tuned to hear the difference; so it would be silly for us to sacrifice the look of a room we love for the sake of a sound quality we can't distinguish.

Many hobbies—and especially collections—do have decidedly decorative properties. Stephen Sondheim's collection of antique games and puzzles includes several giant chessmen that dignify his garden. My sister-in-

The Personal Sound of Music

The Pleasures of Collecting

law Wilhelmina is fascinated by egg shapes; she has lapis lazuli eggs, egg drawings, egg paintings, colored eggs and sculpted ones, and they are most entrancing to look at and to hold. In contrast, back in my Repairs, Inc., days, a man once commissioned me to incorporate his hobby in the decor of his den; an amateur aviator, he ordered furniture built of the planes he had-cracked up; the ceiling was hung with plane models with coordinated spotlights and sound effects. The finished room was impressive but not altogether cheery.

Some people accumulate almost casually the things they love; the John Herseys' house gains great warmth and charm from books and paintings done by friends. A dedicated collector aims to make a point, often to tell the story of the thing he loves. Frequently he is so totally unable to

resist a piece that fills a historic gap that he completely loses sight of aesthetic values.

I have always felt that beautiful things of all ages belong together. To me, rigidly contemporary homes look raw and antiseptic; the furniture is so patently functional that you suspect it is screwed to the floor, and walls are often so conscientiously unadorned that you almost expect plasterers to dash in for a little final smoothing. There is frequently an almost geometric rigidity about the furniture and its arrangement; to draw a chair up

Same mantel, different treatment

to the sofa for a cozy talk or to leave a magazine on a table destroys "the look" of such a room. People living in these glassy houses seem to feel they must give up anything they love from the past. To me, that seems terribly wrong—there are such wonderful things of so many periods to choose from. We all differ in the things we consider beautiful, but an Eighteenth-Century porcelain piece and an ancient fragment of Greek sculpture—both bathed in good Twentieth-Century light—can be delightful in the same room if you enjoy seeing them there.

The closest I have ever come to serious collecting is my quest for antiquities and primitive art that clearly show an influence on contemporary artists: two Cycladic figures and some Persian pieces done about three thousand years ago, for instance. Not long ago I discovered a piece of Coptic embroidery when I was looking for a birthday present for Dick; it is more than a thousand years old, yet you would almost swear it had been created by Dubuffet in the 1960's. In the past few years we've found several such interesting pieces.

Still, on the whole I am eclectic. I have not the discipline to be a true collector; I am drawn to too many different kinds of beauty. I have never wanted to own a great number of any particular thing; I find it impossible to hang pictures three deep or to stack them away in a closet. I am not bound by rules. I fill in no sequences. I buy things for only two reasons: because I love them and because I know I can make a place for them. This way I indulge any number of tastes: for Eighteenth-Century furniture, for Battersea enamel, for the wonderful miniature chests (they were actually salesmen's samples) apprentices made in the days of the great cabinet-makers. Through Dorothy Hammerstein I became fascinated with porcelains. (She has yet to intrigue me with her favorite antique silver.) I am also free to be beguiled by things that fit into no particular category; a case in point is our beautiful Directoire porcelain stove in the sun room at Rockmeadow. I find it a great deal of fun to poke around in fields not especially fashionable at the moment. And my kind of collecting leaves room for frankly sentimental souvenirs—like the bits of needlepoint and paintings friends have made for us, a little silver pitcher Larry Hart gave me, photographs of the grandchildren and Dick's favorite picture of the two of us with a group of Manhattanville nuns—that are, in a sense, the most precious things of all.

Perhaps it is simply that I find enthusiasm more appealing than dedication. If you limit yourself to one kind of object, sooner or later you find yourself buying pieces not for their charm or beauty but for their significance. The next step is the home museum—surely the dustiest and dreariest of answers to any decorating problem. In contrast, there is nothing scientific about the enthusiast's collecting; his only criteria are beauty and personal interest. He may know nothing of the background of a particular piece (though he usually investigates when he gets around to it), but he manages to convey to you his special affection for any number of things. I can't think of a better example than Roy Neuberger, President of the American Federation of Arts, who collects on quite an impressive scale, but whose collection is also delightfully catholic. In his home there are impressionist pictures and contemporary sculpture; there are ancient Egyptian pieces, Greek pieces, Roman and Etruscan fragments. His evident feeling for all these things unites them with a special appeal.

Living with
Collections

I find glass cases or self-conscious displays unappealing. The charm is not necessarily in putting things with their like, but in scattering them and grouping pieces that harmonize rather than match. I like to see lovely things used: antique boxes for cigarettes or candies on a table, old tole pieces for flower containers, porcelain plates as ashtrays (with so many people giving up cigarettes, smoking accessories, like snuff boxes, may soon achieve new status as interesting antiques), candlesticks with candles in them ready to be lit. I don't, on the other hand, believe in letting possessions take over. We know one hostess who freezes her guests; "Cold," she explains, "is so good for the furniture."

One of the most wildly wonderful rooms I have ever seen was, of all things, a bathroom. It belonged to Mrs. Kenneth Keith, who was in those days Slim Hayward; it was huge and it was full of astonishing things she had unearthed goodness knows where. There was a life-sized mahogany bear who held towels in his arms, a white porcelain lion crowned with fresh flowers and a handsome white porcelain stove. There were floor lamps, a magazine rack and wall-to-wall carpeting. (Somehow the all-over carpeting seemed right for this living room-bathroom.) The toilet was screened off, and the tub was so well concealed that I can't remember where it was. The washstand was a lovely old porcelain basin sunk in the center of a long French provincial table. It didn't look much like a bathroom, but it was marvelous because Slim had used so many things she had had fun finding and putting together.

At the same time, I do not think you should feel compelled to set out every single pretty or interesting object you own at the same time. After a few years of pursuing several enthusiasms, it is wise to prune occasionally, to put some things away for a while so that others may have the space and attention they deserve. Insatiable collectors might well take a leaf from the Japanese, who are so economical in their use of beautiful things that they allow you to admire one branch, one flower, one jade bowl at a time. We know a woman who has a great collection of truly beautiful objects, but because there is so much and it is so badly put together, you can spend a whole evening in her house almost without realizing that there are lovely things around you. Yet this same woman would never wear all her jewelry at once. If there is too much, you see nothing. The space around beautiful objects is important. Besides, the practice of putting things away permits you the very special pleasure of rediscovery, of literally seeing the things you love in a new light.

Almost everything that applies to collecting in general is especially true of paintings. Paintings need space and light to be fully appreciated;

still, as with every rule, there have been great experts who paid not the slightest attention. I will never forget being taken to see the paintings Chester Dale kept in his apartment at the Plaza. Though this was only part of his fantastic collection, there were so many pictures that they were hung, unlighted, one above the other, and Mr. Dale would focus a powerful portable spotlight on one painting at a time as he showed visitors through. Our friend Leonard Hanna, a member of the family that did so much to make the Cleveland Museum one of the top museums in the country, did not crowd his paintings; but he made no effort to light them. He always said he knew them so well that it was enough for him to know that they were beautiful and that they were there.

When it comes to hanging paintings, each collector has his own approach. Edward G. Robinson, who has an extraordinarily good eye, started acquiring his pictures long ago; his collection became so fine and so extensive that in order to accommodate the hundreds of people who asked permission to see it each year, he built a separate gallery on his property. The rooms in which Enid Haupt has hung her exquisite collection of impressionist artists (Cézannes, a glorious Gauguin and a superb Van Gogh apple orchard, for examples) are very French and very beautiful, but also very formal. The effect is one of perfection.

We have always bought paintings primarily because we loved them, but from the beginning we have bought with existing rooms in mind rather than with the idea of building the setting around the picture. We have never been willing to crowd walls or hang one picture without regard to the others. When we find ourselves becoming so accustomed to paintings that we no longer see them, we rearrange them. At this point in our collecting lives, buying something new almost always means moving something old to make a place for it. We like to lend paintings to museums and to charity exhibitions as often as possible because we feel art should be shared. But occasionally this practice presents problems. Some of our paintings occupy such dominant places on our walls that it is terribly hard to let them go unless we are going to be away. And every time the problem presents itself, I'm envious of Mrs. Gilbert Chapman, a former president of the Arts Club of Chicago, who owns a number of important, very popular paintings. She is such a talented painter in her own right that she has made copies of her Cubist Picasso, a Braque and others to hang in her home while the originals go on tour.

Many paintings that I find fascinating in museums would be impossible for me to live with. The ones we have bought seem to remain lively and exciting to us year after year. A few have, figuratively, paled and

Traditional furniture, contemporary painting

become boring after a while. For us, whether a picture is large or small, the life-giving quality seems to be strength. Our first painting was a little Chirico of Greek ruins and white horses that we bought in California years ago; at the same time we found two Jean Charlots, one of a pair of lovers, the other of two Mayan figures. The Chirico seemed to lose its power and we sold it; the Charlots, which Dick now has in his bedroom at Rockmeadow, still have remarkable staying power.

We have found that the best work of a minor painter stands up better than a mediocre work by a great painter. The former may approach true greatness; the latter's weaknesses make it dull in time. In the Fauvist period, Braque, who was at other times great, was far from his best; for Vlaminck, on the other hand, these were his finest days.

In painting as in all things, tastes change and grow. My first loves were the Old Masters that my mother introduced me to in those European summers. I have never stopped loving them. It was not hard to add an understanding of and love for the impressionists when I discovered them;

and as time went on, we even acquired a few impressionist and postimpressionist paintings ourselves. But as more and more Renoirs and Monets and Degas took up permanent residence in museums, and prices on the remaining privately owned ones soared, it became evident that if we were going to continue buying paintings, we would have to shift our sights to a new and perhaps less sought-after school. Frankly, the change proved awfully difficult for me. In spite of the words of experts, I had never managed to dredge up the least bit of affection for abstract painting. Yet museums were buying it, some of our best critics liked it, and I felt I had to try. It literally took years. For the first long months of dutiful trudging from gallery to gallery, I saw and felt nothing. After the boredom came outrage. Then one picture here and another there began to get through to me. And finally, after two or three years of eyework and footwork, I honestly came to see what some of the enthusiasm was about. I remain entirely untouched by what I call "mechanical" art; for me, Léger, for example, is too intellectual to inspire emotion. On the other hand, I can now truly love and live happily with such non-objective contemporaries as Jackson Pollock, James Brooks, Riopelle and Soulages.

The Personal Joy of Discovery

Some collections are "made for" people by experts who advise "now you ought to have this" or "the next step is So-and-so," in the old Duveen tradition. And, while this form of collecting is entirely respectable, it has never seemed to me to be much fun. I think discovery is one of the great joys of collecting; and I wouldn't delegate that pleasure to anyone else, even if he were to offer me a free Picasso with every third purchase.

Some people who buy art as an investment buy only established names. But I feel it is wrong to treat paintings like stocks and bonds. Pictures should be bought for pleasure. Your time and money yield a much more satisfying return when they are invested in searching out an unknown work you feel is exactly right for a particular spot than when you accept a name for a name's sake. People who start their serious collecting this way may even reap the extra reward of having their judgment endorsed by the critical powers-that-be over a period of years. We felt very daring and avant garde—for us—when we bought a Nicolas De Staël painting a number of years ago; at the time he was relatively unknown, but he has since been recognized, with Pollock, as a major influence in modern art. The painting is now worth considerably more than we paid for it, and that is nice to know; but the knowledge that we discovered it on our own is almost as rewarding.

A sequel to this story is the pattern of the moves this De Staël we love has made through our apartment. It started at the top of the stairs, where

I always had the feeling it carried me up the steps. When we remodeled the dining room, it was given the place of honor over the sofa. When the living room needed a lift and I suggested moving the painting again, Dick said, "You don't spoil a good first act to fix up a weak second." I agreed in principle, but we tried it anyway, and it looked absolutely wonderful. It is still there, where we have yet to take it for granted. And it is such a great picture that it has done something extraordinary for each of the three places in which it has been hung. Apparently the position at the top of the stairs works as a tryout for the dining-room spot, because the painting by Riopelle that followed the De Staël there now hangs in the dining room, where it looks its best.

Art Buying on a Budget   There is no denying the fact that paintings are expensive. So is sculpture—especially when you consider that an original bronze is usually one of six or eight castings. But paintings and sculpture are not the only kinds of original art in the world. Even if your heart belongs to the classics, you need not give up the thought of collecting. Though the oils of Titian and Michelangelo are securely anchored in museums, it is still possible to find drawings by lesser-known masters and etchings by the top masters within a conceivable price range. What is more, there are limited-edition prints, engravings, colored lithographs, woodcuts, silk-screen prints—the whole range of reproductions which are signed, numbered and, most important, designed by the artist himself to be reproduced in a particular fashion. For these reasons, although they are not enormously expensive, they do have real value and are, in quality, vastly superior to the muddied, mass-produced reproductions which, in terms of artistic merit, are seldom worth the molding it takes to frame them.

In recent years the Museum of Modern Art in New York and many museums throughout the country have operated very imaginative programs through which it is possible to rent original works of art for a period of a few months. If you decide you want to buy, you may apply the rental fee against the purchase price. Among other obvious advantages, the museum staff has made the selection from which you choose, giving you the benefit of its judgment and knowledge.

Auction Buying   On rare occasions we have bought art at auction—a head of Renoir by Maillol and three watercolors (a Dufy of Taormina where we spent our honeymoon, a Boudin *plage* and a Jongkind). But for the most part we do our art buying through established galleries. While an auctioneer cannot guarantee authenticity, a reputable dealer generally stands behind each thing he sells. There is no pressure. Most dealers are willing to let you try out paintings in your own home before you make a final decision, and they will usually arrange for you to pay for your purchase over a period of time.

Though you do sometimes find art bargains at auctions, we don't rely on them as a source of paintings or sculpture. And because you have little control over the price, I am reluctant to sell anything at auction. (You can put stop bids on the items you sell, but then you are charged a commission even if the pieces aren't sold.) Still, I must admit I think auctions can be great fun and a source of worthwhile bargains in other categories. You can, for instance, often make very good buys in upholstered furniture, which is so expensive when it's new.

Auctions can be extremely instructive. By examining pieces carefully at the exhibition and listening closely at the sale, you discover what kinds of things the public wants and what prices they will bring. I cannot be too emphatic about the importance of the pre-sale exhibition. If you have missed it, don't buy at the sale. It represents the only chance you have to examine the merchandise closely and in an atmosphere of relative calm. It is then you should set a firm ceiling price on each object you'd consider buying, and that figure should be what the piece is worth to you, not some theoretical amount the world at large might be offering at the moment. If the lot includes several pieces of which you can use only one, then the price that is right as far as you are concerned is the value of that piece alone. I once came across a lot of fifteen old watercolors done by itinerant amateurs; nine were enchanting enough to make wonderful Christmas presents. I bought the lot at a price that was right for the nine and was lucky enough to find a buyer for the other six. Even framed, my gifts cost very little. But since resale is such an iffy proposition, it should never figure in the limit you set.

Unless you do set limits in advance, it is terribly easy to be carried away in a burst of competitive zeal when the actual bidding starts. Auctions often produce a kind of mass hysteria not unlike gambling fever. Suddenly it's a game to beat. Losing touch with real value, you find yourself bidding, not to buy the object on the block, but to win, or to keep "that revolting man with the mustache" from getting it. Three dollars is no price at all for a stuffed horse—if you need a stuffed horse. If you don't, you've not only lost three dollars, you've gained a problem of no mean proportions.

As a matter of fact, I've found I make my best buys when I stay away from the sale itself. At any reliable auction gallery, when you don't plan to be present, you can leave an order bid—which is to say, you may register the maximum you are prepared to pay for a particular item; on the day of the sale the gallery becomes, in a sense, your agent, honor-bound to buy the piece at the lowest possible price up to the limit you have set. Frequently by order bidding I have bought things for less than I was actually willing to offer. I remember an occasion when the contents of a most elaborate household were put up for sale. There were seven sets of flat silver in my pattern. The gallery sold them separately, and I left a bid of approximately a third of what the auctioneer estimated each would bring. Though I didn't go to the sale, I got my silver—the seventh lot—for exactly half my own price.

On the rare occasions when a well-publicized important personal collection of paintings or porcelain or furniture goes up for sale, snob value tends to inflate prices. A big name brings out top dealers and collectors on an international level. And though you may be able to buy a handsome status symbol, you won't find any bargains. Although a sale may be referred to as an offering of paintings or furniture, it is rare that an auction consists exclusively of one kind of item. Sale pieces may come from one source or several, and the gallery fills out the catalogue with pieces it has been given to sell on consignment. Knowing this can often lead you to bargains since, for example, the porcelain at a sale of paintings generally brings less than it would have brought at a sale advertised to attract porcelain buyers.

You can never tell what you may find at an auction. You may follow sales of antiques for months without coming across the remotest approximation of a chest that would be right for your living room. Yet in the course of your search you may unearth a Regency clock that is perfect for the hall.

Wherever you shop—whether at auctions, small galleries or big stores —your greatest personal treasures will most often be happened on; they cannot be commandeered. You cannot pick up the phone and order them from a list. The highboy that doesn't exist this week may quite possibly turn up next. Tomorrow's find may be that porcelain box you love; or that bowl that is perfect for peonies. Never do such things conform to a schedule—and that's part of their charm.

PART TWO

ENTERTAINING
AT HOME

Parties Large and Small

I LOVE parties in all shapes and sizes: big ones and little ones, the formal occasion that you know has taken weeks of planning and the wonderful evening that just happens when two or four or six friends get together. Invitations are exciting whether they are engraved or hand-written or phoned. They mean that nice things are about to happen. And much as I look forward to the pleasure of being someone else's guest, sending out invitations of my own gives me a happy feeling of anticipation.

I enjoy my own parties because all the things that contribute to an evening—the thinking, the planning, the menu-making—are fun. I like the way my house looks just before guests arrive: the lights, the bowls of flowers, the place cards in place and the tables prettily set. But it is at its best, I think, a few minutes later, when the rooms are filled with friends who are having a good time.

In the thirty-four years we've been married, I suppose we have given hundreds of parties and entertained thousands of people. Yet it's no easier for me to say exactly what makes an evening go than it is to explain a great night in the theatre. I'll never know why it is that at one performance sixteen hundred people have the time of their lives and the next night the audience reacts to the same lines and the same songs as though it were dumb and blind. It is everything, and it is nothing you can quite put your finger on.

Parties are remembered for many different reasons. I remember one particular evening at Paul Gallico's apartment in Cap d'Antibes because the view of the Mediterranean was so especially beautiful. I remember a chamber-music evening at Alfred Newman's in Hollywood, when the musicians wore Eighteenth-Century knee breeches and perukes. And I remember a lunch with Countess Elsie Lee Gozzi in Venice. She picked us up at the hotel in her own *motoscafo*. The meal was perfect, but I can't remember, specifically, what we ate. I do remember her apartment in detail —the huge and very elegant living room–dining room, and the beautiful rose garden; and I'm sure that the reason I recall its tremendous chic so vividly is that it all existed within the walls of the Fortuny fabric factory, which she owns.

If we are lucky enough to be asked, I enjoy knowing I am going to see the Averell Harrimans' marvelous collection of paintings or the view from Katharine Cornell's house in Rockland County (at night the trains across the Hudson look like something straight out of F. A. O. Schwarz). But these are fringe benefits; the basic reason for going to a party is people. No matter how good the food or the wine or the music, if the people are dull, the party is a failure. And, when it comes to entertaining, beginning with a real liking for people is the best guarantee of success.

If there is a single key, that is it.

Neysa McMein will always be thought of as a great hostess. But I can't remember anything I ever had to eat at her apartment. Food was a matter of tremendous unimportance to her and to us—when we were her guests. What mattered was her gift for filling her house with gay and amusing people: Beatrice Lillie, Harold Ross, Jane Grant, Alexander Woollcott, Robert Sherwood—writers and theatre people and artists. Her special kind of warmth (everything at Neysa's seemed to turn into a game) kindled more life and spirit in all of us than we ever had any place else.

Guest Lists   The most important decisions a hostess has to make have to do with the guest list. Numbers are pretty much dictated by the size of the dining and living rooms, the formality of the occasion and the amount of available help. Somehow it is fine to crowd forty people at an informal buffet party but uncomfortable to crowd ten in a space meant for eight at a seated dinner.

Your guest list usually starts with the people you want most to see. Next come people who, in addition to being good friends, are people to whom you are obligated, people who have entertained you. Then comes the analyzing. I try literally to imagine my guests meeting each other. Do they have interests in common? Will they enjoy knowing each other? Keeping the picture in mind, I fill out my list with people I think will add the most life to that particular evening. A party made up exclusively of people you

(96)

"owe" is bound to be a little sticky because, from the beginning, you think of it as a duty, not a pleasure.

Everyone has close friends whom others find difficult or dull. In spite of the fact that you love them, you are tempted to leave them out. Personally, I have finally realized that the guilt I feel when I do is simply not worth the gain. Usually they blend into a largish party. And the few times when they have discovered kindred souls and blossomed, their pleasure has been more than enough reward for any worry involved. Sometimes the most unlikely combination of guests results in a highly successful party. But when this happens I think it comes under the heading of great good luck. At any rate, don't plan to invite an odd mixture of people to insure a happy time for all.

Once in a great while, I feel two people—a man and a woman—would particularly enjoy knowing each other, and I find myself putting one and one together hoping to get a couple instead of two. But I never make their pairing off the point of the evening. And when they do come face to face, I try to keep my introductions reasonably subtle. (I once was so subtle that neither party got the idea at all, and each went home with someone else.)

Uneven numbers are not ideal, but they don't spell disaster either. I have, as does everyone, a number of friends who are single or widowed or divorced. And I refuse to cut them out of my life just because they don't come with partners. I invite extra men when I can, and I welcome women friends singly when that is impossible. After all, as George Kaufman and Edna Ferber put it in *Dinner at Eight*, "They're invited for dining, not mating."

I try to avoid collecting the same faces for every party. The most scintillating people on earth get bored with each other after too-constant companionship. A really complete guest record book (date, menu and fellow guests) helps avoid duplications, but I have never had the patience to keep one up to date. In a small pocket diary I do keep a day-by-day record of our engagements, including lists of guests we entertain, and I find it a tremendous help. As it happens, I don't make a note of what we've served each evening. But recording the key dish along with each group of guests can save you from too frequent repetition.

The liveliest parties mix crowds, interests and professions. Too often a whole party full of lawyers or brokers or insurance men withdraws into shop talk, leaving wives deserted. In groups where everyone knows everyone else too well—at parties of movie people in Hollywood, for example— such men-women splits are almost sure to take place.

New faces make a party more interesting. I've always liked the quotation: "Be not forgetful to entertain strangers, for thereby some have entertained angels unawares." While you will seldom find yourself serving souf-flés to saints, I do believe you should entertain new people whenever you can.

If you live in a city, there are foreign consulates; in New York there is the UN and all its missions. In each of these there are men and women long-ing to know more about us and our country—not just the Very Important People, whose calendars are crowded with diplomatic engagements, but the everyday echelons, easier to meet and often more fun to know.

Special Guests Living in New York, we've met a number of UN people. We've come to know Madame Pandit through my sister-in-law; Paul Hoffman and Henry Cabot Lodge through other friends. The UN Hospitality Committee has in-troduced us to any number of other interesting delegation members. On several occasions we've given luncheons and dinners for them before an art show. The guest list so far has included Greeks and New Zealanders, Colombians and Indians, British and Chinese and Turks. Once the date and time are set, the Committee makes the contacts. We always know that there will be six at a time, but we are never sure who our guests will be until a few days before they arrive. It's suspenseful, but we've always been delight-fully surprised. (I remember boning up on Indonesia one time for a lunch at the UN itself, only to end up seated next to one of the most articulate, best-informed men that I have ever met—not Indonesian, but English.) The

talk never fails to be fascinating, and we've kept in touch with several Committee-introduced guests who've gone on to other jobs and, sometimes, other countries.

The first step toward meeting new people from overseas is usually a letter. If there are foreign consulates in your city, write the consul general or, in the case of the UN, the chairman of the Hospitality Committee at the UN Secretariat or the head of an individual national mission. Explain briefly that you would like to entertain guests from abroad; follow your note with a call for an appointment. The consul himself may offer to introduce you to visitors or members of his staff; or he may suggest other individuals and organizations you will find helpful. In any case, a person-to-person meeting gives both of you the chance to explore the possibilities fully. And a little firsthand knowledge of your interests, your home and family, can help him arrange for you to meet people you'll really enjoy knowing.

If there are no consulates where you live, there may be clubs like the Alliance Francaise or the American-Scandinavian Foundation. They are listed in the phone book, and their officers are usually very gracious and anxious to be helpful.

Recently, with the help of local women's clubs and civic groups, the United States Travel Service has launched a hospitality program called "America at Home." It arranges for tourists from abroad to spend evenings with American families, and it now operates in more than twenty cities across the country.

In smaller towns, especially where there are colleges or universities, you will often find newcomers from other parts of the world who bring with them new viewpoints that can mean a refreshing change for everyone. The public- or community-relations director of a school can often advise you. And the minister of your church, knowing of your interest and of new members of the congregation, will certainly be happy to help.

Teatime or the cocktail hour is a pleasant time to ask foreign guests to your home for the first time; that way neither of you is forced to commit yourself to a whole evening's companionship until you are at least slightly acquainted. You might also take a page from the UN Hospitality Committee and plan your first meeting as a prelude to some other event—a play or a concert or an exhibition of paintings. In any case, keep the group small and make sure that your new guests don't feel they're invited as part of the entertainment. There's a vast difference between a guest and a guest speaker.

When in doubt about food or drink, ask. If we're having luncheon, I usually plan to serve fish and I always make sure there is chilled orange juice on hand. Several religions forbid their members to drink alcohol or eat meat. Your guests might be, as mine have been, among them.

I think you should invite new people whom you find attractive to your house as soon as you can. It is a mistake to wait for them to make the overture. The attraction has almost surely been mutual. And no one is too old or too young or too important not to be flattered by such an invitation.

Parties also gain a great deal from a blending of age groups. Our annual Christmas Eve party is wonderfully mixed that way. On the guest list are our children, our grandchildren, our friends, their parents, older members of our own families, children of our friends and friends of our children. The ages run from nine to over eighty. And though all these people may have very little in common except us, there is a warm family feeling everywhere, a depth of affection that exists only among generations, that makes Christmas Eve, for me, one of the very nicest nights of the year.

Guests of Honor

If you are giving a party in someone's honor, plan with the guest of honor in mind. Though that rule sounds elementary, it is often ignored. Without thinking, a hostess may announce a party *for* a visiting aunt, then proceed to invite guests as though the aunt were not going to be there. Aunt Sophie's friends might be quite different from those you would invite under other circumstances. But after all, if the party is for Aunt Sophie, her friends should head the list. Even if you have never met them face to face, the fact that your guest of honor would be happy to see them is introduction enough.

The list need not be limited to her intimate friends. You'd include, as a matter of course, friends of your own whom you think she would enjoy meeting. But your guest's enjoyment should be uppermost in your thoughts as you make your plans.

The same rule applies to entertainment. I remember a party given for us in California years ago. It was a large lovely dinner at an awfully elaborate beach house. It was all very pleasant indeed until we got up from dinner. The host announced poker. As at most Hollywood parties, there were two games: A Big Game for the men, *a little one* for the women. Well, we don't play cards very often, and we're not very good at gambling. And it developed that even the little-game stakes were too high for our inexperience. So the evening ended with our sitting on a sofa talking to each other while everyone else played.

Business Guests

Business entertaining at home presents somewhat special problems. If it is a "command performance," the people involved may quite possibly be older or lead lives quite different from yours. Assuming that the business guest is someone you have never met, the logical place to begin is by finding out as much about him as you possibly can. What is he like? Is he a hail-fellow-well-met type or a man who frowns on lunchtime martinis? Is he a golfer, a poker player, a collector of first editions? Can your husband tell you anything about the man's wife?

Presumably it's to be dinner and a chance to get better acquainted. If so, numbers are important. An evening for just the four of you may be too strong a dose. In such a situation, dinner for six seems just about ideal. If you know a couple whose interests jibe with your business guests', wonderful. If not, choose friends who are pleasant rather than boisterous and who really like meeting new people.

Then keep your planning as relaxed as possible. Think of the most successful dinner you've ever given and try to give another just like it. Don't aim for new heights of elegance to match a scale on which you think your guests live. An unsure hostess is never at her best. Besides, your guess about their life may be absolutely wrong. So set your table with the pretty things you already own, pick a menu you know you do especially well, and plan to enjoy your guests. Chances are the evening will turn out to be great fun.

Out-of-Town Guests

Acquaintances in town for a visit are special guests of a quite different kind. Often they have entertained you in their own home towns, and you want to do something particularly nice for them. But their time is limited, and it hardly makes sense to devote a whole evening to helping them get to know fellow dinner guests they may never see again.

Because visitors to New York almost always want to go to the theatre, we like to ask them up to the apartment for drinks (not a cocktail party), then take them out to dinner. If it is someone brand new to town, we are apt to choose a restaurant for its uniquely New York atmosphere, rather than for its *haute cuisine*. And even if it is someone who has been here many times, the most expensive, most exclusive places can be so stiff and formal that they spoil the occasion. On the other hand, I'm not mad about arty little places that say they serve Italian food when what they really mean is pasta with lots of garlic. A French restaurant where the food is excellent and the mood is gay and a small gem of a coffee house that serves good Northern Italian food are among our favorites for entertaining, and much more fun for us and our guests than the really pretentious places.

Many people feel it shows great thoughtfulness for the host to order dinner at a restaurant in advance. But ordering ahead puts a premium on split-second promptness, and it also limits the meal to the less exciting dishes you're sure everyone will like. The host may suggest a particularly good appetizer or recommend a house specialty; and he should suggest a wine. Personally, I think it is nice to let guests select the things they themselves like best. In any case, you should allow them the fun of picking their own desserts.

Wherever you live, there are sights that belong to your town alone. Whether a theatre or restaurant or museum, or simply a place from which there is an extraordinary view, your guests will be delighted and flattered to be shown. Don't spoil their good time and your own by apologizing that "this isn't as big" or as grand or as what-have-you as something they've seen before. First, you could be wrong. And second, it's embarrassing to everybody present. The newness and your hospitality are the real pleasures of the day.

Setting the Style

We know a number of wonderful hostesses, and each has her own sure style. Parties at the Joshua Logans' are usually very large, but some of our pleasantest evenings have been spent dining alone with them. Edna Ferber's dinners are small (eight guests, usually) and exquisitely planned; the food is delicious; the talk, of the very best. Betty Furness invites fifty or sixty of the most interesting people in the world (at her last, there were politicians, a plastic surgeon, lawyers, television writers and performers), crowds them quite a lot, makes sure there's plenty of good food and a piano player or two, and everyone talks and eats and sings and has a marvelous time. Our two daughters entertain differently and each very successfully in her own way. Mary will have a gang descend—that's the only way to describe it—on a moment's notice, and the party will be crowded and gay and everyone will serve himself. Linda, who likes the planning part as much as Mary finds it tedious, concentrates on small dinners with a perfectly delicious meal and everything looking inviting.

No amateur I know is as good at telling stories as Johnny Green; and very few people are as enthusiastic fanciers of food. He loves to take a creative hand in the preparations of dinner for guests. As for the single men I know, most of them are so terribly spoiled that they simply don't feel obligated to entertain. The few who do either give cocktail parties (which I am inclined to skip) or, because they live in small apartments that are neither arranged nor equipped for it, entertain in restaurants.

Holiday Parties

We've been to some wonderful holiday parties. I remember one marvelous Russian Easter party George Balanchine gave in Boston. There was fantastic food (even bear-liver *pâté*) and the wildest variety of liqueurs ever assembled. The most spirited Independence Day celebration we've ever been invited to took place at the Joseph Cottens' in Beverly Hills; it had everything a Fourth of July party should have—bunting, beer, children and grandparents, movie stars, and a brass band and Ethel Merman singing *The Star-Spangled Banner*.

But holiday parties don't have to be all that elaborate. One of the nicest things that happens to us in any year is the dinner Dorothy and Howard Lindsay give when they are in New York on Christmas night. It is never a big party, never noisy. Almost the same people are there from year to year. Dorothy's collection of animated antique toys has been brought out for the season; there's a snow scene, a ship that sails the ocean and a collection of old music boxes. If Arthur Schwartz is there, he plays the piano. People are pleasantly tired and very happy to see each other. It's a very *gemütlich* evening.

Betty Comden always asks people for New Year's night, which is especially nice because although it is usually a big party, it is a relaxed, easing-down kind of time. On the other hand, I think that New Year's Eve is the most ungrateful night of the year for entertaining. It is difficult to make a success of gaiety because everyone is trying so hard to have a good time. You accept invitations out of desperation because you're afraid you may not have anything to do—although 364 other nights of the year, you wouldn't care. People have a compulsion about getting around, and they're apt to walk out on your dinner to be on time for a midnight toast somewhere else. The most delightful New Year's Eves we've spent have been in the country with eight of us for dinner, all pretending it was another night.

If, having faced all the drawbacks, you still feel you must ask guests for New Year's Eve, it's best to keep things very informal: a bar set-up and simple food that can survive being left set out on the sideboard through the evening. Sandwiches curl up and die with the passing of time; an assortment of cheese and meats and breads has greater staying power. You might also offer brownies and *Schnecken* and hot coffee. It's important, this night above all, to have plenty of whatever you serve; for often guests who start on the party round in midafternoon may have missed a meal or two en route to your house.

No two hostesses, no two homes, are exactly alike. And any number of factors determine the way you like best to entertain. Do you like large groups or small ones? Would you rather be your own chef or have someone else do the cooking? Can you hire helping hands if you need them? (There are parts of the country where extra help is hard to find even when you are quite able to afford it.) What can you buy? A cake from the Woman's Exchange? Casseroles from a specialty kitchen? Is there a party service ready with chairs and china and coffee urns to supplement your own? Do you have your best times entertaining informally outdoors or inside by candlelight? The answers to these and questions like them shape your favorite kind of party.

Formal or Informal

I can remember lots of perfectly beautiful formal parties. But I can also recall several complete with footmen and candlelight that were terribly, terribly dull. The success of a party rarely depends on formality or the lack of it. Two of the pleasantest memories I have are of one night when Danny Kaye cooked steaks outdoors in Palm Springs and another—also in Palm Springs—when Dinah Shore concocted a delicious chicken dinner. Once we were invited to President Roosevelt's home at Hyde Park for lunch. I've never spent a more fascinating afternoon, and the menu was hot dogs and hamburgers.

To me, the ideal way to entertain is at a small seated dinner for six or eight friends. It is the most fun for me as hostess, and I think my guests enjoy it most, too. In these days when lives are so busy and there isn't enough time to see all the people you love and want to keep up with, there's something particularly flattering about being included in a small group. It's odd that the difference between eight and ten is so great; conversation that includes everyone is possible with eight, but when there are ten it tends to split into two groups. So, while you can expand a dinner to ten or twelve or more if you have a large household, I think you sacrifice intimacy. And the pleasure of being able to meet and get to know a small group of interesting people far outweighs the uncertain excitement of a big party where, however fascinating or amusing the guests may be, you never really talk to a soul.

Only last week end two consecutive parties brought this truth home to me sharply. The first was a birthday party for thirty-five; the assembled names were brilliant, their owners extraordinarily bright and witty. Yet much as I would have loved real conversation with any of them, there was time for only superficial chitchat. The next night, Dick and I had dinner with a young publisher, Larry Hughes, and his wife, Rose. They had invited two other couples, a young novelist and a well-known critic and their wives. The party was small enough for each of us to feel he could get to know the others, and we became so engrossed in getting acquainted that the evening raced by. Suddenly it was one o'clock, and we'd had such a good time we really hated to leave even then.

A small dinner can be very formal. But it can also be done with tremendous charm in an informal way. Dick and I often go to dinner at the home of Georgann and Stanley Prager, a young couple in the theatre. They have three small children, they have no help, and Georgann, who is as pretty as can be and makes many of the very smart clothes she wears, manages everything beautifully. She starts by inviting people who, she feels, would enjoy meeting each other. When we first knew them, she served drinks and

simple hors d'oeuvres in the living room. Then we all moved on to a wonderful big round table in her kitchen for a delicious casserole, a first-rate salad and a dessert she had translated from a fine French cookbook. Everything was passed from one person to another, the talk was good and we never failed to have a delightful evening. The same informal atmosphere prevails even though the Pragers have moved to a new apartment which has a proper dining room.

Brunch or Lunch

But depending on time, place and people, there are all sorts of parties that are great fun to give and to go to. Brunch is perfect for a summer Sunday in the country or on a wintry city week end. The timing is flexible, the service is casual—often a buffet menu highlighted by a chafing dish—and your guests (twelve or fourteen is just about right, I think) come and go as

they please. The plan has a great deal of charm to recommend it, particularly in the country, where you may have a shaded terrace to serve on or a swimming pool to repair to before and after.

Luncheons are another pretty summer thought. You might have a seated party—a mixed group on Sunday or women friends during the week. In any case, you'll suit your food to the season: refreshing salads, cold meats and fruits in the summer; in winter, *crêpes* with a crabmeat curry or some other dish that's substantially warming but has a certain flair as well. If there are more than six or eight of you, you'll probably make it buffet.

Buffet is an elastic term. In a broad sense, it simply means that guests fill their own plates. In practice, it may mean a dinner with no serving help at which six guests serve themselves from a sideboard; or a party for fifty or sixty with all sorts of extra servants. It may mean tremendous variety or no more courses than you would serve at a regular seated dinner. Your guests might all eat at the same time and be seated at tables according to plan. Or they might help themselves as the spirit moves them and sit anywhere they please—dining room, living room, even on stairs in the hall.

When your winter dinner guests number more than twelve, a seated buffet is often the most satisfactory answer. Really large numbers of people can be entertained at a cocktail-buffet (no formal seating arrangement, greater variety of food). I remember a wildly successful one that Moss and Kitty Hart gave. There were all sorts of people: diplomats, UN delegates, actors, writers and directors, doctors and lawyers and a sprinkling of great beauties. When they felt hungry, guests simply helped themselves from the buffet and sat down where they chose. An omelet specialist named Rudolph Stanish set up his portable equipment, including a tantalizing array of fillings—*fines herbes*, cheese, bacon, sour cream and caviar—and turned out omelets to order in a matter of minutes. It was fascinating to watch, and the smell was simply heavenly. Though there were other dishes—cold meats, lobster salad, smoked salmon and so on—it was the omelets that made the menu special.

A seated buffet requires more planning. The food is prepared with greater care. And guests are not expected to ferret out little corners in which to perch while balancing plates on their laps. There are tables and a seating scheme. The tables should be completely set with glasses, salts and peppers, ashtrays, napkins and silver; only the plates for the main course should be on the buffet. When it is time for dessert, the buffet table should be cleared and dessert plates, silver and coffee set out.

If you have a really large group in mind, you might have a late-evening party. Ask guests to drop in for drinks at about nine-thirty and set

Evening Parties

out a buffet supper around half past eleven. The menu should be simple—perhaps a cold Danish ham, a big bowl of potato salad, a board of assorted cheese with bread and crackers plus some little cakes and coffee. If you're ambitious and fairly expert, you might even turn omelet chef yourself. Mix your eggs in a great bowl; set out the fillings (sliced mushrooms, chopped shrimp, caviar, sour cream or whatever you like best) on or near the buffet table, then with a warm pan and a cool head, go into production. Guests leave this sort of party with a sense of having had the hostess's personal attention.

Cocktail Parties

I don't think the same feeling exists at the end of a giant cocktail party —to me, a form of legalized torture. However gracious the hostess's motives, there is always a faint air of paying off obligations *en masse*. There are too many people and too few places to sit. And conversation is shallow or fragmented or both.

Guests are uncertain about the hours involved. If they arrive too late, they are apt to run into a lot of left-over canapés and people—all of them on the soggy side. The hostess, by this time exhausted, has planned to invite the few people who show no signs of leaving to stay for some food although she has had only the sketchiest notion of how much to prepare. Meanwhile guests who aren't sure they'll be asked to stay either search for friends with whom to have dinner or wander home to forage in an empty icebox.

Cocktail parties can't be all bad. Nor can all cocktail parties be bad. When visiting out-of-towners with crowded schedules can't fit in lunch or dinner, it can be very pleasant to have six or eight or ten good friends stop by for drinks in the early evening. In a group that small, everyone does have a chance to talk and catch up.

Smallish cocktail parties can also be good fun before a dinner dance or after a football game or just as a way of getting together during the Christmas holidays. And they are often an especially good way for college-age members of a family to entertain. The guest list can be kept flexible enough to accommodate almost any number of last-minute invitations, and even a young host or hostess with very little experience in party giving can run things, as is rarely true in the case of a seated dinner.

Whether she intends it to or not, a party reveals how its hostess feels about her guests. A carelessly organized party shows a lack of interest. A hostess tangled in her own problems is usually too distracted to consider, much less enjoy, her guests. Genuinely thoughtful planning puts guests at ease, and guests who feel at ease have a good time.

Invitations and Timing

To begin at the very beginning, planning the party itself starts with the invitations. The engraved, formally worded kind are appropriate, I think, only for very large, very special parties. And I don't like telegrams unless there is an awfully good reason—usually a can't-reach-you-any-other-way sort of emergency; whatever the message, they seem businesslike rather than social. If dinner is to be informal, I phone. If it is black tie, and there will be a dozen or more guests, I write short notes ("Will you come to dinner at seven-forty-five . . . ?") on small message cards with our name and address engraved at the top.

Clarity is a thousand times more important than form. Both hostess and guest must have the same date, time and place in mind. This may sound too elementary for words, but confusions do crop up. There have been evenings when we have stepped out of the door only to collide with tomorrow's dinner guests arriving a day early. And once we ourselves turned up for cocktails a week ahead of schedule. Written invitations are always safest. Those passed along via middleman or maid invite trouble along with the guests.

In California it is the custom to issue what I call "two-timed" invitations, and I think they make awfully good sense. The cards read, "Cocktails, seven-thirty; dinner, eight-thirty." Knowing this, guests can time their arrival: on the dot if they like, later if they are of the one-not-two-cocktails persuasion.

What the invitation involves should also be made absolutely clear. Simple as this may seem, it's not. Recently one of our daughters got a note from a friend which said only "Buffet, eight o'clock." Assuming that this meant dinner, she and her husband arrived, unfed, at ten minutes after the hour. They were both understandably faint when the supper was laid out at eleven.

Such miscalculations, while they are uncomfortable for the guests, are not disastrous for the hostess. But it can be miserable for the hostess when a guest's misunderstanding makes him late enough to ruin the saddle of lamb or deflate the soufflé.

This is a subject I feel very strongly about. It has always seemed to me that food at a really fine restaurant gains tremendously from the fact that the diner waits for the food. Be it soufflé or sole, it arrives *au point*—when it is its most delicious. At home, the food waits for you and your guests, and few great dishes can be their best after more than a short delay. It is, therefore, perfectly reasonable to expect dinner guests to arrive within a quarter of an hour of the appointed time.

I also hope guests will be prompt because I believe there is such a thing *Drinks* as a too-long cocktail hour. It is a risky business to expect guests to extend drinking time much beyond sixty minutes. For while cocktails do give a lift to proceedings at first, they tend to cause a let-down later, and at that point the going gets heavy. A writer friend of ours, who admits he feels the thing has really got out of hand, says that after drinks plus dinner his guests are so apt to be drowsy that he dims the lights and shows old silent films with coffee to permit them to catch cat-naps.

To keep such sleepers awake, we ask dinner guests to come at seven-forty-five, sit down at eight-thirty; allowing a quarter of an hour for arrivals, this leaves thirty minutes for cocktails. If we are going on to the theatre, the party gathers at seven and dinner is served at twenty past. We get to the theatre on time and enjoy the show more because of the shortened cocktail hour.

While we are on the subject of cocktails, the well-stocked bar usually contains scotch, bourbon, rye, gin and vodka, a dry and a sweet sherry. These days, dry and sweet vermouths are often served on the rocks as well as being used as cocktail components, and the two Dubonnets—red and blonde—also appeal to gentle tastes. (I buy vermouth in half-bottles, so that it can be used up before it turns vinegary.) In addition to tonic and club soda and such soft drinks as ginger ale and cola, cold beer and chilled, seasoned tomato juice should be on hand. A choice of brandy or crème de menthe will please most people who like a liqueur after dinner.

This is not as large an order as it sounds when you consider how markedly the consumption rate varies from item to item, season to season. And with such a wide choice, the quantity of each bottle consumed on any given evening will be small. There seems to be a growing taste for mild drinks, a waning demand for mixed ones. Martinis are often the only cock-tail people ask for; so, to save time and confusion, I stir up a batch ahead of time in a big jar on which I've hand-painted a label.

Guests are always happiest when offered a reasonable choice. I'm against serving one ultraspecial "new" drink and nothing else. And most punches are, to me, sickly and vicious. Since you never know just what is in them, they can sneak up on you. Strong highballs or cocktails served with-out food are also a mistake. Drinks should be offered, never urged. And a nondrinker, whatever his reason, should be allowed to remain so until he himself decides otherwise.

Dress   The hostess who says, "Come seven-ish and wear something pretty," is not being really helpful. I'll never forget one time when I was vague on this score. We were expecting Mary and Dick Halliday for dinner at our house in the country. When they arrived, Mary made an entrance in a weirdly concocted costume—a mink coat, a satin stole bound in fur and two Indian saris. "You said I could wear what I like," she reminded me sweetly, "and these are the things I like the very most."

Everyone knows pretty much how to react to an invitation that says "black tie." But when men don't wear dinner clothes, you will probably have to be a bit more explicit in answer to questions about what the ladies are wearing. The degree of dressiness usually depends on the size of the party: the bigger the "do," the more formal.

More and more it has become the custom across the country for women to "dress" for dinner even though men wear business suits. At first this seemed strange; but now, I confess, it seems to make sense. The fact of the matter is that even though starched shirts and dickeys are gone, many men hate "dressing" as much as women love it. Women feel prettier in cocktail or dinner dresses; and feeling prettier, they actually look prettier; and looking prettier, they have a better time.

The hostess may, if she likes, be even a bit more specially dressed than her guests. She may wear a long skirt though her guests wear short ones, or, depending on the party and her figure, pants. (I'm convinced that no one who needs a size larger than twelve should wear tapered pants except on the beach; they really only look well on slim long-legged people.) Hostess pajamas—the ones that are cut like culottes—are a different proposition, kinder to most figures. I have a blue-and-gold sari that I've learned to drape the way Indian women do, and I like to wear it every now and then when we have guests. As a matter of fact, current at-home clothes offer a number of delightful choices in style. There's only one real rule where a hostess and her clothes are concerned: she should look and feel as pretty as she can. She owes it to her audience.

When you open the door to your first guest, your house should be looking its very best: flowers in place, lights glowing. So just before people are due, I make a quick check.

Making the House Ready

In the pantry, canapés, ice and liquor should be ready. Try to have adequate closet space with a full complement of coat hangers. If you're renting or borrowing coat racks, they should be in place. A mirror in an outside hall is especially thoughtful simply because it lets a woman get a last look before she makes her first entrance.

The bathroom should look as though you were expecting guests. Family pajamas and dressing gowns should be nowhere in sight. In addition to a good supply of guest towels, make sure there's aspirin, tissues, cotton balls, combs, emery boards and safety pins in several sizes within reasonably easy reach. Incidentally, don't forget the bedrooms and the bathroom when you're planning for flowers; miniature arrangements where they may not be expected are a pretty touch.

(*111*)

The living room should look its most inviting. Flowers work magic. So do candles, but make sure the light bulbs are in working order, too.

The air is terribly important. Since people contribute heat, your rooms should be especially cool and fresh before your guests arrive. And a ventilating scheme to clear smoke and warm air should be ready to operate when it is needed. I often use "burning perfume," a special sort of essence, not terribly well known in this country but widely available. When vaporized in tiny lamps or applied to asbestos rings that are warmed by light bulbs, it releases a delightful fragrance, but, if used extravagantly, it can be overpowering.

Try to avoid a stiff temporary look about furniture that may have been rearranged for the evening. Shift ornaments and photographs if you need extra table-top space for glasses.

There should be matches, filtered and nonfiltered cigarettes, ashtrays (for your guests' and your carpets' sake, have plenty of these).

Introductions   If the party is large enough so that introductions run on, I arrange to have each guest's drink order taken as he comes in and brought to him as he's making the rounds of handshakes and hellos. I have never understood the British custom of skipping introductions entirely (that two people share the same host is enough, say Englishmen) or mumbling one name and shouting the other (usually yours) so the whole effort is wasted. The fact that Americans like names and do try to remember them makes it doubly important to pronounce each one clearly and, whenever at all possible, to make sure that each guest meets all the others. When the surname is a common one, a first name often helpfully distinguishes this Jones from his co-Joneses. I believe that after people have reached maturity, they are entitled to be introduced by their correct titles, be they doctors or professors or Mr.'s or Mrs.'s. Thus, while I might say, "Mr. and Mrs. Thompson, I'd like you to meet Mr. and Mrs. John Mason Brown" rather than simply "Mr. and Mrs. Brown," I would never present the Browns as "John and Cassie." If the Thompsons and the Browns become first-name friends later on, I'm delighted. But I feel that *that* decision and its timing are personal matters beyond my province as a hostess.

In New York, especially, when one couple frequently means two careers, a wife often uses her maiden name in business. Yet almost without exception, women very well known for their own names' sake much prefer their married names on social occasions. So the lady who at the theatre was Claudette Colbert is Mrs. Joel Pressman when she arrives at our apartment for supper twenty minutes later.

An introductory word about mutual interests, a visitor's home, a book he's written or the business he's in helps fix one guest's name in the minds of others. But such verbal footnotes, whether given on or off stage, should never be so pointed that they seem to push people together, nor so long that there's nothing left to talk about.

While I'm all for unpremeditated mingling during cocktails, the seat-   *Seating Plans*
ing of guests at dinner is a matter to which I give a good deal of thought. If I am entertaining ten or fewer, I don't use place cards, but I do plan the seating ahead of time and make a small diagram to refresh my memory just before we sit down.

I think people like place cards. To a guest it is a compliment, a sign that his hostess has given personal thought to his pleasure. For the hostess, using place cards guarantees that there will be no table with either all ex- troverts or shy souls only. And a pre-set plan prevents all the young people from gravitating to one table while the older ones gather at another or the women from collecting in one place while all the men cluster around the prettiest girl present.

When guests come to our house for the first time, I try as often as practicable to place them next to my husband or to me. This, I hope, makes them feel especially welcome and wanted. Otherwise I simply try to put people next to others with whom they will enjoy talking. Wherever I can, I put listeners next to talkers and vice versa. And while it is physically im- possible to put everyone next to the most glamorous, the wittiest, the brightest or the prettiest, I do my best to see that one man doesn't get two inarticulate, retiring women to cope with. Every guest, it seems to me, should be happy on one side at least.

I find that the shape of the table can make a tremendous difference in the liveliness of party conversation. I always prefer a round or square table to an oblong one. And two tables are better than a single really long one. At small tables, conversation is a common pleasure. Otherwise, it is a routine left-and-right affair with an occasional effort at catching the atten- tion of the person across the centerpiece.

Incidentally, I'm all for integration of the sexes where buffets are con- cerned. If, following tradition, the men hang back, the ladies have finished eating by the time their escorts reach the table. Ask the women to take the men with them, and reassure the men that they are helping to make the party a better one by this break with custom. When men and women alter- nate in line and sit down in mixed company, it all works out much more sociably.

One further thought. Later in the evening the sexes may separate when the men stay with cigars and brandy, but it's both host and hostess's job to bring them back together again. If the split becomes permanent, the party—for me, at least—is ruined.

Table Settings   The sight of a charmingly set table always pleases me especially. It is a promise of a dinner that has been carefully planned and prepared. And this, again, is a subtle form of compliment.

In planning my own table settings, I think first of color: in the linens I use, the china I choose, in the centerpiece and the flowers. I admit I am partial to delicate colors and to candlelight just because I feel nothing is more flattering to a woman than candleglow reflected from a rose-tinted cloth. But pink cloths aren't the only pretty ones. On several small tables you might mix cloths and napkins: do two tables pink with blue napkins and two tables blue with pink napkins. If you have a particular shade in mind, you might have a white damask cloth dyed professionally to your order. (Home dye treatment is risky; the result is too often streaked or prone to fade.)

Bright white cloths play up the strong or subtle color of flowers or a centerpiece of delicate antique porcelain. Or, if you have sheer white organdy or very fine linen cloths, you can create any number of frosted color effects by spreading them over bright-hued liners; try red or turquoise or green color-fast sateen or felt.

The great advantage of felt is that it also acts as a silence cloth, an accessory of which I am all in favor, not only for its quieting qualities, but because it protects table tops from heat and cold and spills. You can buy such pads ready-made or buy the feltlike fabric and make your own by cutting them to fit your table and favorite place mats.

Place mats are lovely on a large table, whether it is round or long or square. But for small tables I prefer cloths. They help disguise bridge tables. And, combined with such essentials as salts and peppers, cigarette cups and ashtrays, not to mention a candle or two and a centerpiece, individual mats tend to cut up the space and lend the whole a cluttered, busy look. The same principle applies to the use of flowered tablecloths; they can be beautiful providing the pattern does not compete with the design of the china.

I like white organdy napkins, but napkins with a touch of color, like the charming new printed linens, add gaiety to a table. Whatever the color, napkins should be folded in a simple straightforward fashion—no lilies, no boat shapes, no miters with treacherous dinner rolls lurking inside ready to spring out and roll across the floor. Friends of ours have a butler who is a past-master of this diabolical art, and every time he catches me—and it always seems to be my roll that goes skipping off—I swear to myself I'll remember and be more cautious in the future.

Ideally, centerpieces add the color and shape that make a whole   *Centerpieces*
setting lovely to look at. And they should be planned with great care. They
should never hide guests from each other or usurp needed space. Basically
their shape should follow that of the table: round if the table is round or
square, elongated or extended with candles or compotes if the table is oval
or rectangular. There should be a pleasing relation between the height of
the centerpiece and that of glasses, candles and other accessories.

Most centerpieces are flowers, too often dully handled or taken for
granted. The other extreme is just as bad. I remember a party in Los
Angeles where calla lilies grow like weeds around everyone's back door.
Feeling they were too common in their natural state, our hostess had
painted them gold, never realizing, that she was, quite literally, gilding the
lily. On the other hand, I've never seen any prettier centerpiece than the
roses garlanded with ten-cent-store pearls Mildred Hilson designed for the
party she gave on our thirtieth wedding anniversary.

To put together an arrangement that is both appropriate and pretty
takes taste and imagination. Standard vases almost never do the job.
(Depressingly, this is true no matter where in the house you plan to use the
arrangement.) The container you choose should be low, and it need not
always be china or porcelain or glass. It might be a silver vegetable dish
or a basket with a hidden glass "liner." It could be an oval tole mold. Georgia and Ralph Colin, whose dining table is oval, have a lovely old epergne
with graceful, spreading arms that create a wonderful feeling of airy space
around the bouquets they hold. It takes looking, but there are similar
beauties, enchanting for arrangements of flowers or fruits or both, in
antique shops across the country.

On small tables a cluster of little arrangements is often more successful than a single large one. Choosing small containers is fun and a great
challenge to the imagination. Almost all pretty objects that hold water
qualify. In them, small flowers make the most delightful bouquets. I love
the delicate look of pink verbena in white urn-shaped candle holders; of
pink or blue cornflowers or violets combined with any small pink or white
blossoms massed in little liqueur glasses. Finger bowls work well provided
they are not too deep. So do handleless teacups of Eighteenth-Century or
modern patterns.

One of the most striking centerpieces I've ever seen was a basket of
anemones in those wonderfully splashy scarlets and purples and blues used
by Pam Hayward on a luncheon table. They were fake and they were fine.
But this is not true of all artificial flowers. To be right, they must be bold

and strong and make a point of color. There are floral specialists who deal only in imitation flowers. Working with blooms and candles and greens, they design decorations to fit a holiday season or a special setting or perhaps a table cloth you like particularly. I have a Christmas set made of bright-red carnations, geraniums, holly and red velvet ribbon, and I've enjoyed using it year after year. But I have a horror of those waxy roses that pretend to be really real. For much of the beauty of delicate flowers, roses or narcissi or lilies of the valley, lies in their fragility. And when they are turned sturdy and start collecting dust, for me the beauty is gone.

But centerpieces need not be all flowers. Stacked on dark green leaves, a pyramid of lemons with tiny white flowers between the fruit looks charmingly springlike. So do bunches of dark red cherries with candytuft on a footed compote. (Use transparent tape to hold them in place on a chicken-wire base.) In the fall there are marvelous vegetables to work with —squash and eggplant and pumpkins and shiny green peapods.

I am especially fond of tureens in porcelain or pottery. Gleaming silver and silver gilt have tremendous elegance. A handsome covered silver vegetable dish polished within an inch of its life can stand on its own good looks, too. There are, of course, porcelain baskets filled with porecelain fruits or flowers and designed expressly to be used as centerpieces. And whenever we have a buffet with several small tables, I find myself ransacking the house for china flowers and birds and figurines that are normally part of another room's decor but look lovely on dining tables too.

Crystal, China, Accessories   I like the look of matched crystal. My water goblets, wine and champagne glasses are all of the same extremely simple stemmed shape. Although our silver is in the style of the Queen Anne period, it has a time-

(*118*)

less quality that adapts gracefully to both contemporary and antique settings. In the country we use stainless steel, now so well designed and easy to care for. We do no formal entertaining there, and especially in summer I'd much rather the time was spent arranging flowers than rubbing silver.

But I think it is a mistake to feel that everything must match. If you are using several small tables, their settings need not be identical. I don't especially care for sets of china. I prefer different patterns used at the same dinner, but you should have enough matching pieces for each course. For small tables the old plates you unearth at auctions and antique shops

have a great deal of charm, and they are often less expensive than newly bought porcelain. You need only make sure that the pieces that are on the table at the same time—the butter and dinner plates, the dessert plates and coffee cups—harmonize.

Keep a picture of the whole table in mind as you add the final accessory touches: small boxes or porcelain cups for cigarettes, the ashtrays, compotes or candy dishes for mints. Red or white wine in crystal decanters adds color at an informal lunch or buffet.

Whether they are silver or enamel, crystal or porcelain, low or medium-high, candlesticks can add beauty to table settings. As for candles, my own taste runs to classic white or ivory; complicated shapes and bright colors look distractingly fancy. And the scented kind compete with your food, as do strongly scented flowers. For small tables I much prefer single candles surrounded by flowers to more conventional pairs.

One of the most beautiful tables I have ever seen was in the Paris home of the Duke and Duchess of Windsor. The decorations were all Chelsea porcelain—a tureen surrounded by fruits and flowers and vegetables;

even the knives and forks had Chelsea handles. The cigarettes were in jeweled gold-and-enamel boxes. It was the most elegant and expensive kind of decoration, but it also represented great taste and thought in the assembling of all its many rare and beautiful pieces.

Help Needed

Service takes planning, too. Basically, it is a matter of reconciling the help you need with what is available and what you can afford. If your household includes servants, the problem is relatively simple. You decide where your own staff needs augmenting and hire extra people to answer the door, take coats, make drinks, serve or clear away. With a bit of advance notice, you can usually find assistance either among friends of your own staff or through an agency.

For a big party, you may want to have a caterer provide some of the food while your own cook oversees the meal and prepares only those dishes that are her particular specialties—a delicious soup, perhaps, or a spectacular dessert. Only in the case of an extremely large party, a wedding or a reception, would I ask a catering service to take over all the arrangements. For while such companies are certainly equipped with all the china, glass, chairs, and tables, linens and food necessary to serve tremendous numbers, it is a most impersonal as well as a very expensive way of entertaining.

I feel I should say a word here about the advantages and disadvantages of a live-in staff. For many years our New York household has consisted of a cook, a waitress and a chambermaid. Our cook, Elna Muinonen, and our waitress, Inez Johanson, have been with us for many years, and I could not manage without them. So I make certain adjustments in the interest of their happiness. I plan menus several days ahead to allow time for Elna to market and make her own preparations; I try not to change our dinner hour at the last minute; and I try to avoid adding extra guests without notice. We seldom decide to dine out on the spur of the moment because nothing is so demoralizing to a cook as to hear there will be no one home to enjoy the *coq au vin* she's taken such trouble to fix. To sum up: our house runs smoothly, as I like it to, but we must sacrifice some of the flexibility I envy in servantless homes.

If, like most hostesses, you rely on part-time help, your party's success depends more than ever on planning. First you must know clearly what jobs you want done. If you'd like to and can afford it, you can simply hire enough help to take over from start to finish: to mix drinks, prepare the dinner, serve and clean up afterward. On the other hand, if you love to cook, you may much prefer to "do" the food yourself, then have professional help take over to serve and clear away. If budget makes a difference, begin by asking yourself which jobs you like best and which you really hate. Ideally, your temporary staff takes over the latter tasks and leaves you free to concentrate on cooking or table setting or flower arranging— the things you enjoy doing.

The amount of help you need varies tremendously. For an exquisite formal dinner you need two to serve six, three to serve eight to twelve, four people if there are fourteen to eighteen. At such a dinner, the wine must be poured, bread, sauces and vegetables served almost simultaneously with the main course. With less help, it takes too long. However, I repeat, this size staff is needed only for an exquisite and very formal dinner. At a less formal party, sauces and small items can be placed on the table to be passed by the guests themselves. The host might pour the wine. And for a small buffet you need even less help, since your guests can serve themselves in a matter of minutes.

For a buffet party of forty or fifty, you can get by with one person to make drinks plus three to pass canapés and hors d'oeuvres, empty ashtrays and remove and wash glasses and return them to circulation. The most efficient system is to set up a bar to which the guests go to be served. (Note of caution: make sure you've protected the floor beneath your temporary bar from falling ice, splash and spill by covering it with a rug or plastic or both.) Possibly you have children who can be recruited to help with serving. It is most important at a large party for the host and hostess to be left reasonably free to circulate, perform introductions and generally get things going. If they must be responsible for getting drinks, they are almost certainly going to be forced to neglect some guests while filling glasses for others.

On a part-time basis, expert help is the only sound investment because it leaves you time and mind to do your own job well. Help you have to worry along with from start to finish can leave you as frazzled as you would be if you had done everything yourself.

However, sometimes you are limited by the kind of help available. In your community you may know only women who cook and perform wonders behind the scenes but feel awkward waiting on table. Less often you know men who are good at drink making and serving but no one who is able to cope with a kitchen. There is only one solution: adapt. Hire the available talent to do what it does best. Be realistic. Whatever the limits of budget or circumstances, it is far better to change your party plan, to simplify the menu or the serving scheme or to cut down the number of guests, than to attempt the impossible with less than enough help or help that can't do the job.

People whose work you know, either from having first seen them in the homes of friends or because they have helped you before, are of course the most reliable. Occasionally a cook you know and like can suggest a waitress, one with whom she enjoys working. Even for part-time help, an agency will give references if you ask. And for your own peace of mind, they are worth checking through. Though it is purely a matter of personal taste, I have found women more helpful than men on both a full- and a part-time basis. I feel they are more patient, more careful with glasses and china I prize. While a man may mix drinks and serve expertly, he is less often willing to take over the cleaning-up chores; women are more adaptable.

Though it may sound overcautious to ask, you must be certain that no one whose job includes working with liquor has a drinking problem himself; the situations that might result are too unpleasant to risk. Once at a birthday party we were giving for Mary, a waiter-bartender we'd hired for the evening suddenly found his legs impossibly limp and crashed to the floor with a big tray of glasses. His brother, whom we had also hired for the evening, had, naturally, to drop what he was doing and take the fallen home. We were left with a room full of thirsty people and a staff of none. I remember several days later relating the whole sad story to a friend who lives on a rather grand scale. "But, my dear," she said, astonished, "why didn't you use your *own* men?" I let the subject drop there. It just goes to show that no matter how well you think you live, someone always lives weller.

You are responsible for making what you want done absolutely clear. Is the cook to handle both canapés and dinner, or will you take over in the hors d'oeuvres department? What plates will you use for the salad, which for the main course? Make sure the man who tends bar knows not only how you like your drinks made, but also that you would like him to straighten up the living room while you and your guests are at dinner. Will you need him to serve highballs later? (We prefer to set the makings out on a cloth-covered table and let our guests help themselves.) A check list of what's to be done is insurance against skipped details.

Everyone has her own pet theories about serving. I have several, too. I think guests are more comfortable if the hostess is served first—not only because she helps set a standard by which to judge portion sizes, but also because very few guests enjoy being the first to break into a mold or a fancy tart. A good hostess, constantly aware of her guests' needs, should also always have a way of summoning help. Without giving the man at her side the feeling that she is too distracted to listen to what he is saying, she should be able to indicate that a water glass is empty or that the bread should be passed. If you can be extravagant about help, all this should be accomplished without bells but with the aid of a waitress who keeps a watchful eye on the hostess in order to receive signaled instructions.

Most part-time help supply their own uniforms. But I have found it helpful to keep several matching apron sets on hand. That way, when I have more than one waitress for a party, though the black uniforms may not be identical, they appear to be the same because of the matching accessories.

In some cities there are services that almost take the place of servants. *Special* *Services* There are kitchens that deliver specialized main courses with or without hot rolls and a salad, and such food usually has a bit more personality than that offered by standard caterers. If you aren't wild about cooking and don't care to hire anyone to do it for you, you can still serve an awfully good meal: offer a simple first course like smoked salmon; for the main course, order a *boeuf Bourguignonne* sent in and serve it bubbling hot; add crisp French bread and a salad of your own making (mixed greens with sliced raw mushrooms, for example) and a strawberry tart from a bakery or your own oven. Prices for this sort of service are really quite reasonable when you consider the time and work involved in an authentic French *cassoulet* or a really good beef in wine sauce.

Modern equipment, ingenious though it is, will never replace the kind *Helpful* *Equipment* of animate help that knows when the stew needs a splash of wine or that one more minute will make a good soufflé perfect. But today's mechanical marvels can make work many hands lighter. Rotisseries and cookers and steamers help beginners turn out expert results in remarkably short order. Burners that turn themselves off and on refuse to let food burn. An electric blender makes thirty second's work of puréeing that, over a hot wire sieve, takes considerably more time. Freezers let you do party cooking weeks ahead if you like, store leftovers at their party best and help stockpile party-sized supplies of ice cubes. And, to move to the seating and serving area, stools and cushions that stack and tables that fold expand your capacity yet practically disappear when not in use.

Every hostess has her favorite pieces of equipment, those that suit her party plans best. Personally, I find electric food-warming trays wonderfully useful. They are perfect on buffet tables, fine for keeping a casserole just right while it waits in the pantry or for warming plates to just the proper degree. (I've found these trays so effective that I've had them installed in the top and bottom of a metal cabinet in the pantry to give me a most efficient warming oven.) I find a thousand uses for those big folding aluminum tables. And I also have a weakness for serving carts that fold flat for closet storage between parties. As canapé carts, as movable bars, for serving and clearing, they can't be beat.

Some of these wonderworkers you use every day. Other equipment is either so specialized or takes up so much storage space that it is wiser to rent it than to buy it. You can rent almost anything these days. One firm that started with drive-yourself cars now has a Madison Avenue branch that lend-leases everything from baby feeders to silver punch bowls to portable dance floors. In a somewhat more down-to-earth range, you may find yourself in need of extra chairs, plywood tops that turn square card tables round, a big coffee maker (the seventy-cup size), extra glasses or other practical wares. Your classified directory lists sources for them all under "Party supplies."

You can rent coat racks, unless you prefer to buy the collapsible kind that can be stored in a closet or behind your draperies. (The management of the New York cooperative building where we live has invested in several coat racks plus extra chairs and tables to loan to tenants. It's a great convenience and one that other buildings might well copy.)

Whether you have help or not, a plan for clearing away is just as essential as one for setting out. Plates don't evaporate between courses. Particularly if you are giving an informal party, make sure you know whom you can count on (a cooperative husband, a friend, the children?) and just where there is space in which to store the china until it is time for dishwashing.

When Guests Go

Ever since our girls were small, I've tidied up before going to bed after a party. I never could bear the thought of those scrubbed childish faces coming upon all those tired highball glasses and dead cigarettes first thing in the morning. I still plump up the pillows and carry out glasses and empty and wash the ashtrays. I also dry off table tops. (I've always felt there was something unwelcoming about the act of shoving coasters under guests' glasses. I have found that if the tables are sufficiently waxed and dampness is not allowed to remain on the surface too long—overnight, for instance—there is no permanent damage.) If a tablecloth or a table needs repair, I make a note to tend to it immediately. That way everything will be ready the next time we have people in.

In a way, I'm very fond of the end of the evening, when Dick and I enjoy the party in retrospect. Long ago I learned that even when things do go wrong, they never go as wrong as the hostess thinks. There was that time we ran out of ice cream at a cast party (by this time I should know how hungry actors are on Sunday evening), and the time the finger bowls were presented without water in them. Just recently I miscounted the number of guests and we were one place short at the table. But these incidents didn't spell catastrophe. I once watched Edna Ferber hypnotized by the spectacle of one of her guests ingesting a fine lace doily with her dessert. It was very hard on Edna, but it still was a lovely party. So, while the memory of roast beef that was underdone or a chocolate soufflé that wasn't may plague you, chances are your guests remained happily undisturbed.

Again it is like the theatre. Every show has its ill-starred moments: an actor blows a line; a singer forgets a lyric; a stagehand does an impromptu walk-on within full view of the audience. It's shattering, it's the end to anyone connected with the production. Then the curtain comes down and the lights go up and you realize, always with surprise, that the audience hasn't been bothered in the least. Being generous, intelligent, understanding souls, they have put things in perspective. And a fluff hasn't spoiled the play for them any more than the little things that so worry a hostess have ruined her party for her guests.

So, after making a brief mental note of any necessary corrections, I savor the nice things: I remember the tables with all the candles lit; the note in the conversational hum that meant dinner talk was going well; the friends who finally met and seemed to enjoy each other; the singing at the piano, the conversation by the fireplace, the smiles of people I like.

When an evening has ended in this way, I feel that our guests have had a good time. And because they have, we have, too.

CHAPTER

6

Foods Various and International

W H A T E V E R the hour, the day or the season, the food you serve plays a tremendously important part in your guests' good time. And for every ounce of creative energy you invest in it, you can count on being repaid a thousand percent in terms of your party's success.

Once upon our grandmothers' time—even yesterday, for that matter—guests for dinner meant bringing out the "good" plates and "fancy" foods reserved for special occasions. Too often all this was followed by an over-stuffed feeling almost as acutely uncomfortable as starvation would have been.

I don't think there is any such thing as a "company menu" today, any more than I believe you should hide your beautiful things when you are not expecting guests. And if I ever needed evidence to back me up in this theory, I found it once many years ago when we were honored by an invitation to dinner at the Duke of Kent's London town house. The silver, the china, the table were magnificent and, though it all may have been "everyday" in a ducal household, to us it looked very formal. There was one liveried footman for every two guests. It was the Duchess's birthday, and there were several courses, each accompanied by the appropriate vintage wine. But the main course, beautifully cooked and presented, was unmistakably pot roast.

Times have changed in several ways. Except for oysters, "the season" for most delicacies lasts twelve months of the year. We have Florida aspar-

agus in March, California strawberries in December. Markets carry man-
goes, avocados and soft-shell crabs all year long. Then, too, Americans are
traveling more and discovering gourmet territory they have never before
explored; foreign dishes and foreign seasonings have a new and apprecia-
tive audience. The strictly steak-chop-or-chicken eater is becoming a rare
bird.

Every day new food products—frozen and canned and dried, in an
incredible variety—are introduced in the markets. Not all these inventions
are good, but some are marvelous time and labor savers: frozen chopped
chives and parsley, refrigerated croissant dough and puff pastries, canned
and frozen soups that, while quite bland in their unadulterated states,
respond admirably when blended with one another and doctored with
herbs and a dash of sherry. Canned black bean soup, for example, becomes
quite sophisticated when you add sherry, a slice of hard-boiled egg
and a slice of lemon. There are all sorts of frozen hors d'oeuvres, but I'm
partial to the little Mexican meat-filled *tacos*, to cheese puffs and *quiches*
you warm and serve cut into small wedges. And I've even found a superb
bouillabaisse—wildly expensive, except when you consider all the work
and the ingredients involved—which, served with French bread and salad,
makes an awfully satisfying lunch.

Finally, more American women everywhere and with every sort of
income are doing their own cooking. Consequently they are searching out
more interesting recipes, trying more unusual dishes, making a creative art
out of what was once a chore. I don't think there is any doubt that home
cooking is better for the change. For one thing, the woman who once had
servants and is now her own chef is more capable intellectually of following
a complicated recipe than any but the most exceptional general house-
worker.

Inevitably, the kind of help available plays an important part in the
party menu you plan. Because part-time help is more plentiful than full-
time live-in servants, buffets are more common than formal seated dinners.
And when help is limited, it is only good sense to simplify menus
accordingly. Many hostesses, for example, plan hors d'oeuvres that replace
a specially served first course.

I remember a dinner at the Whitney Darrows' in Connecticut that was
a good example of this kind of planning. There were very good canapés
with the drinks. In the dining room we helped ourselves to the main course:
a fine beef casserole with rice and salad and hot bread. We carried our
plates back into the living room, where the host filled our wineglasses. A
maid cleared away, and dessert—assorted fruit tarts and pastries—was

wheeled in on a cart with coffee. Obviously Middy Darrow had done considerable cooking beforehand, but because her menu and service were so beautifully coordinated, fourteen of us enjoyed a delicious dinner entirely unconscious of the mechanics involved. Given the same space, guests and help, a seated three-course dinner would have been impossible.

International Cuisine

In terms of nationality, there are hundreds of wonderful dishes to choose from. French cooking is, of course, the definitive *haute cuisine*—the subtlest, the most sophisticated. Still, as a steady diet I prefer the kind of food you find in northern Italy; it is simpler, not quite so rich as the French. My tastes cross all sorts of geographical boundaries. I think Scandinavian food is delicious, and some German cooking is marvelous, although I find some of it pretty heavy going. Viennese cooking, with all that lovely cream and butter we're so leery of these days, is hard to equal when it comes to pastry and desserts. There's an inventiveness about Chinese dishes that is as fascinating as it is delectable; they have tremendous variety and delicacy of flavor that is impossible to duplicate at home. And I love good American soups (oyster stew, chicken gumbo, turkey—the kind that is simmered for hours with lots of giblets and hearts in it) and desserts like rice pudding and Brown Betty.

This is not to say that a party menu must be all American or all Danish or consist entirely of recipes you've smuggled out of Tibet. We have had wonderful German buffets at the Dore Scharys', and Marisa Erskine, who was born in Italy, serves delicious Italian meals—cold meats with wonderful sauces, tomatoes with lots of basil, *pasta* that is positively airy. But specialization isn't essential. Italian *prosciutto* with melon and Danish chicken go beautifully on the same menu because, in the final analysis, balance of flavor and texture and color are always more important than the national origin of the recipe.

Where foreign foods are concerned, I have only one limiting suggestion to make: don't serve *pasta* to an Italian or curry to an Indian. You mean it as a compliment, of course; but it is often embarrassing to a guest whose standards for his native cuisine are higher than you can achieve. I've seen only one successful exception to this rule: my sister-in-law Sue Rodgers did give an awfully good curry party for Indian guests once, but she had it catered by Indian cooks.

A few years ago, Betty Marcus worried for weeks over the menu for a lunch in honor of Parisian dignitaries who were visiting Dallas during a Neiman-Marcus promotion. She pored over every gourmet cookbook known to woman. Then, hours before D-day, she threw over her all-French lunch plan in favor of one that was pure Texas—including barbecued beef, black-eyed peas, banana bread and fried pies. For those who were not so adventurous she also offered cold filet of beef, green salad and fresh fruit. And the party was a triumph.

The moral of the story is: you may serve anything any time to anyone —just so it tastes very good. There is no gourmet appeal to badly cooked grouse or squab. And, French or American, the things you cook most often are the things you probably cook best. A fine stew is always better than a mediocre steak. And really good beef hash preceded by cold wine soup attains a sophistication that shrimp cocktail followed by filet mignon will never have. The only real rule is: whatever you do, do it well.

Expanding Your Repertoire

Just as successful menu plans start with a repertoire of the dishes you do best, they expand with recipes you discover here, there and everywhere. I have a very small purse notebook in which I keep track of ideas about seasonings, sauces and foods in general. Over the years I must have filled thirty or more books, and to them I have to give credit for some of my favorite things: the *fraises* in orange juice we first tasted in Italy; a seafood sauce (also Italian) made of tomatoes, sour cream, mayonnaise and brandy; a cocoa-flavored layer cake like one we discovered in Aix-en-Provence.

Unless I know a restaurant well, I'm hesitant about asking for a specific recipe. Chefs aren't terribly enthusiastic about giving away their secrets. However, I am not at all above a discreet bit of idea stealing, and I've become pretty expert at tasting and guessing and experimenting with a particular dish until I have successfully simulated it at home. Unlike professional cooks, friends are usually complimented when you ask them about the recipe for a dish you've especially enjoyed. To such amiable sources I owe the recipes for Georgann's pork rolls, Wilhelmina's veal with ham and cheese, Georgia's hot fruit dessert and others I've used in menus later on. Some of the hearty "Old Country" recipes I like best have come from foreign-born women with a real knack for preparing their national dishes. Jenny, who was our caretaker in the country for many years, gave me one of the most delicious: *Palacsintas*, Hungarian *crêpes* filled with cottage cheese or jelly.

I find just reading cookbooks can give you lots of ideas for working your own variations on a recipe theme; I've become so practiced at it I actually taste the ingredients as they're spelled out. I love to experiment with herbs and seasonings. There is great satisfaction in mastering the art of using them to enhance rather than blanket the flavors your food was born with. Some hostesses feel that enough wine or herbs or garlic can conceal any cooking mistake, but it simply is not true. That kind of reasoning, I suppose, is responsible in part for my own prejudice against garlic. I also believe many people who don't like the taste themselves suffer almost as acutely when their friends eat it. Whenever garlic is called for, I substitute shallots, which contribute a wonderful flavor without the unwelcome consequences.

Considerate Planning

Although people everywhere are more receptive to unfamiliar dishes than they once were, there are still some "odd" foods for which tastes have to be acquired. It is best to avoid these on party menus. I happen to love tripe—especially tripe *poulette* with onions—but very few of our guests would share my enthusiasm, and Dick says he would just as soon eat boiled bath rug. Except for our son-in-law, Danny, who claims he can hear them "baaaaaaa," our family thinks of lamb tongues as a treat, but I'd never serve them to uninitiated guests. I save such special dishes for my own enjoyment and plan less controversial fare for company. As far as party menus are concerned, the trick is to discover dishes that are unusual enough to be interesting without being so exotic that they are frightening.

Whether or not acquired tastes are involved, it is the most flattering thing in the world to go to someone's house for dinner and realize that your hostess is serving a dish she remembers you have particularly enjoyed or that you have mentioned as being one of your favorites. One of my oldest friends and I share a passion for chocolate; we wouldn't dream of offering each other anything else for dessert. Oscar Hammerstein adored snails; his wife, Dorothy, has never liked brown sauces. We have friends who dote on lobster and another who loves mussels the way our cook does them. I always try to keep such facts in mind when these friends are coming to dine with us.

This kind of consideration is especially appreciated when doctor's orders enter into the picture. It is thoughtful to have a slice of melon or a cup of consommé ready for the guest who can't eat the shrimp Newburgh because he's allergic to seafood; but it is even more gracious (and that's a word I use sparingly) to plan a first course of asparagus vinaigrette that he can enjoy along with everyone else.

Another point of considerate planning is so simple it may sound silly to mention it: keeping your serving scheme in mind, you should serve food that is easy to cope with. While Cornish hens are fine for a seated dinner, they are difficult to handle while balancing a plate on your lap at a buffet. And by the same token, you'll never be better loved than when you serve boned squab to men who like fowl but hate the skidding and swordplay involved in dealing with the intricate little birds whole.

Roasts should be carved through so guests won't be obliged to do desperate hacking on their own. And, though small bunches of parsley or watercress look crisp and appetizing, no one should have to fight his way through a forest of grass to get to the food on the platter. Serving spoons or ladles or forks should be of the greatest possible help (spoons for cooked vegetables, flat forks that pick up sliced meats without tearing, and so on). When in doubt, two spoons are almost always better than one.

Balancing the Menu

In course-by-course menu planning, contrast is probably the most important factor. For years college students have griped about tasteless Friday dinners—fish, boiled potatoes, creamed cauliflower. Even when perfectly cooked such a meal couldn't be tempting; its all-white face is against it. A menu that is all one color or texture can't help but be boring although each individual dish is as perfect as Escoffier could have made it. At dinner the other evening we were served a delicious vichyssoise, very good chicken in a creamy sauce and a wonderful cheese cake. I dearly love each one of the three, but together they achieved a creaminess so overwhelming that my tastebuds drowned in it.

After a bit of practice, the process of juggling for contrasts' sake becomes almost automatic. If you plan a meal with a rather rich first or main course, you keep the other things you serve light. When you decide on a meat with a rich sauce—veal birds with sour-cream sauce, for instance—a "light" vegetable like French-cut string beans comes to mind almost automatically, along with a first course like melon and *prosciutto* that has a certain crispness or tang to it.

Every hostess has her pet theories about the foods she serves and the way she plans. I am no exception. So the thoughts that make up this chapter are the guidelines I've tested and found to hold up for entertaining at our house. They won't fit anyone else's life exactly. Still, I hope you'll find some ideas among them you'd like to try blending in with your own schemes.

For example, I've found that the order in which you put together a menu can give you a kind of built-in balance. I plan as I'd choose food at a restaurant rather than starting with the appetizer and following the menu's serving order. First I decide on a main course, then on a first course, then on the dessert. After these basic decisions have been made, I add the wine, the vegetables that accompany the meat, the salad that is served as a separate course with a formal meal or with the main course if I am serving a casserole, the cheese if it is to be offered with the salad, and the bread. Canapés are a thing apart; I leave them for last because I find I have a much clearer idea of exactly which varieties will work best after I've settled on my dinner menu.

Obviously a planning scheme as detailed as this covers every course you'd serve for the most elaborate dinner. And, to be sure, it is meant to be tailored and adapted to the occasion. For an evening on which you feel a fish mousse would make a perfect first course, you simply start planning with it and pick your main course accordingly. The menu for an informal buffet often includes only a casserole, bread, salad and dessert, plus hors d'oeuvres substantial enough to take the place of a first course. Whatever the style of your party, the important point is this: keep the total picture in mind as you plan. You'll find it makes it much easier to avoid the dullness that results when the same color or texture is repeated in dish after dish.

Main Courses   Everyone has favorite main courses. At our house, if beef is the choice, I may pick filets or a stew, a pot roast or a short loin; I'm especially fond of a short loin's texture and flavor (some butchers refer to this cut as a "shell"). Veal has no competition when it comes to versatility; it is basic to so many great recipes. I like ham if it is not too salty (which, to me, Virginia hams are) and providing it is sliced as you slice smoked salmon—very, very thin. This accounts for my preference for hams that come canned and boned, whether from Denmark or Poland or Iowa; I'm convinced that only a surgeon, and a brilliant one at that, can do more than hack away when the bone has been left in. I rarely serve lamb at parties. I find plain leg of lamb dull, but a coffee sauce makes it something special. A saddle of lamb is delicious, but it must be served still pink and juicy, and this takes split-second timing, and the delicate-tasting legs of spring lamb serve only four or five. I love lamb flavor in hash, stew or curry or in stock for a soup thick with barley and dried mushrooms.

Meats fall into one of two categories: those served with a natural kind of gravy and those with rich sauces, usually creamy. It is, basically, the difference between a roast of beef and a beef Stroganoff, a roast chicken and Chicken Supréme. A rich creamy sauce is often an integral part of the recipe for the making of the whole dish, as in *vitello tonnato* or curried lamb. With broiled or roasted meats a natural brown gravy made from drippings left in the pan is usually served with, rather than on, the meat. My only strong conviction about such "pan gravies" is that they should always be thickened with cornstarch or arrowroot—never flour. Non-floury sauces not only taste better, but they have a clear shiny look that is especially appetizing.

Casseroles

For an informal seated dinner, for a small buffet or whenever help is limited, casserole main courses are ideal. They are so good and so easy to serve. By casserole I mean any dish—beef or veal or chicken or lamb, even stew or a curry—that is prepared in advance and reheated at serving time. In many cases, reheating actually enhances the flavor. Casseroles can be as irresistible as the goulash we've had at buffet suppers at Florence and Harold Rome's or the wonderful *blanquette de veau* the Fredric Marches (Florence Eldridge) sometimes serve at their buffet dinners. Simple or fancy, casseroles are the mainstay of many hostesses I know who, rather than hire a cook who might only be so-so, like to prepare the party food themselves, let the help take over to warm, serve and clean up afterwards.

First Courses

Theoretically, if a dinner is extremely formal, the main course is preceded by both a soup and a fish course. But it has been years since I've served all three. People aren't in the habit of eating the enormous meals they reveled in years ago. Besides, the only soups that are suited to such an occasion are the clear harmless consommé kind of thing my grandmother always dismissed as "hot and wet." In general such concoctions seem so refined and unexciting that I don't think they add much to a meal. There are a few exceptions; turtle soup with sherry, beef consommé julienne and borscht served hot and clear with little strips of beet are all as good to the taste as they are appropriate to very formal menus. Still, on most formal evenings I skip the soup entirely and choose another kind of first course.

There are so many great ones: hot or cold fish *mousse* with lobster sauce and any number of other wonderful dishes. Fresh-caught regional fish and seafood are particularly delicious: the lobster in New England, the stone crab in Florida, Lake Superior whitefish, Gulf Coast pompano and red snapper. With a *mousse* of filet of sole or salmon, I often serve a mousseline sauce, which is like hollandaise in color and taste but airier in texture. Any number of cold sauces are good with fish; you might, for instance, try cold curried sauce or a mustard or dilled mayonnaise.

In the summer, when the weather is warm, I try to plan a first course that can be fixed in advance or one that doesn't even have to be "done" in the serious cooking sense: melon or pear with *prosciutto*, cold soup, a tomato aspic ring with lobster or crab meat in the center, artichokes or asparagus vinaigrette—anything that won't heat up the kitchen just before mealtime.

For small dinners and luncheons, my menus often begin with soup. Crab or lobster bisque can actually be quite formal; and clam broth with a dab of whipped cream on top is a nice change when you prefer something a little less hearty. But there must be hundreds of soups to choose from, including all those that can be served both hot and cold, like vichyssoise or borscht or senegalese. And with a salad and bread and dessert, such substantial informal standbys as clam chowder and the bean soups can literally be the greatest part of a meal.

Desserts   Dessert plans are determined by what has gone before. If it has been a rich meal, I almost always serve fruit in one form or another—oranges in wine, for instance, or a compote with custard sauce or, in summer, a wined watermelon. If the meal is simple, then I can choose a rich dessert like a *crème brûlée* or a ginger roll or one of my chocolate favorites. I love ice cream or sherbet surrounded by fruit, vanilla ice cream with brandied cherries or blueberries on lemon ice. I have a few personal taste quirks where sweets are concerned: I'm not crazy about chocolate and liquor flavors mixed; for me, jam between the layers spoils a chocolate cake and coconut spoils everything.

Perhaps because dessert seems a more frivolous course than the others, it tempts some hostesses to whimsy. Forgetting that this course, like any other, must be eaten to be enjoyed, they stuff whole apricots into skinny parfait glasses, present orange sherbet in hollowed-out orange skins (I don't even think this looks pretty) or devise other serving arrangements featuring a wide assortment of vessels like tiny-mouthed brandy snifters, from which it is nearly impossible to extricate the food. While their guests may be slimmer for the experience, they are scarcely ever grateful—particularly if such ingenuity leads to ice cream in a velvet lap.

From baked beans to pheasant, almost any meal served after noon is enhanced by wine. Yet until recently, the volume of chi-chi wine talk has been so great that hostesses have often hesitated to serve it. Forty years ago, the recommended glassware alone was intimidating. A setting for a full-dress dinner included a glass for the sherry that accompanied the soup, another for the white wine that went with the fish, a third for the red wine served with the beef, a champagne glass to go with dessert and a Port or Madeira glass for the savory course. With the "proper" crystal assembled, there were all sorts of rigid serving rules to master—so many that people gave up before they started.

Wines

Today's attitude toward wine is more relaxed. It helps when you realize that for almost every "Thou shalt" handed down by a wine authority, you can probably unearth another expert source that says just the opposite. In considerable digging, I've come up with only one commandment on which all agree: red wine must never be served with ham or fish.

With the mumbo-jumbo gone, wines become the pure pleasure they were always meant to be. I serve them frequently and very simply. Only on formal occasions do we serve more than one. If we are being quite formal, I serve red and/or white wines plus a dessert wine in thin-stemmed clear glass goblets. I have three sizes of glasses (the white-wine glasses are smaller than the ones for red, and then there are glasses for the dessert wine); but it's perfectly possible to get along nicely with a single set of wine goblets plus matching champagne glasses—preferably tulip-shaped rather than *coupe* design. A large wineglass not only looks attractive, but it actually makes the wine taste better. Pour it half full, so that guests may most easily savor the wine's bouquet.

Your only real obligation is to learn which wines you like best. The first step in any basic wine education is to locate a good wine merchant. He should be something more than a neighborhood liquor dealer. His stock and his talk should give evidence that he has more than a label-dropping acquaintance with the subject. Such a man is to be trusted, if only because

his business improves with each new wine buyer he converts and pleases. And to accomplish this he must keep in mind both palates and, within reason, pocketbooks. He begins by suggesting likely wines to serve with specific menus. Then, as each customer develops her own list of favorites, he may point out bargain buys, even offer to store bulk purchases where storage problems exist.

Partly because so few people knew them, distribution of domestic wines was once quite limited. Recently, since more and more people have discovered how really good they are, they are found everywhere. Red and white and rosé, full-bodied and light, their variety is impressive. But when you stop to realize that America's wine-producing traditions as well as its vines literally spring from European roots, their quality is not so surprising.

Most American wines come from California or New York State, with New York known especially for its sherries, its champagnes and dryer wines. As with foreign vintages, some will please you more than others. But contrary to the popular notion, with a few exceptions the price difference between a good imported wine and a domestic wine of comparable quality is not tremendous. So the only valid reason for choosing any wine—domestic or imported—remains a genuine liking for the wine itself.

Although I am willing to admit that wine in half-bottles may not be quite as good as the same wine in a full-sized bottle, I like to keep a selection of the smaller size on hand. The difference in taste is so slight that only an unusually sensitive expert can detect it. And for dinners when there are just two of you or for informal meals when two guests like red wine while the other two prefer white, half-bottles are the perfect answer. When there are no opened larger bottles on hand, halves are useful for cooking, too.

As a rule, I think "cooking wines"—which is to say, wines of less-than-table quality bought solely to use in food preparation—are an extravagance. Aside from the injustice they may do other ingredients, they are wasteful. Regardless of quality, opened bottles of wine keep only two or three days (whites, refrigerated; reds at room temperature). Table wines can be used for either drinking or cooking during that time. Leftover cooking wines, however, must either be used in food or let go to vinegar. And wine vinegar—of which no cook can use unlimited quantities—becomes terribly expensive when produced this way.

There are really no set rules, except for the ham-and-fish one, when it comes to what wine is served with any particular dish. The one thing to keep in mind is that the flavors should complement, never compete with or overpower, each other. For example, wine and salad dressing are highly incompatible. Also for flavor's sake, when more than one wine is served, the lighter should come first—the white before the red, the dry before the sweet—so that both can be appreciated fully. Red wines are usually served at room temperature; white wines are chilled, and rosé wines are cool but not iced.

In general, most people discover that they like the substantial flavor of red wine balanced against the hearty red-meat flavors and prefer the more delicate taste of white wine with the subtler flavors of fish or fowl. But no rule says you must combine these or those. And occasionally a full-bodied white wine is just the thing to serve with a fine cut of beef.

There is more to learn about red wines than there is about whites because there are more of them. Among French red wines, there are two basic classifications: Bordeaux and Burgundy. Bordeaux, known as "claret" in England, is the lighter of the two and is usually served with beef, veal, fowl of all kinds and simple foods with light sauces.

If you want to simplify your life among the Burgundies, ask for Beaujolais—any one of a number of wines from the Beaujolais district of France, especially good with beef, veal, lamb, chicken, game or cheese. Since these wines are best when less than two years old, the date on the label is important.

On French wines the label points out a number of things worth knowing. As a rule, the more details given, the better the wine inside. The phrase *Appelation contrôlée* means that the French government guarantees the wine's origin as stated on the label; any good wine will bear this marking. With Bordeaux, vineyard names are significant; and Château Ausone, Château Latour, Château Lafite, Château Haut-Brion, Château Mouton-Rothschild and Château Margaux are among the best-known. A less costly but delicious Bordeaux is Château Lascombes. Usually a township name and owner's name in addition to "Beaujolais" on a Burgundy indicates a superior wine; so does the phrase *mis* or *mise en bouteilles au château* or *au domaine* or *à la propriété*, because it shows that the wine within is bottled on the estate where it is made, not shipped off to be mixed with other miscellaneous wines in the bottling process. Since the French word for cellars is *caves* and all wines are bottled in cellars, the phrase *mis en bouteilles dans nos caves* means little or nothing.

Italy's best-known red wines are Chiantis, and there are two kinds, both similar to France's Beaujolais. The first, sold in tall bottles, is a full-bodied wine right for hearty roasts and stews; it is aged in casks for four or five years, then bottled. The second comes in the short, straw-covered bottles; it is younger (about two years old) and a great favorite with *pasta*.

Burgundy is famous for dry white wines, too—some of the best in the world. These include Chablis, Montrachet, Pouilly-Fuissé and white Châteauneuf du Pape (lovely with curries and egg dishes)—all especially nice with fish, seafood, veal, pork, ham, cheese dishes, casseroles and highly spiced foods and meats.

White Bordeaux are sweeter than white Burgundies. Best-known are the sauternes—of which Château d'Yquem is one perfectly delicious example—that are so good with desserts. Other white wines worth investigating are such popular Italian dessert wines as Asti Spumante and Lachryma Christi; Neuchâtel from Switzerland (light, dry, nice with lunch); excellent Alsatian Rhine wines like Riesling and Gewürz-Traminer; Chilean Riesling (not only dry and good, but inexpensive) and dry Italian wines like Soave, Verdicchio and white Chianti.

The best known of the light pink wines called *rosés* are Tavel and Anjou from France; I find them particularly delightful with summer lunches. Another personal favorite is a sparkling Portuguese rosé called Lancer's Crackling.

There are at least twenty brands of imported champagne that are always good. Among the most popular: Piper-Heidseick, Bollinger and Mumms, to name only three. Remember champagnes can be either sweet or dry, too; and although the dry is best if you are serving it all through the meal, sweet champagne, in spite of the fact that it is harder to find, is actually a better dessert wine.

Beers   And don't forget the pleasures of beer. Though my own beer palate is not as highly developed as it might be, beer-loving friends tell me the very best are imported from Holland and Denmark. They also recommend an American beer which used to be available only on draft but is now bottled to take home.

Pasta and   Whether you are building your menu around a roast or a casserole,
Vegetables   you are almost expected to serve something starchy. If your casserole has noodles or rice built in, you need nothing more. If it is a goulash or curry, the starch usually comes along as a side dish. There is no doubt that on a buffet rice waits best. I've made herbed rice the morning of the day of a dinner party, then spread it on a cookie sheet and slid it into the oven to heat and dry just before serving time; the result was perfect. With *pasta*, the only real sin is overcooking. I've come to the conclusion that in most cases the ideal boiling time is just about three quarters of the minimum recommended on the box. The key phrase is *al dente*, which in Italian means firm to the bite, never soft or sticky. If you have the help to do it, cooking two half batches rather than one large one makes second helpings tastier. I find that noodles stay quite tasty in a warmer if you add a bit of light cream,

(*138*)

butter, freshly-ground pepper and some grated Parmesan cheese when you prepare them.

Roasts generally mean potatoes, which I like done in the very simplest way. I love little boiled potatoes—the kind you cut out with a scoop and serve buttered and sprinkled with parsley or small new potatoes boiled and served in their jackets; and I can make a whole lunch of a baked potato, especially if it keeps company with sour cream and chives. I love baked potatoes in all sizes, down to and including the tiny one-inch new ones, the runts of the crop really, which we often have baked in their skins, opened, buttered and seasoned. Good soufflé potatoes are sometimes exactly what is called for, and I prefer them to French-fried or mashed potatoes.

I sometimes plan to have puréed peas in place of potatoes, but basically I feel legumes and starchy vegetables should be served with simple roasts rather than with rich main dishes. I love almost any vegetable that is tender and young and not overcooked. Actually, with a few exceptions such as corn, asparagus and tomatoes, I think frozen vegetables are generally more delicious than the so-called fresh things you can buy in most markets. The frozen varieties are processed so quickly and so near the place where they are harvested that they almost always taste younger and better. They are certainly much easier to prepare. To serve six, you'd have to buy an enormous quantity of unshelled peas to equal the number of tiny sweet ones you get in two frozen packages.

I am fond of root vegetables like carrots and beets when they are young and tender. And I love big blanched canned asparagus, artichoke hearts and bottoms and, best of all, the kind of artichokes you get in Italy, where you can eat every morsel including the leaves. Though I sometimes include them in menus, I am not wild about aromatic vegetables like broccoli and cauliflower; and since I've grown up, no Brussels sprout has ever crossed my lips.

People seldom use enough imagination when it comes to preparing vegetables. Some really cook the flavor out by simmering them too long and in too much water. Spinach is often drowned because so few people realize that after it has been washed, the leaves hold all the moisture you need to cook it to perfection. Neutral-flavored vegetables take on a real distinction when you add a sauce or herbs or even the proper garnish; witness string beans in dilled sour cream or with chopped toasted almonds on top; peas with some shallots and lettuce, tomatoes with basil. Hollandaise makes a marvelous dish of poached zucchini. And even cauliflower deserves something better than the standard *au gratin* treatment. Cookbooks are full of ideas when you are looking for new ones.

I like to serve roasts surrounded by little bouquets of mushrooms, peas, string beans and potatoes, not only because the whole platter looks so tempting, but also because in that way guests can help themselves to meat, potatoes and vegetables all at once while they are hot and taste their best. Again, because food stays warmer, at a seated dinner I like to divide things so that each serving dish is passed to only six or eight guests. And I do think, with the exception of meats like squab or game hen that come in one-portion sizes, everything should be offered to everyone twice—if only because people have grown to expect it and may serve themselves sparingly at first with a second chance in mind.

Salads I like cold vegetables, cooked or raw, in salads with a French or a vinaigrette dressing or, if it's beet salad, with a creamy one. But as you may have guessed, I love salads in general. We serve lots of variations: mixed green salad with sliced raw mushrooms (they have a wonderful texture), artichoke hearts, hearts of palm and, of course, lettuce and tomatoes, romaine and lettuce, endive and romaine or endive and lettuce. I'm particularly partial to spinach salad—the young leaves—with bits of crisp bacon sprinkled through it. I don't like to see salads "arranged" but tossed in a big wooden bowl; nothing could look more inviting.

For me, salad dressings are French—by which I mean three parts of oil to one of vinegar, salt and freshly ground pepper plus several flavor ingredients: shallots and mustard and herbs (tarragon is my favorite). Some people add a touch of mayonnaise instead of mustard.

Cheese At our house, when salad is served as a separate course, I offer a selection of cheese with it. Only at a very large party do I serve four or five kinds. As a rule, I think a choice of two—one soft and one firm—provides everyone with a taste and texture that tempts him. Depending on the season and the cheese you have found best in your part of the country, you might pair a Brie and a Port Salut, a Camembert with a Bel Paese, or a Crème Chantilly (a Swedish cheese not quite so well known as the other two soft varieties, but delicious all the same) and a Tallegio. There's another marvelous cheese from Denmark called Crema Danica; it could share honors with an Oka cheese from Canada.

We tend to think of the best cheese as being imported, and this is often true. However, I think that our own counterparts are frequently superior. (European cheese must withstand not only the trip but also the pasteurization process required for export to this country.) Even our native varieties have improved steadily over the years.

Breads With the cheese, of course, go crackers—*un*salty ones, like soda biscuits or toasted sesame crackers or matzóth. I usually have crackers passed with the first course, too; and with the main part of the meal I like French or Italian bread or small croissants (the authentic French kind are so rich and flaky you really don't need butter with them) or crisp rolls. The breads and rolls you can buy all ready to brown are not only easy and good; they have an appealing "baked specially" quality, too. All soft and rubbery breads—the kind that are chilled and served at some banquets—leave me cold, and I think it is a crime to let white bread come to the table any way but toasted. Very thinly sliced pumpernickel and salty rye are awfully good with fish and seafood; so are little cucumber sandwiches; and thin rye toast is not served often enough.

A buffet, as I have said before, may be only a way of solving a serving problem, in which case the menu would be the same as that for an informal seated dinner though guests simply help themselves. The large buffet is another thing entirely—sort of a vaudeville show, a variety party. You start with a list of guests that is simply too long to make the passing of platters practical. Then, instead of assuming that every one will eat every dish that is offered, you plan on a wide enough choice of different dishes so that each of your guests will find one or two that tempt his taste especially. Here, too, food balance is part of the plan. Instead of a single main dish, there are three or four. At least one is hot; at least one is fish or seafood, and at least one is cold meat. Curried chicken and lobster, beef or tarragon chicken in jelly, sautéed veal marengo, risotto with chicken livers, paella—all these have been great buffet successes. Obviously, an important consideration with any buffet dish is its waiting power. An aspic that comes unjelled or a cooling filet that should have been served sizzling hot is no more appealing than ice cream running to soup.

Buffets

(*141*)

To the main courses you add a salad, breads, cheese and dessert. If it is at all possible, I like to have dessert and coffee passed. I always plan on a fresh fruit (mixed fruit with rum or kirsch or brandy, oranges in red wine, a hollowed melon filled with fruit) and cake or *petits fours* for guests who like something sweet. For nondieters, there might be a *crème brûlée* or a Bavarian cream as well.

Brunches   Brunches are almost always buffets, but their menus can be approached in two ways. Our daughter Linda, who has had some delightful ones, starts with a sort of smorgasbord in mind and offers six or eight different good things to eat at a time; there's plenty of everything, but no huge amount of any one dish is called for. (One of her menus is given on page 212.) Or you may treat the whole thing as a spectacular late breakfast built around lavish quantities of a single very good main dish. Scrambled eggs or omelets, pancakes or waffles that should go from griddle to plate with no chill platter between can be done on the spot in the dining room, a production hungry audiences applaud.

Either way, it's an informal party that owes part of its fun and its character to the in-between hour. The food you serve has a slightly breakfasty feeling; and there should always be lots of good hot coffee. But because it is also lunch time, you serve something a bit dessert-like and offer drinks beforehand. The usual drink choice is between fruit or tomato juice plain and fruit or tomato juice doctored—as in Bloody Marys, Screw Drivers and Whiskey Sours, all of which make very good pre-brunch drinks. Another vodka concoction called the Bull-Shot (bouillon on the rocks with a shot of vodka) is fine, too; but remember to use non-jelling consommé for your base.

Canapés   Taking your dinner menu into account, you should follow the same rules of balance in planning hors d'oeuvres. There are so many good ones. I love crab fingers or shrimp or chunks of lobster meat with a curried mayonnaise or *sauce vert;* smoked salmon (sprinkled with freshly ground black pepper) on thin, unbuttered slices of pumpernickel; raw mushroom caps filled with caviar and sour cream; cherry tomatoes with paté inside; little raw meat balls (about an inch in diameter); and quail eggs with freshly ground pepper. I always offer several kinds of raw vegetables (zucchini and carrots with seasoned salt, cauliflower with mustard mayonnaise), not only to keep dieters happy, but also because they taste so good. Hot canapés, such as tiny frozen pastries, are marvelous if you are geared to serve them and disastrous if they turn cool and rubbery. But although I like hot cheese puffs and small wedges of *quiche* as hors d'oeuvres, I'm not a great devotee of strong cheese before a meal. And I am downright opposed to gooey canapés and those garnished with chopped egg, not only out of consideration for my own carpets and upholstery, but because it takes no more than a trickle on a guest's pretty new dress to ruin her whole evening. For most parties four or five good ideas are plenty; and there are hundreds of wonderful ones to choose from.

In general, whether it is brunch or a white-tie dinner served standing or seated or reclining on Roman couches, the thing to serve is a dish you've tried before. When things are unfamiliar, mistakes are more likely to happen. I know a bride who served green shrimp cocktail to guests (she didn't know that they turn pink only with cooking) and another who built a towel into her chocolate roll (well, the recipe did say "roll in a towel"). And we once had a cook who proudly informed me she'd "cut all the legs off those bugs," by which she meant some prize soft-shell crabs I'd managed to find for a party. I was crushed and then astounded later when they appeared on the table, legs attached—that is, until I saw the black thread with which she'd painstakingly sewed each one on again.

I don't mean it is wrong to try anything new. You can work all sorts of variations—add sherry, substitute herbs—on a recipe you know. But you should be reasonably sure of the basic dish: of the time it takes to prepare it, how long it will wait for guests and the handsomest way to serve it. More than anything else, the knowledge that your meal will be delicious gives you the sense of ease every hostess should feel about any party she plans.

CHAPTER
7

Menus with a Sense of Balance (and Recipes)

THE MENUS in this chapter are designed only to set your own imagination going. There is nothing inherently formal about curried shrimp with rice or invariably informal about turtle soup with sherry; the turtle soup might very well be the first course at a formal dinner, while the curried shrimp would make a delicious main course at lunch. Because availability varies with geography, my wine suggestions are general rather than specific. Assuming you have favorite cookbooks at hand, I've given only those recipes I feel might be hard to find or those for dishes that come straight from friends' kitchens or my own. All of them are yours to try, to experiment with, to enjoy.

Formal Dinners

FORMAL DINNER 1

Curried shrimp with rice
Rock Cornish hens
String beans with almonds   Soufflé potatoes
Spinach-and-bacon salad   Assorted cheese
Crème brulée with crushed strawberries *

A simple natural gravy with the main course goes well between the hot curry and the blandness of the *crème brulée*. Use young raw spinach and bits of very crisp bacon for the salad. The sharp flavor of the strawberries keeps the *crème* from being too sweet.

Serve a red Bordeaux with the hens and Chateau d'Yquem with dessert.

CRÈME BRULÉE
(*Serves 8*)

8 egg yolks, slightly beaten
2 tablespoons granulated sugar
Pinch of salt
4 cups light cream, scalded
¼ cup brandy (4 tablespoons)
1 cup brown sugar
2 lb. home-stewed strawberries or 3 packages frozen sliced straw-
    berries

Combine the slightly beaten yolks of 8 eggs with 2 tablespoons granulated sugar and a pinch of salt. Stir in gradually 4 cups scalded light cream and
cook over boiling water for 5 minutes, or until mixture coats a wooden spoon,
stirring constantly. Pour into large, round, shallow oven-proof dish and cool,
then chill slightly. Pour ¼ cup brandy over top and chill thoroughly. About 30
minutes before serving, preheat broiling unit to very hot. Cover the surface of
the custard with a thick layer of soft sifted brown sugar, using at least 1 cup.

Place dish on tray of cracked ice, reduce heat of broiling unit to low and broil until top of sugar melts to a brown glaze (be careful not to let the sugar catch fire—it browns very quickly). Serve a bowl of home-stewed or defrosted frozen strawberries with the *crème*.

FORMAL DINNER 2

Cold filet of sole mousse with lobster sauce *
Breast of chicken on tongue with tarragon sauce *
French peas   Parsleyed potato balls
Raw mushroom and lettuce salad   Assorted cheese
Strawberry tart

You might vary this dinner in several ways. The mousse can be served hot or cold, or it can be made of salmon instead of sole. For a change of hot sauces, try a mousseline (a lighter version of hollandaise) or a curried one; a mustard sauce or dilled mayonnaise are excellent cold ones. I prefer tongue to the ham more usually served with the chicken breasts. Cook some lettuce and tiny onions with the peas. A soft cheese—Camembert, Brie or Crème Chantilly—should be offered, as well as a firm one like Bel Paese, Port-Salut or Taleggio. Keeping color in mind, you might substitute a cherry or blueberry tart for dessert.

If you serve two wines, try a Montrachet with the fish and chicken, a champagne with the tart.

COLD FILET OF SOLE MOUSSE WITH LOBSTER SAUCE
(*Serves 8*)

1½ lbs. fresh filet of sole or flounder
2 cups (1 pint) heavy cream
2 egg whites
Dash of pepper
Dash of cayenne
Salt to taste (about 1 teaspoon)
Preheat oven to 350° F.

Put 1½ lbs. fresh filet of sole or flounder through the meat grinder three times, using first the coarse, then the medium and last of all the finest blade. Place this purée in a bowl and stir in 2 cups heavy cream, a dash each of pepper and cayenne and about 1 teaspoon salt. Place half the mixture in an electric blender and run for a minute or two, stopping to press the fish down into the bottom of the blender. Remove mixture to bowl, and repeat the process with the remainder. Blend the two lots together. Stir 2 unbeaten raw egg whites into the mixture and run through the blender again, half of it at a time. Butter a 1½-quart mold and fill with the fish mixture. Tie buttered brown paper over the top. Place mold in a pan of boiling water in preheated 350° F. oven and bake until set (about 18 to 20 minutes). Cool and chill thoroughly. (This mousse can, of course, be served hot as well.) Unmold and serve with the following Lobster Sauce. Sprinkle with finely chopped parsley before serving.

Lobster Sauce

2 large shallots
2 tablespoons butter
1 tablespoon flour
½ cup milk
¾ cup tomato juice
1½ lbs. boiled lobster meat
2 to 3 tablespoons dry sherry
½ cup heavy cream (optional)

Peel and chop 2 shallots very fine. Lightly brown them in 2 tablespoons butter. Stir in 1 tablespoon flour and cook for a minute or two. Heat together ½ cup milk with ¾ cup tomato juice and add slowly while hot to the shallots, flour and butter. Stir until smooth. Remove from fire and add to the sauce 1½ lbs. fresh boiled lobster meat, cut into small pieces. Cool and chill. Just before serving, mix in 2 to 3 tablespoons of dry sherry, and if added richness is desired, stir in ½ cup heavy cream.

BREAST OF CHICKEN ON TONGUE
WITH TARRAGON SAUCE

(*Serves 8*)

10 chicken breasts, boned (halved breasts of 5 chickens)
¼ lb. butter, clarified
½ cup dry white wine
1 cup chicken stock
2 tablespoons fresh chopped tarragon or 1 tablespoon dried tarragon
4 teaspoons cornstarch dissolved in 1 tablespoon cold water
10 slices of cooked smoked tongue
3 truffles, peeled and chopped (1 ⅞-oz. can)
Salt, pepper to taste

Brown 10 chicken breasts slowly in large iron frying pan, in ¼ lb. clarified butter. Turn until golden on both sides. Pour over the chicken ½ cup dry white wine and 1 cup chicken stock and add 1 tablespoon of dried tarragon or 2 tablespoons of fresh chopped tarragon. Cook over low heat until tender (about 1 hour). Remove skin from breasts. Keep chicken hot in top part of double boiler over boiling water. Add 4 teaspoons cornstarch dissolved in 1 tablespoon cold water to the remaining chicken broth. Stir until thickened and bubbling hot. Heat 10 slices of cooked smoked tongue in this sauce and place on hot platter. Place 1 chicken breast on each slice. Add the chopped truffles. Season sauce to taste with salt and a dash of pepper. Pour sauce over the chicken and tongue and serve.

FORMAL DINNER 3

*Lobster with special sauce ***
Filet of beef with truffles, sauce Béarnaise
Bouquet of vegetables
Green salad   Assorted cheese
*Oranges in red wine ***

The fish dish can also be made with mixed seafood—crabmeat, shrimp, lobster and, when available, small bay scallops and mussels, or any two or three of these. A short loin of beef may be substituted for the filet; I actually prefer it because it has more texture and flavor. The vegetables look attractive on the meat platter: little clusters of peas, mushrooms, string beans and small boiled potatoes with parsley. The simple dessert provides a refreshing contrast to the rich sauces of the dinner.

If you serve two wines, try a Pouilly-Fumé with the fish and a red Burgundy with the beef. If you serve only one wine, make it Burgundy.

LOBSTER WITH SPECIAL SAUCE
(*Serves 8*)

8 small lobsters (about 1 lb. each)
6 tablespoons butter
16 shallots, finely chopped
2 cups dry white wine
1½ cups heavy cream
1 lump sugar
Salt, paprika to taste
3 tablespoons English mustard
1 tablespoon finely chopped parsley

Plunge 8 small lobsters, head first, into a large pot of actively boiling salted water. Cover the pot and boil about 12 minutes, counting from the time the water comes to a second boil. Remove lobsters from water and place on a large wooden board, shell side up, pulling tails out flat. Cool, turn over and split the undershell lengthwise with a sharp knife. Remove and discard the dark vein, the sac near the head and spongy tissue, but save the green liver and coral, if any. Remove the tails and claws from the shells and cut into bite-sized pieces. Melt 6 tablespoons butter in large saucepan. Add 16 finely chopped shallots and cook for a minute or two without browning. Add the lobster meat, 2 cups of dry white wine, 3 tablespoons of dry English mustard, dissolved in ½ cup cream, 1 lump of sugar and salt and paprika to taste. Cook over very low heat for 10 minutes, add another cup of heavy cream into which you have stirred the green liver and the coral, and continue simmering on very low flame for another 10 minutes. Place in hot serving dish, sprinkle with 1 tablespoon of finely chopped parsley and serve.

ORANGES IN RED WINE
(*Serves 8*)

8 to 10 navel oranges
3 tablespoons orange rind cut in fine shreds
1 cup red Bordeaux wine
1 cup water
2 slices lemon including the rind but without seeds
2 sections tangerine
¾ cup granulated sugar
1 3-inch stick cinnamon
2 whole cloves

Prepare the thin shreds of orange rind and set aside. With very sharp knife cut away rind and white bitter part from 8 to 10 navel oranges, exposing the fruit. Slice between each section, making moon-shaped pieces, minus membrane. Place in serving dish and sprinkle with shredded orange rind.

Pour 1 cup red Bordeaux wine in pan and add 1 cup water, 2 slices of lemon, 2 sections from 1 tangerine (seeds and tough white part cut away with scissors) and ¾ cup granulated sugar. Tie up a 3-inch stick of cinnamon bark and 2 whole cloves in a piece of cheesecloth and add to pot. Bring to a boil, stirring until sugar has melted. Pour over the orange sections, discarding lemon, tangerine and spice bag. Cool and chill for several hours before serving.

FORMAL DINNER 4

Crêpes filled with crabmeat and mushrooms in cheese sauce *
Boned jumbo squabs stuffed with wild rice
Puréed spinach
Hearts of palm salad　　Assorted cheese
Peaches in red wine *

Because the first dish is a filling one, I have eliminated rich sauces from the other courses. Have you ever watched a man struggle to get meat from a squab? Do have your butcher bone the birds, and be rewarded by the delight of your guests when they find they can eat every bit.

Try a red Burgundy with the squabs and a dry champagne with the dessert.

CRÊPES FILLED WITH CRABMEAT AND MUSHROOMS IN CHEESE SAUCE

(Serves 8)

For the batter

¾ cup unsifted flour
Pinch of salt
1 egg
1 egg yolk
1 cup milk
2 tablespoons melted butter
1 tablespoon brandy
6 tablespoon butter, clarified

Sift into a small bowl ¾ cup of flour with a pinch of salt. Beat lightly 1 egg plus 1 extra yolk into 1 cup milk. Add this to flour slowly. Add 2 tablespoons melted butter and 1 tablespoon brandy. Mix well and strain. Clarify 6 tablespoons butter. Heat a 6-inch iron frying pan and when hot add a little clarified butter, tilting the pan so that the inside is coated; drain off excess butter and pour into the pan 2 scant tablespoons batter. Tilt pan again so that the bottom is completely covered with a thin coating of batter. Cook until lightly browned on one side (about ½ minute), then with the aid of a small, thin spatula turn crêpe over and brown the other side. Turn out bottom side up onto dish towel. Repeat process until all the batter is used, making about 14 to 16 crêpes. Then make the filling.

Filling

¾ lb. small fresh mushrooms
3 tablespoons butter
1 tablespoon flour
½ cup milk
½ cup dry sherry
¾ cup grated American cheese
½ lb. fresh lump crabmeat
¼ teaspoon salt
Dash of pepper
Preheat oven to 250° F.

Wash, stem, and if necessary peel ¾ lb. small fresh mushrooms and slice fine. Sauté these quickly in 2 tablespoons butter until they form their juice. Set aside. Melt 1 tablespoon butter in top part of double boiler on direct low heat and stir in 1 tablespoon flour. Cook for a minute or two without browning, then add gradually ½ cup hot milk, making a smooth white sauce. Add ½ cup sherry and ¾ cup grated American cheese and cook over low heat, stirring constantly with wooden spoon, until thickened, then add the mushrooms and their juice and ½ lb. fresh lump crabmeat, carefully picked over to remove all cartilage. Season to taste with about ¼ teaspoon salt and a pinch of pepper. Butter a large rectangular oven-proof dish and place in oven to warm. Put two scant tablespoons of the mushroom and crabmeat mixture on each crêpe and roll up; use as little sauce as possible. Raise oven temperature to 350° F. Remove crêpes to warm dish. Pour remaining sauce over the whole; replace in oven until hot, and serve.

PEACHES IN RED WINE
(*Serves 8*)

1½ cups granulated sugar
2 cups red Bordeaux wine
2 cups water
4 slices lemon
1 3-inch stick cinnamon bark
4 whole cloves
12 large freestone peaches
4 sections orange

Place in pan 1½ cups granulated sugar with 2 cups red wine and 2 cups water. Add 4 slices lemon and a cheesecloth bag containing a 3-inch stick of cinnamon bark and 4 whole cloves. Bring to a boil, skim off foam and simmer; meanwhile split in half and remove pits from a dozen large peaches. Drop them into a small quantity of boiling water, one at a time; then plunge into cold water and remove the skins, which should slip off easily. Drop peaches into the syrup as you peel them, and when all have been added, skim foam off again. Add the orange sections, and cook until peaches are just tender (10 to 15 minutes). Remove cheesecloth bag and the orange and lemon slices and place peaches in a serving dish.

Strain wine sauce over the peaches, and serve hot or cold.

INFORMAL DINNER 1

Prosciutto and melon
*Danish chicken with rice **
String beans
Salad with artichoke hearts   *Cheese*
*Chocolate roll **

*Informal
Dinners*

(*151*)

Prosciutto is delicious, too, when served with pears instead of melon. The chicken recipe is my own reconstruction of a marvelous dish we had at the Danish Pavilion at the 1939 New York World's Fair. I have chosen a simple first course because the chocolate roll is so wonderfully rich.

Serve a Chablis with the chicken.

DANISH CHICKEN WITH RICE
(*Serves 8*)

10 large chicken breasts (halved breasts of 5 chickens)
5 cans chicken broth
4 stalks celery
4 small carrots
2 onions
6 cups hot boiled rice

Wipe chicken with damp cloth and place in large pot. Add 5 cans of clear chicken broth and bring very slowly to the simmering point, skimming from time to time. Add 4 stalks of celery, 4 small peeled carrots and 2 onions. Cover partially and simmer gently until tender (about 1¼ hours). Strain off and reserve stock, and as soon as chicken is cool enough to handle, pull meat from bones in as large pieces as possible, discarding bones and all the skin. Place chicken in top part of double boiler and cover with part of the broth. Keep warm over hot water while you make the sauce.

Sauce

6 tablespoons butter
6 tablespoons flour
4 cups reserved chicken stock
1 cup sauce (made with 3 egg yolks, 3 tablespoons cold water
  and ¾ cup butter)
2 teaspoons granulated sugar
2½ to 3 tablespoons freshly grated horseradish, or about the same
  amount of dried powdered horseradish
Salt and white pepper to taste
2 tablespoons freshly chopped parsley

Melt 6 tablespoons butter, without browning, in top part of large double boiler. Stir in 6 tablespoons flour, cook over direct low heat for a minute or two, stirring constantly with wooden spoon, then gradually add 4 cups of reserved hot chicken stock. When sauce is smooth and thickened, place over boiling water and continue cooking, stirring occasionally. Keep sauce warm while you mix 3 egg yolks and 3 tablespoons of cold water in the top part of a small double boiler. Melt ¾ cup butter in separate pan. Place the pan containing the yolks and water over small quantity of boiling water, over medium heat, and stir briskly with wire whisk until slightly thickened; then remove from fire and slowly add the melted butter, stirring constantly. Now gradually blend the first sauce into the second. Season cautiously to taste with salt and a very little white pepper. Add 2 teaspoons granulated sugar and 2½ to 3 tablespoons freshly grated horseradish (or about the same quantity of dry powdered horseradish). Strain and keep sauce warm over warm, not hot, water.

Drain the chicken thoroughly and place in center of large hot serving platter. Surround with hot boiled rice and pour part of the sauce over the chicken. Garnish with finely chopped parsley and serve the remainder of the sauce separately.

CHOCOLATE ROLL
(*Serves 8*)

6 oz. dark sweet chocolate (6 squares)
3 tablespoons water
5 egg yolks
¾ cup granulated sugar
5 egg whites
Vegetable oil
Granulated sugar
Unsweetened cocoa
1 cup heavy cream, lightly whipped
2 tablespoons light rum
Confectioners' sugar
Preheat oven to 350° F.

Melt 6 squares of dark sweet chocolate with 3 tablespoons water in top part of double boiler. Beat 5 egg yolks with ¾ cup granulated sugar until pale yellow and creamy. Beat 5 egg whites until stiff. Cool chocolate slightly and blend with egg yolks and sugar. Mix and gently fold in egg whites.

Oil a jelly-roll pan and lay on it a sheet of waxed paper extending about 4 or 5 inches at both ends. Lightly oil paper. Pour batter onto paper, spreading evenly.

Bake in preheated 350° oven for 12 to 15 minutes, or until just set. Remove from oven and press damp cold towel on top of cake and allow to cool. Put in refrigerator for about 4 hours.

Spread overlapping pieces of waxed paper on kitchen table and cover with a mixture of fine granulated sugar and cocoa in the approximate size and shape of the jelly roll pan. Remove towel carefully from cake and turn cake out onto cocoa-and-sugar mixture, peeling off waxed paper gently. Lightly whip 1 cup heavy cream to which you have added 2 tablespoons light rum and a little confectioners' sugar. Spread whipped cream on cake and roll lengthwise, using waxed paper to help shape roll. (Don't worry if it breaks in places.) Transfer roll to serving platter or long board by lifting paper. Trim paper with scissors close to roll. Sprinkle cocoa-and-sugar mixture on any breaks. Chill in refrigerator until time to serve.

INFORMAL DINNER 2

Chicken gumbo soup with crabmeat *
Paupiettes de veau * *with purée of peas* *
Mushroom rice *
Asparagus hollandaise
Macedoine of fruit with Kirsch

The veal has a tomato sauce and looks especially appetizing served on the puréed peas. After the rich hollandaise, the fruit is particularly refreshing. Serve an Alsatian wine with the veal.

CHICKEN GUMBO SOUP WITH CRABMEAT
(*Serves 8*)

4 10½-oz. cans chicken gumbo soup
1 cup dry sherry
1 lb. fresh lump crabmeat

To four 10½-oz. cans of chicken gumbo soup add 1 cup sherry and 1 lb. fresh lump crabmeat which has been carefully gone over to remove any cartilage. Heat to scalding point and serve.

PAUPIETTES DE VEAU WITH PURÉE OF PEAS
(*Serves 8*)

Filling
1½ pounds ground lean veal
4 teaspoons chopped fresh tarragon or 2 teaspoons dried tarragon
4 teaspoons chopped parsley
¼ teaspoon ground cloves
Pinch of cayenne pepper
¼ teaspoon salt, pepper
2 tablespoons egg whites
2 tablespoons heavy cream

Veal Rolls
2 pounds veal cutlet, cut in 16 very thin even slices
Salt, pepper

8 slices boiled ham, cut in two (or 16 thin slices of tongue)
¼ pound butter, clarified
4 tablespoons dry sherry
3 tablespoons flour
2 teaspoons tomato paste
1½ cups clear chicken broth
2 bay leaves

Mix 1½ pounds ground lean veal with 4 teaspoons chopped fresh tarragon or 2 teaspoons of dried tarragon, 4 teaspoons of chopped parsley, ¼ teaspoon ground cloves, a pinch of cayenne, and ¼ teaspoon salt and pepper. Soften with 2 tablespoons unbeaten egg white and 2 tablespoons of heavy cream.

Pound slices of veal between 2 pieces of waxed paper, dividing the meat to make 16 small uniform pieces. Spread them out on waxed paper and sprinkle lightly with salt and pepper. Place a thin slice of ham or tongue on each. Spread the filling over the meat, dividing the mixture equally. Roll up and tie with string. Place ¼ pound of clarified butter in a large heavy frying pan, and when it is sizzling hot, add the veal rolls and brown them lightly on all sides (about 15 minutes). Place the rolls in a heated casserole. Pour over them 4 tablespoons heated sherry. Add to the residue in frying pan 3 tablespoons flour and 2 teaspoons tomato paste, stir with wooden spoon and cook 2 or 3 minutes. Add gradually 1½ cups hot clear chicken broth, and stir until smooth. Pour over the veal rolls, add 2 bay leaves, cover and cook over low heat about ½ hour longer.

PURÉE OF PEAS

3 pounds fresh peas
½ teaspoon salt
3 tablespoons butter
5 tablespoons flour
¾ cup heavy cream

While the meat is cooking, cook the peas in small quantity of boiling water with ½ teaspoon salt. Drain and rub through a sieve. Melt 3 tablespoons butter in a saucepan, add 5 tablespoons flour, and cook over low heat, stirring constantly with wooden spoon, until the mixture is lightly browned. Add the puréed peas and mix well, then gradually stir in ¾ cup heavy cream.

Spread the purée over the bottom of a large serving platter. Remove strings from veal rolls and lay them on top of the purée. Strain sauce, pour over all, and serve.

MUSHROOM RICE

(Serves 8)

1 lb. fresh mushrooms
1 bar and 2 tablespoons butter

Salt, pepper to taste
1½ cups long-grain rice
1 tablespoon parsley, finely chopped

Wash, stem, peel and slice fine 1 lb. fresh mushrooms. Melt 8 tablespoons butter in a frying pan and, as soon as the butter has stopped foaming, add the mushrooms. Toss and shake the pan over moderate heat and cook the mushrooms about 5 minutes. Remove from heat and season to taste with salt and a very little freshly ground pepper.

To 4 quarts of rapidly boiling salted water add 1½ cups unwashed rice slowly (so that water does not stop boiling). Boil for exactly 13 minutes. Put rice into collander and rinse under cold running water. (This may be done in advance.) Twenty minutes before serving, cover rice with towel and steam over boiling water. Fluff rice with fork while it is warming. Add the sautéed mushrooms and mix lightly with two forks. When very hot, add 2 tablespoons butter cut in small pieces. Place in hot serving dish, sprinkle with 1 tablespoon chopped parsley, and serve.

INFORMAL DINNER 3

Smoked salmon with lemon wedges and capers
Veal in lemon butter *
Zucchini   Fettucini
Raspberry water ice surrounded by black brandied cherries

Except for the salmon, this is a northern Italian kind of dinner. The fettucini is rich, but the veal and dessert are simple and balance well.

Serve an Alsatian wine with the salmon and veal.

VEAL IN LEMON BUTTER

(*Serves 8*)

2½ lbs. veal cutlet cut in thin, even slices
¼ lb. butter, clarified
1 cup chicken broth
2 tablespoons additional butter
Salt, pepper to taste
Juice of 2 lemons, strained
2 tablespoons chopped parsley

Pound veal between two pieces of heavy waxed paper until slices are very thin. Clarify ¼ lb. butter. Place 1 cup chicken broth and 2 tablespoons butter in top part of large double boiler, over boiling water. Let veal whiten (but do not brown), one piece at a time, in small amount of clarified butter in frying pan. Place in top of double boiler and proceed in the same manner until all the veal has been whitened. Sprinkle lightly with salt (about 1 teaspoon) and about ¼ teaspoon freshly ground pepper and pour over all the strained juice of two lemons. Cover and allow to cook over boiling water until very tender (about 30 to 35 minutes), basting occasionally with its own juice. Place on hot platter, sprinkle with 2 tablespoons of chopped parsley, and serve, accompanied by fettucini (Italian noodles) bathed in cream and butter and sprinkled with black pepper.

INFORMAL DINNER 4

Onion soup
Beef stew with onions and mushrooms *
Mixed green salad   *Cheese*
Gâteau mousse *

This dessert, based on one I discovered in a French restaurant, is always a big success at our house. Although it is quite complicated, it can be made well in advance.

Serve a full-bodied red Burgundy with the stew.

BEEF STEW WITH ONIONS AND MUSHROOMS
(*Serves 8*)

4 lbs. top round beef, cut into 1½-inch cubes
¼ lb. butter, clarified
2 additional tablespoons butter
3 tablespoons dry sherry
½ lb. small mushrooms
4 tablespoons flour
2 cups beef stock
1 tablespoon tomato paste
Salt, pepper
1 large bay leaf
18 small white onions
1 tablespoon chopped parsley

Spread 4 lbs. top round of beef, cut into 1½-inch cubes, onto paper toweling and sponge dry with another paper towel. Brown the beef in ¼ lb. clarified butter in large iron frying pan. Put 2 additional tablespoons butter in an earthenware casserole and, as the meat browns, transfer it to the casserole. Pour 3 tablespoons hot sherry over the meat and cover. Allow to cook over very low heat while you add to the frying pan ½ lb. small mushrooms previously washed and with the tough part of the stems removed.

Stir the mushrooms with a wooden spoon and cook for a minute or two before adding 4 tablespoons flour. Continue stirring until the flour is well blended, then slowly add 2 cups hot beef stock. Stir in 1 tablespoon tomato paste and season to taste with about ½ teaspoon salt and a dash of pepper. Add 1 large bay leaf and pour the sauce over the meat. Stir with a wooden spoon, cover and simmer gently for about 1 hour. Skim off excess grease. At this point add 18 small white onions, peeled but left whole. Continue cooking until the meat is tender, or for about 2 hours in all. Sprinkle with 1 tablespoon chopped parsley and serve.

GÂTEAU MOUSSE
(*Serves 8*)

For the Sponge Cake:
4 tablespoons cornstarch
6 tablespoons unsifted cake flour
3 egg yolks
3 egg whites
1 tablespoon cold water
Pinch of salt
2 tablespoons melted butter
6 tablespoons granulated sugar
2 tablespoons unsweetened cocoa
Preheat oven to 500° F.

Note: This amount of batter makes 2 thin sponge cakes, but only one is used for the *Gâteau Mousse* which serves 8. (So for a big party, double the ingredients for the Bavarian-cream filling only.) When serving only 8, use the extra cake for trifle.

Butter 2 pans 13″ x 9″ x 1″ deep. Sift 4 tablespoons cornstarch with 6 tablespoons unsifted cake flour and return to sifter. Place 3 egg yolks in a small bowl, with 1 tablespoon cold water, and 3 egg whites in a larger bowl, with a pinch of salt. Have ready 2 tablespoons melted butter and 6 tablespoons of granulated sugar. Beat whites until they form soft peaks, then gradually beat in the previously measured 6 tablespoons sugar until the whites are very stiff. Beat the yolks and water well, and fold into whites. Sift flour and cornstarch together again and fold gently into mixture. Then fold in the melted butter.

Spread batter evenly in the two buttered tins, dividing it equally. Bake 7 minutes in preheated 500° F. oven. Turn out immediately onto wooden board. Cover loosely with paper and towel to prevent cakes from drying out while you make the Bavarian cream filling.

Chocolate Bavarian Cream Filling

2 tablespoons plain powdered gelatin (2 envelopes)
4 tablespoons cold water
2 tablespoons boiling water
1½ cups milk
1 ounce unsweetened chocolate (1 square)
6 tablespoons granulated sugar
3 egg yolks
1 cup heavy cream

Soak 2 tablespoons plain gelatin in 4 tablespoons cold water for 5 minutes. Stir in 2 tablespoons boiling water; set aside. Heat together in top part of double boiler over boiling water 1½ cups milk, 1 ounce of unsweetened chocolate and 3 tablespoons granulated sugar and stir until chocolate has completely melted. Beat 3 egg yolks until light; gradually beat in 3 tablespoons sugar. Pour chocolate-milk mixture into yolks, a little at a time, return to double boiler and cook, stirring constantly until mixture coats wooden spoon; add gelatin and stir until well mixed. Remove from fire, place over cold water and cool, stirring occasionally, until mixture begins to set (about 1 hour), changing cold water to hasten proceedings.

In the meantime, line the long sides and bottom of a 9″ x 4″ x 2½″ loaf pan with one of the thin sponge cakes cut in 3 strips; put browned side of cake on inside of pan.

Watch the Bavarian cream carefully, and when it is about to set, fold in 1 cup heavy cream which has been beaten to a foam (not stiff). Pour cream into cake-lined pan. Cover with waxed paper and refrigerate for several hours. Unmold on serving dish. Sprinkle with 2 tablespoons unsweetened cocoa, and serve sliced, accompanied by well-chilled custard sauce flavored with vanilla and brandy to taste.

Custard Sauce

¾ quart milk
6 tablespoons granulated sugar
6 egg yolks
1 teaspoon vanilla
3 to 4 tablespoons brandy

Heat together in top part of double boiler over boiling water ¾ quart of milk, sweetened with 6 tablespoons granulated sugar. Beat the yolks of 6 eggs until pale and creamy, add a little of the hot milk to the eggs, then add this to the rest of the milk. Cook over boiling water, stirring constantly, until sauce is well thickened and coats the spoon, or for about 6 or 7 minutes. Remove from heat, cool and flavor to taste with 1 teaspoon vanilla and 3 to 4 tablespoons brandy. Chill before serving with the *Gâteau Mousse*.

INFORMAL DINNER 5

Clam vichyssoise *
Beef tenderloin sauté *
String beans with sour cream and caraway seeds
Potatoes boiled in their jackets
Romaine and lettuce salad   Cheese
Black-and-white soufflé *

The soup is my own variation on a summer favorite. It can be served hot or cold. The dessert, like all soufflés, must be timed, but it is worth waiting for.

Try a red Bordeaux or a Burgundy with the beef.

CLAM VICHYSSOISE
(*Serves 8*)

4 large leeks
1 large white onion
4 small potatoes
1½ cups chicken stock
¼ teaspoon salt, dash of freshly ground pepper
3 cups clam broth (2 12-oz. jars)
2 cups light cream
1½ tablespoons parsley, finely chopped

Remove all green part and root ends from 4 large leeks, split them down the center, wash, and slice fine. Peel 1 large white onion and 4 small-sized potatoes, and slice fine. Put all in pan with 1½ cups chicken stock. Season with about ¼ teaspoon salt and a dash of freshly ground pepper. Simmer slowly until mushy, or for about 20 to 25 minutes. Add 3 cups (2 12-oz. jars) clam broth and bring to a boil. Cool partially, then run through electric blender, ⅓ of the mixture at a time until smooth. Put all together in pan and cool, then refrigerate until very cold. Thin to desired consistency with about 2 cups light cream. Pour into 8 chilled serving cups, sprinkle with parsley and serve.

BEEF TENDERLOIN SAUTÉ
(*Serves 8*)

½ lb. small fresh mushrooms
¼ lb. butter

1 tablespoon brandy
1 tablespoon dry sherry
1 tablespoon Madeira
3 tablespoons flour
1 tablespoon French mustard
1 cup beef consommé
3 tablespoons butter, clarified
8 slices beef tenderloin, cut ¾″ thick
Salt, pepper to taste
1 tablespoon chopped parsley (optional)

Wash, stem and pat dry ½ lb. small fresh mushrooms. Heat 2 tablespoons butter in 10″ frying pan and, when it is sizzling hot, add the mushrooms and shake the pan over moderately high heat until mushrooms begin to brown lightly, or for 3 to 4 minutes. Remove from fire and pour over them 1 tablespoon each of brandy, Madeira and sherry. Set on fire and allow flames to subside and go out. Set aside.

Cream together 6 tablespoons butter with 3 tablespoons flour and stir in 1 tablespoon French mustard. Cook these together over low heat, stirring constantly for a minute or two, then gradually add 1 cup hot beef consommé. When it comes to a boil, remove the pan from heat and set aside.

In a heavy iron frying pan, heat 3 tablespoons clarified butter and, when it is sizzling hot, add 8 slices beef tenderloin cut ¾″ thick. Cook rapidly about 3 minutes on each side, for pink centers, turning only once. Add salt and pepper to taste. Place on large hot platter, add the mushrooms and their juice to the frying pan, stir with wooden spoon and, last of all, add the thickened consommé. Stir and, when the sauce is bubbling hot, pour it over the meat and serve. A little finely chopped parsley may be sprinkled over all if desired.

BLACK-AND-WHITE SOUFFLÉ
(*Serves 8*)

6 egg yolks
10 egg whites
½ cup plus 2 tablespoons granulated sugar
3 squares unsweetened chocolate
1⅓ cups milk
4 tablespoons butter (½ bar)
4 tablespoons flour
2 teaspoons vanilla
¼ teaspoon salt
6 ladyfingers split in two
2 tablespoons brandy
Extra confectioners' sugar in a sifter
　　　Preheat oven to 375° F.

Butter a round 3-quart oven-proof glass baking dish and sugar it with 1 tablespoon granulated sugar. Place 6 egg yolks in a small bowl. Place 5 egg whites in a large bowl and 5 more egg whites in another larger bowl. Measure out ½ cup plus 2 tablespoons granulated sugar. Melt 3 squares unsweetened chocolate in top part of small double boiler over hot water. Heat 1⅓ cups of milk in a small pan. Melt 4 tablespoons butter in top part of a 2-quart double boiler over hot water. Add 4 level tablespoons flour to the melted butter and stir over very low heat for a minute or two, then gradually stir in the hot milk, making a smooth thick sauce. Place over boiling water and stir in the measured granulated sugar. Cook for a minute or two and remove from fire. Beat the egg yolks until very light, and stir into them part of the sauce, then stir the whole into the remainder of the sauce. Flavor with 2 teaspoons of vanilla and ¼ teaspoon salt. Pour half of this into a medium-sized bowl, and to the remainder in the pan add the melted chocolate, mixing with a spoon until thoroughly blended. Beat the whites of 5 eggs until stiff and fold them carefully into the chocolate mixture. Pour into the 3-quart buttered-and-sugared dish. Split 6 whole ladyfingers and sprinkle with 2 tablespoons brandy. Lay the soaked ladyfingers on top of chocolate mixture. Beat the other 5 egg whites until stiff and fold them into the yellow mixture. Cover the ladyfingers with this. Place the baking dish in a large pan of hot water and put in preheated 375° F. oven. Close the door gently, and bake the black-and-white soufflé for 35 to 40 minutes without looking. Remove from oven carefully, sprinkle lightly with confectioners' sugar and serve at once.

INFORMAL DINNER 6

*Boula soup ***

Breasts of chicken in wine surrounded by artichoke bottoms

*with squash ***

Peas with prosciutto   Riced potatoes

Salad

*Hot fruit, custard sauce ***

The hot fruit dish is unusual. We first tasted it at Ralph and Georgia Colin's, and it was so marvelous I begged for the recipe. In the summer, I make it with fresh fruit sprinkled with Cointreau or Kirsch, and it is delicious.

Serve a light red Bordeaux with the main course.

BOULA SOUP

(*Serves 8*)

2 packages frozen peas
2 onions, peeled and chopped

> 1 quart clear turtle soup with turtle meat (2 1-lb.-4-oz. cans)
> ½ cup dry sherry
> Salt, pepper to taste
> 1 cup heavy cream, whipped
>   Preheat broiling unit.

Cook 2 packages frozen peas with 2 onions, peeled and finely chopped, in 3 cups boiling, salted water, until tender, or for about 15 minutes. Cool the mixture partially and run it through electric blender. Add the contents of two 1-lb.-4-oz. cans clear turtle soup with turtle meat, and heat to boiling point. Add ½ cup sherry and salt and pepper to taste. Place soup in 8 individual casserole soup servers and top each with a spoonful of whipped cream. (Work quickly, to avoid chilling soup or melting cream.) Place under preheated broiling unit for a moment, until lightly browned, and serve.

BREASTS OF CHICKEN IN WINE
(*Serves 8*)

> 10 large chicken breasts, boned and skinned (halved breasts of 5 chickens)
> ½ lb. butter, clarified
> 1 bar and 2 tablespoons butter
> ½ to ¾ cup chopped parsley
> 2 teaspoons chopped fresh rosemary or 1 teaspoon dried rosemary
> ½ teaspoon salt
> 1¼ cups dry white wine
> 1½ cups clear chicken broth
> 2 12-oz. packages of frozen cooked yellow squash
> 2 14¾-oz. cans of artichoke bottoms

Place chicken breasts on wooden board which has been covered with waxed paper. Cover chicken breasts with waxed paper as well, and beat flat with heavy wooden mallet; remove paper and set chicken aside. Clarify ½ lb. butter; set aside. Cream together 1 bar and 2 tablespoons butter with ½ to ¾ cup chopped parsley, 2 teaspoons chopped fresh rosemary (or 1 teaspoon dried rosemary) and add ½ teaspoon salt. Spread this over the chicken breasts, dividing it equally. Roll and tie with string.

Heat the prepared clarified butter in a large heavy frying pan and, when it is sizzling hot, add the chicken breasts and sauté to a golden brown on all sides (about 10 minutes). Place a few spoonfuls of the butter in which the chicken was cooked in a separate heated casserole, add the chicken and ¼ cup dry white wine. Cover tightly and simmer gently over low heat for about half an hour. Baste from time to time to prevent sticking. In the meantime, add to butter remaining in frying pan 1½ cups clear chicken broth and stir well to dissolve brown residue. Boil down rapidly to syrupy consistency (about 8 minutes). Add 1 cup dry white wine and boil for another 2 minutes. Pour off into small pan and allow to stand until excess butter rises to surface. Skim off most of the butter. There should be about ¾ cup of rich gravy. Keep gravy hot in double boiler over boiling water. Five minutes before the chicken is done, remove strings, keeping chicken hot over the low heat.

Prepare 2 packages frozen cooked yellow squash, following directions given, and heat in double boiler the contents of two 14¾-oz. cans of artichoke bottoms.

When ready to serve the chicken, place the drained artichoke bottoms around the edge of a large hot serving platter. Fill artichoke bottoms with the squash and place the cooked chicken in the center, along with whatever pot gravy remains. Serve accompanied by the additional gravy in a hot sauce boat.

HOT FRUIT, CUSTARD SAUCE
(*Serves 8*)

1 1-lb.-14-oz. can of Bartlett pear halves
1 1-lb.-14-oz. can of peaches
1 1-lb.-14-oz. can of apricot halves
1 1-lb. can of pitted red sour cherries
5 whole cloves
Shredded rind of 2 lemons
3 tablespoons dry sherry
½ cup seedless raisins
Preheat oven to 450° F.

Mix the juice from canned pears, peaches, apricots and cherries. Add cloves, shredded rind from 1 lemon and 3 tablespoons dry sherry. Cook until well reduced, or for about 1 hour. Arrange fruits attractively in oblong, oven-proof glass baking dish, 12″ x 7½″ x 2″, and sprinkle with remainder of lemon rind and the raisins. Strain the reduced cooked juice and pour 1 cup of it over the fruit. Put dish in preheated 450° F. oven until fruit begins to simmer (about 20 minutes), then place a rectangular dish of water under the fruit on the shelf below to catch the juice, if it should boil over. Cover the fruit with a piece of aluminum foil and continue cooking for about 1 hour, adding additional juice as needed and using it all. Serve very hot with cold custard sauce.

Cold Custard Sauce

8 egg yolks
2 tablespoons granulated sugar
2 cups light cream
4 tablespoons brandy

Beat 8 egg yolks with 2 tablespoons sugar. Heat 2 cups light cream and pour gradually over yolks. Cook in double boiler, stirring constantly until mixture coats wooden spoon, or for 4 to 5 minutes. Be careful not to overcook. Allow to cool. Add brandy and chill.

INFORMAL DINNER 7

Hot beef consommé with slice of lemon
Pork rolls *
Baby lima beans with dill   Soufflé potatoes
Ginger roll *

The recipe for the pork rolls comes from Georgann Prager. They are delicious, but very rich; so I have kept the first course simple. The ginger roll, which I learned to do at the Cordon Bleu, usually comes as a big surprise—people expect chocolate.

A Pouilly-Fumé is excellent with the pork rolls.

PORK ROLLS

(Serves 8)

4 lb. loin of pork, boned, and cut into 16 ½″-thick slices with all
    fat removed
6 slices white bread, crusts removed
2 eggs
½ lb. lean beef
12 slices bacon
6 tablespoons chopped onion
2 tablespoons butter
4 tablespoons chopped parsley
4 shallots, finely chopped
1 cup freshly grated Parmesan cheese
¾ teaspoon salt
⅛ teaspoon pepper
⅓ teaspoon nutmeg
⅓ lb. fresh mushrooms, washed, stemmed, peeled and finely sliced
3 tablespoons tomato paste
3 tablespoons beef consommé
⅔ cup dry white wine
Preheat oven to 350° F.

Pound 16 slices of fat-free pork between 2 pieces of waxed paper until they are very thin; set aside. Remove crusts from 6 slices white bread and moisten with ⅔ cup cold water. Break up with fork and drain off excess liquid. Place 2 whole eggs in large bowl and beat well with fork. Add the bread. Run ½ lb. lean beef through meat grinder, using coarse blade, and do the same to 4 slices bacon. Add both to the bread-and-egg mixture. Mix well. Lightly

(*165*)

brown 3 tablespoons chopped onion in 2 tablespoons butter and add to the bread and meat. Add 2 tablespoons chopped parsley and 4 shallots, peeled and finely chopped. Add 1 cup freshly grated Parmesan cheese and season to taste with about ¾ teaspoon salt, ⅛ teaspoon pepper and ⅓ teaspoon nutmeg. Blend well, and place a heaping tablespoon or more on each slice of pork, dividing the mixture equally. Roll up neatly and wrap each in ½ slice of bacon, securing with toothpicks. Place, toothpick side up, side by side in a roasting pan. Bake in preheated 350° F. oven for about 55 minutes. Transfer to an oven-proof serving dish, remove toothpicks and return to oven. Turn off heat while you make the sauce.

Add to the fat and brown residue in roasting pan 3 tablespoons chopped onion and cook gently until soft, or for about 5 minutes, then add 1 tablespoon chopped parsley and ⅓ lb. fresh mushrooms, previously washed, stemmed, peeled and sliced fine. Cook for another 5 minutes, stirring with wooden spoon. Drain off excess fat, stir in 3 tablespoons tomato paste thinned with 3 tablespoons beef consommé and ⅔ cup dry white wine. Stir well, simmer for a minute or two and pour over the meat. Sprinkle with 1 tablespoon chopped parsley and serve.

GINGER ROLL
(*Serves 8*)

⅓ cup butter
⅓ cup granulated sugar
⅓ cup molasses
1 cup flour
1 teaspoon baking soda
1 teaspoon ginger
1 teaspoon cinnamon
1 teaspoon allspice
1 teaspoon nutmeg
½ cup hot water
1 beaten egg
Confectioners' sugar
1 cup heavy cream
½ teaspoon vanilla
Preheat oven to 375° F.

Melt ⅓ cup butter and mix with ⅓ cup sugar and ⅓ cup molasses. Put flour, baking soda, spices, beaten egg and ½ cup hot water in bowl and combine with molasses mixture, beating lightly until blended. Lightly oil a jelly-roll pan 13½″ x 9½″ x 1″ deep. Line the pan with waxed paper, leaving ends of paper extending about 4 or 5 inches at both ends. Lightly oil paper.

Spread mix on paper evenly and bake in preheated 375° oven until set (about 12 to 15 minutes). Remove from oven, cover with cloth wrung out in cold water, cool 5 minutes, then chill in refrigerator for 25 minutes longer. Put overlapping sheets of wax paper on kitchen table. Dust paper with confectioners' sugar in approximate size of jelly-roll pan. Remove pan from refrigerator and towel from top of roll and turn roll out onto sugared paper. Gently pull off paper. Beat 1 cup heavy cream until just barely stiff. Flavor and sweeten it to taste with about ½ teaspoon vanilla and about 1 tablespoon of confectioners' sugar. Spread evenly over roll and roll up lengthwise, using paper to help shape roll. Holding ends of paper, lift roll onto platter. Cut off ends of paper. Chill roll in refrigerator. When ready to serve, sprinkle with confectioners' sugar. (Keeping a vanilla bean in sugar gives it a delicious flavor.)

INFORMAL DINNER 8

Prosciutto with pear
Pot roast
French peas   Potato pancakes *
Salad   Cheese
Lemon ice with crème de menthe

A Burgundy would go well with the pot roast, or—if it's a very informal evening—beer. Pass a bottle of *crème de menthe* after the ice has been served.

POTATO PANCAKES
(*Serves 8*)

9 medium-sized potatoes
3 eggs, beaten
3 teaspoons flour
2¼ teaspoons sugar
1½ teaspoons salt
1½ teaspoons baking powder
½ bar butter, clarified

Peel and grate 9 medium-sized potatoes, using medium side of grater. Work quickly, since the grated potatoes turn brown when exposed to air. Beat 3 eggs and add to the potatoes. Mix together in a small cup 3 teaspoons flour, 2¼ teaspoons sugar, 1½ teaspoons salt and 1½ teaspoons baking powder, and stir into the potato-and-egg mixture. Heat large heavy frying pan and add a teaspoon of clarified butter. Tilt pan until the whole surface is covered, then drop a tablespoon of the mixture into the pan and cook over moderate heat until brown on one side (about 1 minute), turn and brown the other side. Transfer to the top part of double boiler over boiling water to keep hot while you make the rest, adding a little additional clarified butter as needed to grease frying pan. Serve with pot roast.

INFORMAL DINNER 9

Chicken and turtle soup with sherry *
Curried lamb with rice and chutney
String beans
Asparagus vinaigrette
Miniature jelly rolls *

When fresh peaches are available, use them crushed instead of jelly in the dessert rolls; serve with a sauceboat full of additional crushed, sugared peaches and a pitcher of cream.

A *vin rosé* is good with the lamb.

CHICKEN AND TURTLE SOUP WITH SHERRY
(Serves 8)

3 cups clear chicken broth (2 14½-oz. cans)
2 1-lb.-4-oz. cans clear turtle soup
1 cup dry sherry
8 slices lemon

Combine 3 cups of clear chicken broth (2 14½-oz. cans) with 2 1-lb.-4-oz. cans of clear turtle soup. Add 1 cup dry sherry and bring to a boil. Serve hot, with a slice of lemon in each serving.

MINIATURE JELLY ROLLS
(Serves 8)

3 egg yolks
1 teaspoon grated orange rind
4 tablespoons cornstarch
6 tablespoons flour
3 egg whites
6 tablespoons granulated sugar
2 tablespoons butter, melted
Confectioners' sugar
8 oz. blackberry jelly
    Preheat oven to 500° F.

Lightly oil a jelly-roll pan measuring 17½″ x 11½″ x 1″ and line it with heavy waxed paper, allowing paper to extend beyond the ends of the pan about 2 inches.

(*168*)

Cream together 3 egg yolks, 1 tablespoon water, and 1 teaspoon grated orange rind; set aside. Sift together 4 tablespoons cornstarch and 6 tablespoons flour; set aside. Beat the whites of 3 eggs until almost stiff. Then beat in gradually 6 tablespoons granulated sugar. Fold the egg whites into the yolk mixture. Sift the flour again into the egg mixture and fold in gently. Add 2 tablespoons melted butter, fold it in but stop as soon as the butter disappears. Spread batter evenly into pan and bake in preheated 500° F. oven for about 7 minutes. In the meantime, spread a dish towel on kitchen counter or bread board and cover with a piece of waxed paper. Sprinkle the paper lightly with confectioners' sugar. Turn cake out gently onto sugared paper. Lay a cloth wrung out in cold water over the cake and cool 10 minutes. Remove cloth and peel off the waxed paper carefully. Trim edges of cake with sharp knife. Soften slightly 8 oz. of blackberry jelly in top part of double boiler over hot water. Spread jelly evenly over cake, stopping about 1 inch from edges. Starting with the long side and using the paper to help, form a tight roll and secure by twisting both ends of paper. Refrigerate. When ready to serve, transfer roll to serving platter and remove paper. Cut roll into 8 slices, dust with confectioners' sugar and serve.

INFORMAL DINNER 10

Hot madrilène with slice of lemon
Veal rolls *
Zucchini with mustard hollandaise　　　*Rigatoni in butter*
Beet and endive salad
Lime chiffon pie

My sister-in-law Wilhelmina contributed the recipe for the veal rolls. Because they are made with prosciutto and cheese, I have omitted cheese with the salad. After such a substantial main course, the lime pie is delicate and light.

Serve a Pouilly-Fumé with the veal.

VEAL ROLLS

(*Serves 8*)

16 small scallions
2 lbs. veal cutlet, cut into 16 thin, even slices
8 slices prosciutto ham or boiled ham, cut very thin
2 6-oz. packages Muenster cheese, cut into 16 pieces
½ lb. butter, clarified (2 bars)
1⅔ cups sweet vermouth
1 tablespoon chopped parsley
　　　　Preheat oven to 350° F.

Remove root ends and green part from 16 scallions; wash thoroughly; set aside. Cover wooden bread board or table with waxed paper and spread out over it 2 lbs. veal cutlet divided into 16 pieces, as equal in size as possible. Cover veal with more waxed paper and pound with wooden mallet until very thin. Place ½ slice prosciutto or boiled ham on each slice of veal. Cover the ham with a slice of Muenster cheese slightly smaller than the meat. Put a scallion in the center of each and roll up the veal, tying each piece with string. Clarify ½ lb. butter. Place in large, heavy frying pan and, when it is sizzling hot, add the rolls and brown quickly on all sides. Transfer the rolls to a large heated rectangular baking dish. Add 1⅔ cups of sweet vermouth to the pan drippings and stir with a wooden spoon over low heat to incorporate brown residue; pour the whole over the veal rolls. Place baking dish in preheated 350° F. oven and bake for 20 to 30 minutes, basting occasionally. Remove strings from rolls, sprinkle with 1 tablespoon chopped parsley and serve.

INFORMAL DINNER 11

Cold wine soup *
Chicken vealburgers *
Potatoes boiled in jackets with chopped chives
Beets
Crêpes with orange sauce *

The soup may also be served hot. It and the meat course are my own facsimiles of dishes we have enjoyed at two fine restaurants. If you have the equipment, making the sauce for the crêpes at the table adds a touch of drama.

A light red Bordeaux goes best with this dinner.

COLD WINE SOUP

(*Serves 8*)

4 or 5 leeks
1 large onion
1½ bunches of watercress
1 large potato
2 cups chicken broth
1½ cups dry white wine
1½ to 2 cups light cream
Salt, pepper to taste
2 tablespoons finely cut chives

Cut off and discard all the green part of 4 or 5 leeks. Slice off and discard all the root ends. Split remaining white portions of leeks lengthwise and wash thoroughly. Cut fine; set aside. Peel and chop fine 1 large onion; set aside. Wash 1½ bunches fresh watercress, discarding stems; set aside. Peel, cut and slice fine 1 large potato. Place leeks, onions and potato in pan and add 2 cups chicken broth. Cook until soft (20 to 25 minutes). Add 1½ cups of dry white wine and bring to a boil. In a separate pan, cook the watercress in 1½ cups slightly salted boiling water for 2 or 3 minutes. Add this to soup, cool slightly and run it through blender. When cool, refrigerate and, before serving, add as much light cream as desired (1½ to 2 cups). Adjust seasoning to taste. Serve in chilled bouillon cups and garnish with a few cut chives.

CHICKEN VEALBURGERS
(*Serves 8*)

4 chicken breasts (halved breasts of 2 chickens)
Small bunch of celery leaves
1 carrot, peeled
1 onion, peeled
1 lb. lean veal, ground
Salt, pepper to taste
¾ cup sour cream
Flour
6 tablespoons butter
1 tablespoon parsley, chopped

Cook 4 chicken breasts in 2½ cups of water flavored with a small bunch of celery leaves, 1 carrot, 1 onion and ½ teaspoon salt. When tender (in about 1 hour) remove from fire, and allow to cool in the broth. Remove skin and bones and strain broth over the chicken meat. Chill until ready to use. (This may be done the day before.)

Shortly before time to make the chicken vealburgers, run the chicken through the meat grinder, using medium cutter. Do not include the jellied broth. Add the chicken to 1 lb. of lean veal (ground by the butcher). Season to taste with a dash of freshly ground pepper and about 1 teaspoon salt. Stir in ¾ cup sour cream. Mix well and shape into 24 patties. Dust lightly with flour and pat off excess.

Heat 3 tablespoons of butter in each of 2 medium-sized heavy frying pans. When the butter has foamed and is subsiding, place 12 patties in each pan and cook over moderate heat (about 3 minutes on each side). When patties are lightly browned, cover the pans and continue cooking over low heat for about 15 minutes, turning the patties once. Place the patties on a hot platter and add a spoonful of chicken broth to each pan. Stir and cook down until syrupy, then pour over the patties, sprinkle with parsley and serve.

CRÊPES WITH ORANGE SAUCE
(*Serves 8*)

1 cup unsifted cake flour
Pinch of salt
1 teaspoon granulated sugar
2 eggs
1 egg yolk
1¼ cups milk
2 tablespoons butter, melted
1½ teaspoons brandy
6 tablespoons butter, clarified

Sift 1 cup cake flour with a pinch of salt and 1 teaspoon granulated sugar into a mixing bowl. Combine in another bowl 2 eggs and an extra yolk with 1¼ cups milk and beat a little; gradually add egg mixture to flour, stirring well. Add 2 tablespoons melted butter and 1½ teaspoons brandy. Mix well and strain. Heat a 5-inch iron frying pan and when it is hot, brush with clarified butter. When sizzling hot, add small quantity of the batter (about 2 tablespoons) and tilt pan so that the bottom is thinly coated. Cook until under side begins to brown, flip over with spatula and cook until brown on the other side. Place on cloth to absorb excess butter and repeat the process until you have used all the batter, making about 18 crêpes. Brush the pan each time with additional clarified butter. As you make the cakes, flip them over on the towel to absorb the butter on both sides. These may be made in advance and kept warm neatly stacked on top of each other in the top of a double boiler over boiling water. Before serving, fold the crêpes in quarters and place them on a hot platter.

Sauce

1½ bars butter
4 tablespoons granulated sugar
4 tablespoons strained orange juice
4 tablespoons Grand Marnier liqueur
2 teaspoons grated orange rind
1 jigger brandy (optional)

Melt 1½ bars butter in a large skillet or chafing dish. Add 4 tablespoons granulated sugar, 4 tablespoons strained orange juice, 4 tablespoons Grand Marnier liqueur and 2 teaspoons grated orange rind. Cook for a few minutes. Lay the crêpes in the sauce until they are heated through. At this point 1 jigger of brandy may be poured over the crêpes and set aflame.

INFORMAL DINNER 12

Lobster bisque
Chicken with tarragon sauce *
Small roast potatoes　　*Peas*
Spinach salad　　*Cheese*
Pots de crème chocolat *

Tarragon, fresh or dried, is one of my favorite herbs, and it is especially good with chicken, as in this recipe.

Serve a Montrachet with the main course.

CHICKEN WITH TARRAGON SAUCE
(Serves 8)

4 3-lb. chickens, jointed
2 quarts chicken broth
2 tablespoons fresh tarragon or 1 tablespoon dried tarragon
6 tablespoons butter
4 tablespoons flour
4 egg yolks
1 cup medium cream
Salt to taste
2 tablespoons finely cut fresh tarragon or 1 tablespoon dried tarragon
6 cups boiled rice

Wipe and dry 4 3-lb. chickens that have been jointed. Place pieces in deep pot and pour over them 2 quarts of chicken broth. Bring very slowly to simmering point (this takes at least half an hour). Skim and add 2 tablespoons of fresh tarragon or 1 tablespoon of dried tarragon tied securely in a piece of cheesecloth. Cover pot partially and simmer until tender, or for about 1 hour, counting from time the broth again starts to simmer. Remove from fire and empty into collander placed over a pan to catch the broth. Cool just long enough to enable you to handle the chicken, then carefully remove and discard skin and pull meat off bones in as large pieces as possible. Put the meat in top part of large double boiler and pour over it sufficient broth to cover (about 2 cups). Keep warm over hot water.

Melt 6 tablespoons butter in top part of another double boiler over direct low heat and stir in 4 tablespoons flour. Cook, stirring constantly for a minute or two without browning, then gradually add 4 cups of broth. When the sauce is smooth and thickened, place over boiling water. Beat the yolks of 4 eggs with

1 cup of medium cream, add a little of the thickened sauce, and stir until well incorporated. Add this gradually to the remainder of the sauce, stirring constantly. Season to taste with salt (about 1½ teaspoons).

Drain the hot chicken thoroughly and place in deep, heated serving platter. Pour part of the sauce over all and sprinkle with 2 tablespoons finely cut fresh tarragon (or 1 tablespoon dried tarragon). Serve with boiled rice and the remainder of the sauce in a separate gravy boat.

POTS DE CRÈME AU CHOCOLAT
(*Serves 8*)

13 oz. dark sweet chocolate (13 squares)
½ cup strong coffee
2 teaspoons brandy
6 egg yolks
6 egg whites
4 oz. grated blanched almonds

Melt 13 oz. (13 squares) of dark sweet chocolate in top part of double boiler with ½ cup strong coffee. Stir until smooth, remove from heat and add 2 teaspoons brandy. Add 6 egg yolks, one at a time, mixing well after each one. Beat the whites of 6 eggs until stiff and fold them into the egg-and-chocolate mixture until whites disappear completely. Pour into little covered pots and sprinkle with 4 oz. grated blanched almonds. Chill for at least two hours.

INFORMAL DINNER 13

Turtle soup
Baked fresh ham
Boiled potatoes with caraway seeds
Raw mushroom salad
Ice cream bombe *

The *bombe* has a filling of grated dark sweet chocolate. For a change, try using black brandied cherries in its place.

One of the Alsatian white wines would go well with the ham.

ICE CREAM BOMBE
(*Serves 8*)

3 quarts vanilla ice cream
2 cups dark sweet chocolate, finely grated (½ lb.)

Line two 1½-quart melon molds with a coating of vanilla ice cream, making it about 1½″ thick. Pack it firmly, but work quickly. Fill the center of each with a cup of grated sweet chocolate and fill level with more ice cream. Cover with heavy waxed paper and press on the lid. Place in freezing compartment of refrigerator until ready to serve, at which time remove the lid and paper and run a knife carefully around the edge of each mold. Turn upside down into 2 separate oval well-chilled platters. Place teacloths wrung out in hot water on top of the molds for a minute or two; it should then be possible to lift off the molds. Cut into thick slices and serve.

INFORMAL DINNER 14

Hot borscht with julienne beets
Filet of sole with shrimp and wine sauce *
Rice with sliced truffles　　Puréed spinach
Lettuce and hearts of palm salad
Sour cherry tart *

This seems a pleasant plan for a Friday evening. The subtle flavor of the truffles makes ordinary rice seem something very special.

A nice complementary wine would be a flowery wine from the Loire or one of the Graves whites.

FILET OF SOLE WITH SHRIMP AND WINE SAUCE
(*Serves 8*)

12 filets of sole
Juice of 1 lemon
¾ cup dry white wine
6 tablespoons water
½ teaspoon salt
8 peppercorns
3 small bay leaves
¾ lb. fresh mushrooms
½ bar butter
¾ lb. small cooked shrimp
Preheat oven to 350° F. and preheat broiling unit

Wash 12 filets of sole in 2 cups cold water to which you have added the juice of 1 lemon. Dry on cloth or paper toweling. Butter a large shallow baking dish and arrange the filets in the dish; cover with ¾ cup dry white wine and 6 tablespoons water. Sprinkle with ½ teaspoon salt and 8 peppercorns and add 3 small bay leaves. Place dish on asbestos mat over moderate heat and slowly bring to a boil; let simmer about 2 minutes. Strain off most of the liquid and reserve. Bake the fish in preheated 350° F. oven for about 15 minutes, basting once or twice. In the meantime, wash and stem ¾ pound fresh mushrooms and slice. Sauté them quickly in 4 tablespoons butter. When the fish is cooked, scatter the mushrooms and their liquid over the fish, and keep dish warm while you peel and devein ¾ lb. small cooked shrimp. Place them on top of the mushrooms.

Sauce

4½ tablespoons butter
6 tablespoons flour
1½ cups hot milk
Reserved liquid from fish
1 cup freshly grated Parmesan cheese
2 to 3 tablespoons butter

Melt 4½ tablespoons butter in a saucepan and add 6 tablespoons flour. Cook for a few minutes over low heat, stirring constantly with wooden spoon, being careful not to brown; then add gradually 1½ cups hot milk. Bring to a boil and stir in the strained reserved liquid from the fish. Pour sauce over filets, dot with 2 to 3 tablespoons butter, sprinkle with 1 cup freshly grated Parmesan cheese, and place under preheated broiling unit until the dish is a golden brown (about 3 minutes). Serve with truffled rice. (Just before serving, add a little butter and some peeled sliced truffles to boiled rice.)

SOUR CHERRY TART
(*Serves 8*)

1½ cups flour
1½ teaspoons granulated sugar
Pinch of salt (no salt if salted butter is used)
1 bar and 1 tablespoon butter
3 tablespoons ice water
3 tablespoons graham crackers, crumbled
¼ cup granulated sugar
½ teaspoon cinnamon
2 1-lb. cans pitted sour cherries
8-oz. jar red currant jelly
Preheat oven to 400° F.

Sift 1½ cups flour, 1½ teaspoons granulated sugar and a pinch of salt together. Using pastry blender or two knives, cut in 1 bar and 1 tablespoon chilled butter until a very sandy mixture is obtained. Sprinkle dough with 3 tablespoons ice water; mix dough well and form into ball. Wrap in towel and allow to rest in refrigerator for about an hour. To roll dough, sprinkle board with flour and roll in a circle, starting from center and not rolling to ends. Keep turning dough to retain round shape. When dough is a little larger than tart pan, fold it in half and allow it to fall into place in buttered tart pan. Do not pull down. Cut off excess with rolling pin. Dust bottom of shell with 3 tablespoons crumbled graham crackers. Sprinkle with part of ¼ cup granulated sugar into which you have stirred ½ teaspoon cinnamon.

Drain 2 lbs. pitted cherries well and arrange in pastry shell, placing cherries close together one row deep and, if possible, with pit holes toward bottom. Dust cherries with remainder of sugar and cinnamon. Bake tart in preheated 400° F. oven for 35 to 40 minutes. If fruit becomes too dry, cover tart with buttered brown paper about 25 minutes after tart has been in oven. Melt currant jelly in top part of small double boiler over boiling water and pour while still hot over cherries after the tart has cooled slightly.

INFORMAL DINNER 15

Crab bisque
Broiled filet mignon with tarragon sauce *
String beans with almonds   Small roast potatoes
Crêpes Normandie *

The filets are done very quickly and the sauce can be made in advance. It is not a rich dish and therefore provides a contrast to the bisque and the crêpes.

A good red wine from the Rhône district would taste delicious with the beef.

BROILED FILET MIGNON WITH TARRAGON SAUCE
(*Serves 8*)

1½ tablespoons arrowroot
2 cups beef consommé
2 whole peeled shallots
5 tablespoons fresh tarragon, coarsely chopped, or
    2½ tablespoons dried tarragon
10 individual filets mignon (1½″ thick)
Salt, pepper to taste
3 tablespoons butter

Set broiler pan 3 inches from flame and preheat broiler to high heat.

To make the sauce, dissolve 1½ tablespoons arrowroot in ½ cup of the cold consommé; set aside. Put 2 whole peeled shallots and remaining 1½ cups of consommé in top part of double boiler and let stand at room temperature for 1 hour. Bring to boil over direct heat, remove shallots, add tarragon and cook for 2 or 3 minutes. Add the arrowroot that has been dissolved in the cold consommé and cook for 3 or 4 minutes longer. Season to taste and keep sauce hot over boiling water.

Place filets in preheated broiler and broil for about 5 minutes on one side. Turn them and broil for 4 minutes on other side. Remove filets to warm serving platter, season with salt and pepper and spread with 3 tablespoons butter. Serve accompanied by hot tarragon sauce.

CRÊPES NORMANDIE
(*Serves 8*)

Make 20 to 22 small crêpes according to recipe given for Informal Dinner 11. Keep hot over boiling water. Make sauce as follows:

> 1 cup heavy cream
> 1 teaspoon sugar
> 2 teaspoons Cointreau
> 12 dry almond macaroons finely crumbled
> Additional Cointreau
> Preheat oven to 450° F.

Whip 1 cup heavy cream until almost stiff and season with 1 teaspoon sugar and 2 teaspoons Cointreau. Chill. Fold the crêpes in quarters and lay them overlapping in a large rectangular oven-proof glass baking dish. Sprinkle with 12 dry almond macaroons finely crumbled. Place dish in oven and allow to remain just long enough to heat thoroughly; then pour a little additional Cointreau over the crêpes and spread the whipped cream over all. Return to oven just long enough for the cream to melt slightly. Serve hot.

INFORMAL DINNER 16

Turtle soup with sherry
*Beef Stroganoff ***
Herbed rice   String beans
Romaine and endive salad
Chocolate soufflé

There are many excellent recipes for Stroganoff; this is my own version. Individual soufflé dishes make one of my favorite desserts even more attractive. A Beaujolais would be my choice of wine.

BEEF STROGANOFF
(*Serves 8*)

> 3½ lbs. beef tenderloin
> ½ cup flour
> 1 teaspoon salt, ¼ teaspoon pepper

> 1½ bars butter, clarified
> ½ cup dry sherry
> 1 lb. fresh mushrooms
> 1 to 2 additional tablespoons butter
> 2 cups beef consommé
> Dash of monosodium glutamate
> ½ teaspoon paprika
> ½ cup sour cream
> 2 tablespoons chopped parsley

Ask your butcher to remove all excess fat from beef and cut into pieces about 2″ x ½″ x ½″. Dredge beef lightly in flour seasoned with 1 teaspoon salt and ¼ teaspoon freshly ground pepper. Clarify 1½ bars butter. Brown the meat quickly in a large iron skillet, using half the butter and half the beef at a time. Transfer to a large, heated casserole, discarding excess butter from skillet. Add ½ cup dry sherry to skillet, scraping well so as to use all residue from browning of meat. Pour this over the meat. Wash and stem 1 lb. fresh mushrooms and slice fine. Cook for a minute or two in another skillet in 1 to 2 tablespoons butter just long enough to extract liquid. Reserve the mushrooms, adding their liquid to the beef. Add to the meat 2 cups hot beef consommé, a dash of monosodium glutamate and ½ teaspoon paprika. Simmer meat over low heat for 20 minutes. Add the mushrooms and simmer for another 10 minutes. Allow to cool, remove fat from surface (strips of paper toweling laid for a split second in the gravy will absorb the last bits of fat). Before serving, reheat in top part of large double boiler over boiling water. When the meat is very hot, stir in sour cream to taste (about ½ cup). Place in large hot earthenware casserole, garnish with 2 tablespoons chopped parsley and serve.

INFORMAL DINNER 17

Tomato aspic ring filled with crabmeat
Chicken casserole *
Cold asparagus vinaigrette
Strawberry tartlets *

Use lump crabmeat in the aspic ring. When fresh asparagus isn't available, I love the fat, canned white kind.

Montrachet accompanies the chicken beautifully.

CHICKEN CASSEROLE
(*Serves 8*)

2 small carrots
18 small white onions

12 small fresh mushrooms
1 tablespoon parsley, chopped
18 small potato balls
4 3- to 3½-lb. roasting chickens, jointed
3½ cups clear chicken broth (2 13¼-oz. cans)
½ bar butter, clarified
3 tablespoons dry sherry
2 slices bacon cut in strips
1 tablespoon tomato paste
1½ tablespoons cornstarch
½ cup dry white wine
Salt and pepper to taste
1 bay leaf

Peel and cube 2 small carrots. Peel 18 small white onions. Wash, stem and peel 12 small fresh mushrooms. Prepare 1 tablespoon chopped parsley. From peeled potatoes scoop out 18 potato balls and place these in cold water. Wipe pieces of chicken with a damp cloth and place them in a large pot. Add enough chicken broth to cover. Bring slowly to boiling point over low heat (about 15 minutes). Drain and dry the chicken on paper toweling, reserving the stock. Brown the chicken lightly on all sides in 4 tablespoons clarified butter in large, heavy iron frying pan. Heat 3 tablespoons dry sherry in a separate little pan, flame and pour it over the chicken. Transfer the chicken to a large, heated casserole and add the onions and carrots to the browning pan. When they begin to glaze, add 2 slices of bacon, cut with scissors into narrow strips and add the mushrooms. Cover pan and cook 3 minutes; add 1 tablespoon tomato paste and 1½ tablespoons cornstarch dissolved in ¼ cup cold chicken broth. Add reserved chicken broth and ½ cup dry white wine. Stir until mixture comes to a boil. Season to taste with salt and pepper and add 1 large bay leaf. Pour sauce over chicken and simmer for 1½ hours. About 25 minutes before it is done, add the potato balls. When the potato balls are soft, remove the bay leaf, sprinkle chopped parsley over all and serve.

STRAWBERRY TARTLETS
(*Serves 8*)

3 cups flour
Pinch of salt if sweet butter is used
6 egg yolks
6 tablespoons butter
6 tablespoons granulated sugar
1 quart large strawberries
1 cup heavy cream
1 teaspoon light rum
½ teaspoon confectioners' sugar

1 cup red-currant jelly (1 glass)
Preheat oven to 375° F.

Sift 3 cups flour in a mound on a marble slab or into a large bowl, adding a pinch of salt if sweet butter is being used. Make a well in the center of the flour and break into it the yolks of 6 eggs. Add 6 tablespoons soft butter and 6 tablespoons granulated sugar. With a fork gradually work into a smooth paste. Shape into a flat ball and roll out to about ¼″ thickness. With fluted cookie cutter cut into rounds a little larger than the individual tartlet tins you are using. For tiny tartlets use a 3″ cutter; for muffin tins use at least a 4½″ cutter. Lightly butter the tins and line with pastry circles, allowing them to fall into place gently; press down into tins and up the sides with fingers, so that the pastry comes up to the top of tins. Cut circles of waxed paper the same size as the pastry circles and place on dough; weigh down with uncooked rice. Bake in preheated 375° F. oven until lightly browned (15 to 20 minutes). Remove paper and rice; remove tarts gently from tins and place on cake rack to cool.

Wash, stem and dry 1 quart large strawberries. Whip 1 cup heavy cream and flavor with 1 teaspoon light rum and ½ teaspoon confectioners' sugar. Place 1 cup (1 glass) red-currant jelly in top part of small double boiler and add 1 tablespoon cold water. Melt over boiling water. Shortly before serving tarts, put a spoonful of the whipped cream on bottom of each tart; fill with strawberries and brush tops with cooled red-currant glaze.

INFORMAL DINNER 18

Billi-Bi *
Ham with Madeira sauce *
Creamed spinach   Baked acorn squash
Lettuce salad
Apricot tart

Tinned hams—Dutch, Danish, Polish or domestic—are not only delicious, but also make possible the thin, thin slices that make this dish look as good as it tastes. The tart can be made with fresh or dried apricots; sometimes I alternate them with prunes.

Serve a Pouilly-Fumé with the Billi-Bi and the ham.

BILLI-BI

(*Serves 8*)

4 lbs. mussels
4 shallots, peeled and chopped
4 small onions, chopped

4 sprigs parsley
½ bar butter
1½ cups dry white wine
1 cup milk
2 egg yolks
2 cups light cream
1 tablespoon chopped parsley

Scrub 4 lbs. mussels with wire brush to remove seaweed and barnacles. Wash thoroughly in cold water, discarding any that are open; set aside. Place 4 peeled and chopped shallots in large kettle, add 4 small chopped onions, 4 sprigs of parsley, ½ bar butter and 1½ cups dry white wine. Lay the mussels on this bed, cover tightly and steam 10 minutes, or until the mussels have opened. Drain off carefully all the juice and strain through cheesecloth. Shell the mussels, discarding any that have not opened. Discard the black parts. Carefully pull off the yellow parts and run them, along with the strained juice, through the electric blender. Place in top part of double boiler over hot water; add 1 cup milk and heat to scalding point; beat the yolks of two eggs with 2 cups light cream and add to this gradually part of the soup, stirring constantly, then blend into remainder of soup, stirring continuously until all has been incorporated and the soup has thickened slightly. Remove completely from heat and serve garnished with finely chopped parsley.

If soup is to be served cold, place pan over cold water and cool quickly, stirring occasionally. Refrigerate until ready to serve, thinning if necessary with a little more light cream.

HAM WITH MADEIRA SAUCE
(*Serves 8*)

1 lb. fresh mushrooms
2⅔ cups beef consommé
5 tablespoons butter
5 tablespoons flour
Salt, pepper to taste
1¼ cup Madeira wine
1 3-lb. canned ham
Sprigs of parsley for garnish

Sauce

Wash and stem 1 lb. of fresh mushrooms. Slice the caps very thin. Place in saucepan, add ⅔ cup consommé and simmer gently. Meanwhile melt 5 tablespoons butter in top part of double boiler over direct low heat, add 5 tablespoons flour and stir constantly with wooden spoon, making a light-golden-brown roux; this should take about 10 minutes. Slowly add 2 cups hot consommé and season to taste with a little salt and a dash of freshly ground pepper. Continue cooking over direct low heat for about 5 minutes, then place over boiling water and cook for another 15 minutes. Add the mushrooms and their juice and 1 cup of Madeira wine and keep hot.

Ham

Preheat oven to 350° F.

Half an hour before the ham is to be served place it and any gelatin there may be around it in an oven-proof glass dish; pour ¼ cup Madeira over the ham, cover the dish, and put in oven to warm through, or for about 30 minutes. Place on a large heated serving platter, carve in thin slices, and pour part of the sauce over all, reserving the rest to be passed separately. Garnish the ham with sprigs of parsley and serve.

INFORMAL DINNER 19

Smoked trout with mustard sauce
Roast of beef with natural gravy
Yorkshire pudding   Baby lima beans
Brandy snaps *

The brandy snaps are a great favorite in England, and this recipe came to us from David and Jennifer Gibbs via their cook, Mrs. Sansom.

A full-bodied red Burgundy would be an excellent choice to serve with the beef.

BRANDY SNAPS

(*Serves 8—2 to 3 dozen*)

¼ lb. butter
1 cup light brown sugar (lightly packed)
⅓ cup golden syrup or Karo
⅛ teaspoon powdered ginger
1 cup unsifted cake flour
1 teaspoon brandy
Preheat oven to 375° F.

Place together in saucepan ¼ lb. butter, 1 cup light brown sugar and ⅓ cup golden syrup or Karo. Bring to boiling point over low heat. Remove from fire. Add ⅛ teaspoon powdered ginger to 1 cup unsifted cake flour and sift into syrup mixture. Stir with wooden spoon until smooth and free from lumps. Stir in 1 teaspoon brandy.

Lightly grease 2 cookie sheets and with a teaspoon drop ½ teaspoonfuls of batter on tins, making only 4 mounds on each tin. Place one tin in oven and after 5 minutes add the second tin. Remove first tin after 5 minutes more and allow cookies (which will have spread out paper thin) to cool enough to handle. Working quickly and carefully with spatula, loosen cookies and roll on the handle of a wooden spoon, making cornucopias. Place them on waxed paper and remove second pan from oven and repeat process. Repeat with the rest of batter, greasing tins each time. When all are baked, you will have 2 to 3 dozen cornucopias. Place these carefully in air-tight tins until ready to fill with whipped cream flavored with brandy and sugar. Do not fill with cream more than half an hour before serving, or they may get soggy. (Without cream filling, snaps may be served as cookies.)

Filling

2 cups heavy cream
2 teaspoons confectioners' sugar
2 teaspoons brandy

Beat 2 cups heavy cream until partially stiff, add 2 teaspoons confectioners' sugar and 2 teaspoons brandy and continue beating until stiff. Fill cornucopias about ½ hour before serving.

INFORMAL DINNER 20

Greek egg-lemon soup *
Lamb in pastry *
Puréed spinach   Baby carrots
Chocolate steamed pudding with custard sauce

The egg-lemon soup recipe was given to me by Mrs. Basile Vitsaxis, the wife of the Greek Consul General in New York. The Greek lamb in pastry is made with strudel dough, but my version using frozen puff paste is far easier to cope with.

Try a white Chianti with the lamb.

GREEK EGG-LEMON SOUP

(*Serves 8*)

3 quarts clear chicken broth
¾ cup rice
4 egg whites
4 egg yolks
½ cup strained lemon juice
Salt, pepper to taste

Bring 3 quarts clear chicken broth to boiling point. Wash ¾ cup rice, add to broth and cook until soft, or for about 20 minutes. When rice is cooked, turn off heat.

In a large mixing bowl beat 4 egg whites until stiff, then add 4 yolks and continue beating, adding gradually ½ cup strained lemon juice. Add the broth and rice, a little at a time, beating constantly with large spoon. Pour this mixture back into pot. Place on low heat and bring barely to boiling point stirring constantly. Remove from heat, season to taste with salt and pepper and serve.

LAMB IN PASTRY
(*Serves 8*)

4 lbs. of lamb, cut from leg of lamb in 1½″ cubes
2 tablespoons parsley, chopped
2 small onions, peeled and finely chopped
4 teaspoons dried oregano
½ teaspoon dried rosemary
½ teaspoon dried basil
Salt and pepper to taste
¼ pound butter
3¼ cups beef consommé
2 teaspoons cornstarch
4 packages frozen patty shells
Sprigs of parsley for garnish

Ask your butcher to cut away all the fat from 4 lbs. of lamb and cut the meat in 1½″ cubes.

Allow 4 packages of frozen patty shells to thaw out partially in bottom of refrigerator for about 4 hours, then unwrap them and place them on two plates, to thaw out completely at room temperature, or for about ¾ of an hour while you prepare the lamb.

Prepare 2 tablespoons chopped parsley and add to it 2 small onions peeled and finely chopped, 4 teaspoons dried oregano, ½ teaspoon dried rosemary, ½ teaspoon dried basil and salt and coarsely ground pepper to taste (about ¼ teaspoon of each).

Melt 3 tablespoons butter in a heavy frying pan, and when it is sizzling hot, brown half the meat in it. When brown, remove and set aside. Repeat browning process with rest of meat.

Melt 2 additional tablespoons butter in a casserole which has been placed on an asbestos mat over low heat. Transfer meat to the casserole. Add 3 cups consommé to the frying pan and bring to a boil, stirring with wooden spoon to incorporate residue from pan.

Add the prepared herbs to the meat; add onion and parsley and cook for a few minutes, stirring with wooden spoon. Add consommé from frying pan. Cover casserole and simmer gently for 1¼ hours, at which time stir in 2 teaspoons cornstarch dissolved in ¼ cup cold consommé. Bring to a simmer, stirring well, and cook gently for about 15 minutes longer. (Do not overcook, since the meat will later be baked in dough.)

Remove from stove and allow to cool completely; skim off all fat from gravy. When ready to make the pastry, drain off most of the sauce from the meat into top part of double boiler, over cold water.

Preheat oven to 450° F.

Pile half the patty-shell dough onto center of a lightly floured pastry board or cloth and gently press together to make a thick rectangular lump. Sprinkle lightly with flour and roll out to a rectangle about 16″ by 12″ and about ¼″ thick. Place half of the meat lengthwise down the center of the dough and trickle over it ⅓ cup sauce. Roll up dough quickly, folding in the ends and pinching the two overlapping edges of dough together, to secure the meat inside. With floured hands or with the help of a pancake turner, place the roll, seam side down, onto a lightly buttered cookie sheet with sides. Repeat process with remainder of dough, meat and another ⅓ cup sauce. Place both pans in preheated 450° F. oven and bake until the pastry begins to puff up and brown lightly, then reduce heat to 400° and bake for 25 to 30 minutes longer.

Meanwhile heat the sauce over boiling water. Place the pastry rolls on a large heated platter, slice, garnish with parsley and serve, accompanied by the hot sauce in a gravy boat.

Lunches

LUNCH 1

(SUMMER OR WINTER)

Red caviar soup *
Bay scallops sauté with tartar sauce
Boiled potatoes   *Peas with prosciutto*
Oeufs à la neige *

Oeufs à la neige is the fancy name for Floating Island; I love it no matter what it is called, and, in this sophisticated version, it is also very popular at Le Pavillon Restaurant.

Verdicchio suits the scallops well.

RED CAVIAR SOUP

(*Serves 8*)

4 cans madrilène
2 4-oz. jars red caviar
½ pint sour cream (1 cup)
2 tablespoons parsley, chopped

Jell 4 cans madrilène by placing them in refrigerator for 12 hours. Put 2 teaspoons red caviar and 3 teaspoons sour cream in the bottom of each of 8 bouillon cups. Cover with jellied madrilène, stir. Garnish with chopped parsley and serve very cold.

OEUFS À LA NEIGE
(*Serves 8*)

5 cups milk
⅔ cup granulated sugar
1 teaspoon grated lemon rind
6 egg yolks
6 egg whites
¼ teaspoon salt
½ cup confectioners' sugar
2 teaspoons cornstarch
⅓ cup blanched slivered almonds

Scald 5 cups milk in top part of large double boiler; add ⅔ cup granulated sugar and 1 teaspoon grated lemon rind. Cover and remove from fire. Beat 6 egg whites with ¼ teaspoon salt until stiff, then gradually beat in ½ cup confectioners' sugar. Pour the scalded milk into a 10″ frying pan and bring to boiling point. Lower flame considerably and, using two tablespoons, drop the egg whites in even-sized mounds into the hot milk, making a dozen of them. Cook very gently for 1½ minutes, turn over and cook the other side for another 1½ minutes. With slotted spoon carefully remove mounds to a towel to drain while you make the custard. Return the milk to the top part of double boiler over boiling water. Beat 6 egg yolks with 2 teaspoons of cornstarch and gradually stir part of the hot milk into the mixture. Pour mixture back into the remaining hot milk a little at a time, stirring constantly, and cook until well thickened (about 5 minutes). Remove from fire and cool, stirring occasionally. Pour custard into large round or oval dessert dish and carefully lay egg whites on top. Chill and, when ready to serve, sprinkle ⅓ cup of blanched and finely sliced almonds over all.

LUNCH 2

(SUMMER OR WINTER)

*Consommé with beaten egg ***
*Crabmeat quiche ***
Beet salad
Mixed fruit compote

There are many varieties of quiches, and some hostesses have even created their own. This is one of my favorites. Serve any dry white wine that you enjoy.

CONSOMMÉ WITH BEATEN EGG
(*Serves 8*)

4 eggs
8 cups beef consommé
4 teaspoons parsley, chopped

Break 4 eggs into a 2-qt. kettle and add 8 cups of beef consommé. Beat with rotary beater until well blended. Place pan on direct low heat and stir constantly until just before soup comes to a boil. Remove from fire. (Better to undercook than overcook in this case.) Pour into 8 heated soup cups, sprinkle with chopped parsley and serve.

CRABMEAT QUICHE
(*Serves 8*)

3 cups flour
¼ teaspoon salt (if sweet butter is used)
2½ bars butter
6 tablespoons ice water
1 egg, beaten

Make dough for pastry according to method given for Sour Cherry Tart in Informal Dinner 14 but omitting sugar and using ingredients in amounts given above. (Note: the amount of dough will be double.) Line two 9″ pie plates with pastry; brush pastry with a little beaten egg and chill.

Filling

3 cups crabmeat
4 tablespoons dry sherry
2 tablespoons parsley, chopped
2 tablespoons celery, chopped
2 tablespoons onion, chopped
8 eggs
4 cups light cream, scalded
½ teaspoon salt
¼ teaspoon white pepper
½ teaspoon nutmeg
Preheat oven to 450° F.

Pick over 3 cups crabmeat to remove cartilage; add to crabmeat 4 tablespoons dry sherry, 2 tablespoons chopped parsley, 2 tablespoons chopped celery and 2 tablespoons chopped onion. Mix well and turn into the chilled pastry shells. Lightly beat 8 eggs and gradually add 4 cups scalded light cream.

Season with ½ teaspoon salt, ½ teaspoon nutmeg and ¼ teaspoon white pepper. Pour mixture over crabmeat. Bake in preheated 450° F. oven for about 10 minutes, or until pastry begins to brown very lightly, then reduce heat to 375° F. and continue cooking until knife inserted near centers comes out clean (about 25 minutes longer). Serve warm.

LUNCH 3

(SUMMER OR WINTER)

Cressonnière soup *
Soft-shelled crabs sauté with mustard sauce
Broccoli
Endive salad
Raspberries with custard sauce

The soup may be served either hot or cold. The tiny crabs are by far the best, but allow three or four for each person.

Verdicchio would accompany this meal beautifully.

CRESSONNIÈRE SOUP
(*Serves 8*)

6 small onions, peeled and sliced
6 medium potatoes, peeled and finely sliced
2 tablespoons butter
1 large bunch watercress, stems removed (about 2 cups)
1½ cups milk
2 cups clear chicken stock
¾ teaspoon salt, pepper to taste
1 to 2 cups light cream

Cook 6 small peeled, sliced onions and 6 peeled, sliced potatoes in butter for about 10 minutes, or until mushy, stirring frequently with wooden spoon. Do not allow to brown. Add all but ½ cup of watercress leaves; cook another minute. Add 1½ cups milk and 2 cups chicken stock, and season to taste with a dash of pepper and about ¾ teaspoon salt. Stir over fire until the soup comes to a boil (about ten minutes). Cool slightly and put through blender. Place in top part of 2-quart double boiler over boiling water, add enough light cream (1 to 2 cups) to make the soup a desirable thickness. Chop reserved ½ cup watercress, add to soup, reheat and serve.

LUNCH 4

(WINTER)

Clear hot beet soup
Baked potatoes served with fresh caviar and sour cream
Mixed green salad
Apples maison *

I can serve this marvelously sophisticated lunch only when someone sends us fresh caviar as a present. I'm perfectly willing to give it as a gift myself, but I'm incapable of buying anything so extravagant for our own use. Apricot jam, rum and almonds make something extraordinary out of ordinary apples.

If wine is served, it should be dry, light and white.

APPLES MAISON

(Serves 8)

12 large green apples
6 tablespoons butter
1½ cups apricot jam
3 tablespoons lemon juice, strained
1 to 1½ cups light rum
1 cup finely sliced blanched almonds
2 cups heavy cream, lightly whipped
2 additional tablespoons light rum
1 tablespoon confectioners' sugar

Peel, core, and quarter 12 large green apples, then sauté them in 6 tablespoons butter until they are a light golden brown, or for 5 to 10 minutes. Add 1½ cups apricot jam and 3 tablespoons strained lemon juice and continue cooking, stirring with wooden spoon, for about 5 minutes longer. Arrange on hot serving plate and pour 1½ cups heated light rum over all. Sprinkle with 1 cup finely sliced blanched almonds. Serve with 2 cups lightly whipped cream that has been flavored with 2 tablespoons light rum and sweetened with 1 tablespoon confectioners' sugar.

LUNCH 5

(WINTER)

Sorrel soup *
Double French lamb chops on artichoke bottoms,
served on a platter with puréed peas
Fraises Romanoff *

Cut the meat off the chop bones and arrange the rounds on heated artichoke bottoms. This main course is ideal for a women's lunch.

If you'd like wine, how about Lancers Crackling, a sparkling *rosé?*

SORREL SOUP
(Serves 8)

¼ lb. fresh sorrel
3 large potatoes
6 cups clear chicken broth (4 12½-oz. cans)
½ bar butter
½ teaspoon salt
¾ cup milk
¼ cup heavy cream
1 tablespoon chervil, chopped

Wash ¼ lb. fresh sorrel and remove stems; place in cheesecloth to press out excess water; cut sorrel into small strips. Wash and peel 3 large potatoes and slice fine. Heat 6 cups clear chicken broth. Melt 4 tablespoons butter over low heat in large saucepan. When it is very hot, add the chopped sorrel and cook until mushy (about 3 minutes). Add the chicken broth, potatoes and ½ teaspoon salt. Bring to a boil, lower heat and simmer 30 minutes. Cool slightly and run through electric blender, a small amount at a time. Stir in ¾ cup milk to which you have added ¼ cup heavy cream. Add 1 tablespoon chopped chervil, reheat and serve.

FRAISES ROMANOFF
(Serves 8)

2 quarts large ripe strawberries
1 cup superfine sugar
3 to 4 cups sour cream

(*191*)

Wash and stem 2 quarts large ripe strawberries and dry on paper towel. Place in large serving bowl and sprinkle with 1 cup superfine sugar. Refrigerate for several hours; just before serving, add sufficient sour cream to coat all the berries (3 to 4 cups). Mix gently so as not to bruise the berries.

LUNCH 6

(SUMMER)

Beet and buttermilk soup *
Poached eggs in jelly with ham *
Watercress salad
Sliced peaches and cream

This is really quite a light lunch. Like all buttermilk soups, this one has almost no calories. Iced tea or coffee would be nice—especially on a really hot day.

BEET AND BUTTERMILK SOUP
(*Serves 8*)

2 8¼-oz. cans of tiny whole beets
1 quart fresh buttermilk (4 cups)
Salt, pepper to taste
3 tablespoons finely cut fresh chives

One can at a time, grind beets with all their juice in blender until smooth. Combine two lots. Stir in 1 quart (4 cups) fresh buttermilk. Season to taste with salt and freshly ground pepper. Let stand in refrigerator for 2 or 3 hours. Pour into 8 serving cups and sprinkle top of each with finely cut chives.

POACHED EGGS IN JELLY WITH HAM
(*Serves 8*)

2 dozen tarragon leaves
4 cups beef consommé
2 envelopes plain gelatin
2 tablespoons Madeira wine
8 eggs
1 1-lb. canned ham

Pull 2 dozen leaves of tarragon from their stems. Have some ice water ready. Pour boiling water over the leaves and let them stand for half a minute, drain and then plunge them into ice water. Spread out leaf by leaf on cloth to dry. Refrigerate on cloth until ready to use. Dissolve 2 envelopes of plain gelatin in 1 cup beef consommé. Heat the remaining 3 cups over low heat. Add the soaked gelatin and stir until completely dissolved. Set aside to cool. Flavor with 2 tablespoons Madeira wine and pour 1 cup of it into an oval 12-inch platter. Refrigerate until it is set (15 to 20 minutes). Chill the remaining 3 cups of gelatin in the meantime, and when the gelatin in the platter has set, arrange the chilled tarragon leaves crisscross on the jelly (a pair of leaves for each egg). Spoon a little of the remaining gelatin over each leaf and return the platter to the refrigerator.

Poach 8 eggs in water seasoned with vinegar and a little salt. (It is best to cook only 4 at a time.) When done, lift the eggs one by one with a slotted spoon and lay them on a dish towel to drain. Trim eggs into perfect circles, using a 3″ cookie cutter. Place the eggs, best side down, directly onto the gelatin over the crisscrossed tarragon leaves. By now the rest of the gelatin should be about to set. Remove it from refrigerator. Slice a 1-lb. canned ham into 8 even pieces. Trim off fat and cut into rounds slightly larger than the eggs. Lay one slice on top of each egg and carefully spoon the remainder of the gelatin over all. Refrigerate until completely set. When ready to serve, run a knife around the edge of the platter and place it in a shallow pan of hot water for about ½ minute. Place a serving platter at least 2 inches longer than the one you have used for the eggs on top of the smaller platter and, holding the two together firmly, turn them upside down. Serve chilled.

LUNCH 7

(SUMMER)

Jellied beef consommé
Vitello tonnato *
String bean salad
Strawberries and blueberries with cream   *Palets de dames* *

The *vitello* came to me via a fine Italian restaurant. People who haven't tasted the dish before never guess the mystery ingredient which is, of course, tuna fish.

I think I would serve a Soave.

VITELLO TONNATO
(*Serves 8*)

5-lb. veal roast, cooked and chilled
1½ cups dry white wine

7 oz. canned white tuna (solid pack)
1½ cups heavy cream, slightly whipped
1 2¼-oz. bottle capers in vinegar

Early in the day, roast the veal, following directions given below for hot roast veal, but in this case, do not use the gravy. (Save it for something else.) Allow the veal to cool completely, remove strings, slice carefully and arrange on large serving platter.

Chill wine, tuna, and cream. Pour off all the oil from can of white tuna, and put fish in electric blender, along with 1½ cups dry white wine. Run the blender at low speed for about ½ minute. Place purée in bowl and fold in 1½ cups heavy cream, very slightly whipped. Spread sauce over the cold, sliced veal so as to cover it completely. Garnish with capers which have been thoroughly drained of all their juice. Chill for several hours before serving on cold plates.

Hot Roast Veal

(*Serves 8*)

5-lb. roast of veal, center cut of leg, bone removed, tied for roasting
    but not rolled
Juice of 1 lemon
¼ lb. soft butter
½ cup peeled, sliced carrots
½ cup peeled, coarsely chopped yellow onions
Salt, pepper to taste
2 whole cloves
Bouquet garni of parsley, ½ teaspoon thyme, 1 small bay leaf
1 cup boiling water
1 12½-oz. can clear chicken broth
Parsley or watercress

Preheat oven to 350° F.

Wipe both sides of roast with damp cloth, place in dish, squeeze the juice of 1 lemon over all, turning the roast over so that both sides are bathed in the juice. Allow to stand until ready to roast.

Spread 4 tablespoons soft butter over bottom of roasting pan, and sprinkle over it ½ cup peeled sliced carrots and the same amount of peeled, coarsely chopped yellow onions. Place the roast on this bed and sprinkle with 1 teaspoon salt and a dash of freshly ground pepper and spread top of roast with another 4 tablespoons soft butter. Add 2 whole cloves and a *bouquet garni* (parsley, ½ teaspoon thyme, 1 small bay leaf tied in cheesecloth) to the pan. Add ½ cup boiling water to 1 12½-oz. can of clear chicken broth and pour half of it around the roast. Place in preheated 350° F. oven and roast for about 2½ hours, basting frequently and adding the remaining broth as needed to keep the vegetables from browning too much. About 15 minutes before the roast is done, transfer it to another heated pan and return it to oven. To make clear gravy, add ½ cup boiling water to roast pan, place on fire and bring to a boil, stirring with wooden spoon to incorporate all the brown residue. Strain into small pan and discard the vegetables. Allow to stand, then skim off fat. Reduce the gravy to a syrupy consistency by simmering it while you remove the strings from the roast. Place roast on hot platter, carve, garnish simply with parsley or watercress and serve, accompanied by the hot clear gravy.

PALETS DE DAMES
(*24 Cookies*)

6 tablespoons butter
5 tablespoons granulated sugar
1 egg
1 tablespoon light rum
⅔ cup flour, unsifted
Confectioners' sugar
    Preheat oven to 350° F.

Cream 6 tablespoons butter and gradually add 5 tablespoons granulated sugar. Beat until thick and pale in color. Add 1 egg and 1 tablespoon rum, beat well and fold in ⅔ cup of unsifted flour. Butter a cookie sheet 11½″ x 17½″ x 1″. With teaspoon place batter on tin, making 24 small mounds. Flatten with fork dipped in water, then bake in preheated 350° F. oven until golden brown (about 13 minutes). Remove from oven and take up from pan immediately, using a spatula. Cool and sprinkle with confectioners' sugar flavored with vanilla bean.

LUNCH 8

(SUMMER)

Artichokes vinaigrette
Boeuf en gelée *
Mixed green salad
Stewed peaches with heavy cream   Chocolate cake Aix en Provence *

This whole meal can be prepared in advance—a blessing in really warm weather. I learned about stewed peaches with cream in England; it's curious how much the flavor differs from raw sliced peaches. Anyhow, they're delicious, especially when the cream is very heavy. The cake is really sponge cake flavored with cocoa, but the icing is marvelous bitter-sweet chocolate. It's my version of a cake we first tasted in France.

A Tavel or an Anjou wine would go well with this lunch.

BOEUF EN GELÉE
(*Serves 8*)

6 to 7 lbs. bottom round or brisket beef
2 tablespoons vegetable shortening
2 bay leaves
½ teaspoon thyme
4 medium-sized carrots
4 leeks
2 stalks of celery
8 ripe tomatoes
8 sprigs parsley
1 cup dry white wine
1 slice rye bread
½ teaspoon salt, pepper
2 envelopes plain gelatin
¼ cup brandy
4 cups beef consommé
24 baby carrots
3 cups chicken broth
16 small white onions
Parsley or watercress for garnish
Preheat oven to 400° F.

Sear 6 to 7 lbs. bottom round or brisket beef in 2 tablespoons hot vegetable shortening and remove to covered roasting pan; discard fat. Tie 2 bay leaves and ½ teaspoon thyme in cheesecloth and add to meat. Add 4 medium-sized carrots, washed and peeled; 4 leeks (white part only); 2 stalks celery; 8 ripe tomatoes cut in quarters; 8 sprigs parsley; 1 cup dry white wine; 1 slice rye bread; ½ teaspoon salt and a dash of freshly ground pepper. Cover pan. Bring to a boil on top of stove; place in preheated 400° F. oven and cook until a sharp fork can easily pierce through the meat, or for about 2 hours. (Turn the meat over every half hour and stir the sauce.) Remove the meat and allow to cool, then chill. Discard cheesecloth bag. Strain the vegetables and sauce into a saucepan; press lightly on the vegetables to extract all the juice. Cool and skim off fat.

Soak 2 envelopes plain gelatin in 2 cups beef consommé for 5 minutes, add to sauce, and blend into the remaining 2 cups of beef consommé, or enough to make 4 cups in all. Stir over medium heat until gelatin is completely dissolved. Stir in ¼ cup brandy and set aside.

In the meantime wash and scrape 24 baby carrots, leaving them whole, and simmer them in about 1½ cups clear chicken broth, until they are tender or until no broth is left (40 to 50 minutes). Peel 16 small white onions and simmer them in covered pan in 1½ cups chicken broth until they are tender and all liquid has been absorbed (40 to 50 minutes).

By now the gelatin broth should be cold. Pour about 1 cup of it into large oval serving platter and chill in refrigerator until set (about 25 minutes). In the meantime cut fat away from the meat and slice it thin. Place slices down the center of the gelatin-covered platter and garnish with the carrots and onions. Pour remainder of gelatin over all and refrigerate until set and ready to serve. Garnish with additional parsley or crisp watercress.

CHOCOLATE CAKE AIX EN PROVENCE
(*Serves 8*)

Make a round sponge cake, using your favorite recipe but cutting the amount of flour in half and substituting an equal amount of dark unsweetened cocoa. (Sift flour and cocoa together.) If you have no favorite recipe, here is one of mine adapted for this cake.

Chocolate Sponge Cake

1 cup flour
3 egg yolks
3 egg whites
1 cup granulated sugar
4 tablespoons unsweetened cocoa
¼ teaspoon salt
1 teaspoon baking powder
3 tablespoons brandy
1 teaspoon vanilla
Preheat oven to 350° F.

Sift flour and measure out 1 cup. Sift again with 4 tablespoons unsweetened cocoa. Add ¼ teaspoon salt and 1 teaspoon baking powder. Sift for the third time. Beat 3 egg yolks until thick and lemon-colored and slowly add 1 cup sifted granulated sugar, beating until mixture is very thick. Add 1 teaspoon vanilla, 3 tablespoons brandy and 2 tablespoons water, then fold in flour-and-cocoa mixture, using a wire whisk, until ingredients are well blended. Beat whites of 3 eggs until stiff and fold into batter. Pour batter into lightly buttered and floured 9″ round cake tin (pan with removable bottom is best). Bake in preheated oven until it tests done in the center (about 20 minutes). Cover cake rack with waxed paper, invert cake tin to cool on rack. Run a knife around the edge and gently ease cake out onto the rack.

Bittersweet Icing

6 squares unsweetened chocolate (6 oz.)
3 tablespoons hot water
1½ cups confectioners' sugar, sifted
2 eggs
7 tablespoons sweet butter

1½ teaspoons vanilla
Pinch of salt
1½ teaspoons unsweetened cocoa

Place 6 squares (6 oz.) chocolate in top part of large double boiler over hot water and stir until melted. Add 3 tablespoons hot water and 1½ cups of sifted confectioners' sugar and stir until just combined. Add 2 eggs one at a time and beat vigorously with spoon until the mixture is smooth, keeping pan over hot, not boiling, water. Add 7 tablespoons butter and continue beating with spoon until mixture is smooth. Flavor with 1½ teaspoons vanilla and a pinch of salt. Cool, stirring occasionally.

Spread on top and around sides of cake. Just before serving, sprinkle top of cake with 1½ teaspoons unsweetened cocoa.

LUNCH 9

(SUMMER)

Chicken-caviar soup *
Cold poached salmon surrounded by cucumber salad, dilled mayonnaise
Asparagus vinaigrette
Coeur à la crème with strawberries, raspberries and blueberries *

Garnish the salmon platter with quartered tomatoes and hard-boiled eggs. There are two recipes for the *coeur*—one much richer than the other, but both good.

Serve a chilled Chilean Riesling with this menu.

CHICKEN-CAVIAR SOUP

(*Serves 8*)

4 12½-oz. cans chicken broth
1 4-oz. jar black caviar
½ cup sour cream
2 tablespoons finely cut chives

Jell chicken broth in cans. Put 2 teaspoons black caviar and 1 tablespoon sour cream in bottom of each of 8 soup cups. Divide jellied stock into cups. Stir well, sprinkle with chopped chives and serve.

Note: It is not necessary to use the fresh, unsalted, expensive variety of caviar.

(*198*)

COEUR À LA CRÈME
Low-Calorie *Coeur à la Crème*

(*Serves 8*)

¾ lb. small-curd cottage cheese, creamed
½ lb. cream cheese
Pinch of salt
1 tablespoon confectioners' sugar
1 cup heavy cream
1 large square cheesecloth
1 large (or 2 medium-sized) heart-shaped basket
1½ pints fresh raspberries
1½ pints blueberries
1½ pints fresh strawberries
Additional bowl confectioners' sugar
Additional pitcher heavy cream

Using a fork, mix together in a bowl ¾ lb. of creamed small-curd cottage cheese, ½ lb. cream cheese, a pinch of salt and 1 tablespoon confectioners' sugar. Moisten with 1 cup heavy cream and rub through a fine sieve, using a wooden spoon. Line one large heart-shaped basket (or 2 medium ones) with a square of double-thickness cheesecloth wrung out in cold water. Fill with the cheese mixture, pressing down well, and fold corners of cheesecloth over the top. Place in refrigerator over a bowl to drain and mold.

When ready to serve, turn back the corners of the cheesecloth and turn cheese out onto large, chilled serving dish; remove cheesecloth carefully, so as not to spoil the heart shape. Garnish with bouquets of strawberries, raspberries and blueberries. Pass additional sugar and heavy cream separately.

COEUR À LA CRÈME: FOR NONDIETERS
(*Serves 8*)

10 small *coeur à la crème* baskets or 10 small porcelain heart-
    shaped molds (with holes in the bottom)
10 small squares cheesecloth
1″ piece vanilla bean
1½ tablespoons confectioners' sugar
12-oz. whipped cream cheese
1 cup heavy cream, whipped until almost stiff
4 10-oz. packages frozen sliced strawberries

Line 10 small baskets or molds with the squares of cheesecloth wrung out in cold water. Split a 1″ piece of vanilla bean, scrape out the tiny black seeds, and add these to 1½ tablespoons confectioners' sugar. Blend sugar with 12 oz. whipped cream cheese and 1 cup heavy cream, beaten until almost stiff. Fill the baskets or molds level full and fold the corners of the cheesecloth over the tops. Place on platter and refrigerate until ready to serve; at that time fold back the cheesecloth and carefully turn out the cheese onto a chilled serving platter. Remove the cheesecloth. Serve accompanied by a bowl of defrosted frozen sliced strawberries.

LUNCH 10

(SUMMER)

Individual cheese soufflés
Cold Danish ham
Mixed vegetable salad
Stewed nectarines with Sabayon sauce *

This meal takes some timing for the first course, but it's worth it. Sabayon is a custardlike sauce that can be served with many other desserts. How about cold beer with the ham?

STEWED NECTARINES WITH SABAYON SAUCE
(*Serves 8*)

Fruit

1½ dozen nectarines
2½ cups granulated sugar

Peel 1½ dozen ripe nectarines by plunging them, a few at a time, first in boiling water for about 30 seconds, then in cold water. The skins should peel off easily. Split nectarines in two and remove pits. Moisten 2½ cups granulated sugar with 2 cups water, bring to a boil, skim and boil 5 minutes. Add the nectarine halves, bring again to a boil, remove from heat and cool partially. Serve warm, with the following sauce:

Sabayon Sauce

5 egg yolks
¼ cup granulated sugar
2 cups milk
¼ cup light rum

Beat 5 egg yolks until light and beat in ¼ cup granulated sugar. When the mixture is thick and pale in color, slowly add 2 cups milk. Place over boiling water and cook, stirring constantly with wooden spoon, until thick (4 to 5 minutes). Remove from heat and cool partially. Stir in ¼ cup light rum, and serve warm over the warm stewed nectarines.

LUNCH 11

(SUMMER)
Jellied madrilène
Quiche Lorraine *
Lettuce and tomato salad
Pears in red wine *

Lorraine is the best-known of the *quiche* family—perhaps deservedly so. Serve the salad with it. Iced tea or coffee feels right for this lunch.

QUICHE LORRAINE
(*Serves 8*)

Pastry

1½ cups flour
1 bar and 1 tablespoon butter
3 tablespoons ice water
Pinch of salt (no salt needed if salted butter is used)

Mix dough for 10″ tart as in recipe for Sour Cherry Tart (see Informal Dinner 14), but omit sugar. Chill for at least ½ hour, then roll out and line one 10″ glass pie plate. Crimp the edge, prick the bottom with fork and chill until ready to fill and bake.

Filling

Preheat oven to 450° F.

1¼ cups Swiss cheese, grated (4 oz.)
¼ cup Parmesan cheese
6 to 8 slices bacon
6 eggs
2 egg yolks
1 tablespoon flour
⅛ teaspoon each salt, pepper and nutmeg
1 cup milk
1 cup cream
1 teaspoon soft butter
2 tablespoons butter

Grate 1¼ cups Swiss cheese and ¼ cup Parmesan cheese, but do not combine. Set aside. Cook 6 to 8 slices bacon until very crisp, drain on paper and crumble; set aside. Combine 6 whole eggs and 2 yolks in a bowl. Add 1 tablespoon flour and ⅛ teaspoon each freshly ground pepper, salt and nutmeg, 1 cup milk and 1 cup heavy cream and beat with rotary beater until well mixed but not too frothy. Remove the pastry shell from refrigerator, spread 1 teaspoon soft butter on bottom of shell and sprinkle evenly with crumbled bacon. Cover with the grated Swiss cheese and pour the custard over all. This should just fill the dish. Place in preheated 450° F. oven until pastry starts to brown very lightly (10 to 15 minutes), then reduce heat to 325° F. and continue baking until *quiche* tests almost done in center (about 20 to 25 minutes). Remove from oven while you pour over the surface 2 tablespoons lightly browned butter and sprinkle top with ¼ cup grated Parmesan cheese. Return to oven and bake about 10 minutes longer. Let *quiche* stand for 10 minutes, cut in wedges and serve.

PEARS IN RED WINE
(*Serves 8*)

8 large pears
4 cloves
1 3″ stick of cinnamon
2 cups red Bordeaux wine
1½ cups granulated sugar
4 slices lemon
4 wedges tangerine or orange

Cut 8 large pears in half, peel and core. Put 4 cloves and 1 3″ stick of cinnamon in cheesecloth bag and combine with all ingredients, cooking slowly until pears are tender, about 20 minutes. When done, remove cheesecloth bag, arrange pears in serving dish, strain sauce and pour over pears. Serve either hot or cold.

LUNCH 12

(SUMMER)

Senegalese soup (cold)*
Cold halibut with dilled mayonnaise
Raw vegetable salad
Cheese and pears

Senegalese soup is just as good served hot. The halibut is a refreshing change from salmon. The best cheese to use is a firm, rather mild one —Oka, Bel Paese or Port-Salut.

How about a Neuchâtel with the cheese and pears?

SENEGALESE SOUP

(*Serves 8*)

2 breasts of chicken (whole breast of 1 chicken)
2 quarts chicken stock
3 yellow onions
1 carrot
3 stalks celery
2 large apples
6 tablespoons butter
1 tablespoon flour
1 tablespoon curry powder
1 cup light cream
Salt to taste
Chopped chives for garnish (optional)

Cover 2 large breasts of chicken with 2 quarts of chicken stock. Peel and add 1 yellow onion, 1 carrot and 1 stalk celery. Simmer until chicken is tender (about 1¼ hours). Cool chicken in its juice until it can be handled, then remove all the skin and bones. Cover with a little of the broth and refrigerate while you complete the soup.

Peel, core and quarter 2 large apples. Put them in cold water while you peel 2 yellow onions. Chop onions and 2 stalks celery and add to the drained apples. Sauté the mixture slowly in 6 tablespoons butter in large pan, stirring constantly with wooden spoon until it begins to brown lightly (about 15 minutes). Stir in 1 tablespoon flour mixed with 1 tablespoon curry powder. Cook for a minute or two and gradually add the remainder of the chicken stock. Simmer gently for ½ hour, remove from fire and cool partially. Put the whole through the electric blender and stir in 1 cup light cream. When completely cool, season to taste with a little salt and refrigerate until ready to serve. In the meantime, cut the white meat of chicken into strips. Put a teaspoon of chicken in each cup, cover with the well-chilled soup. (Soup may be served without chicken. Chopped chives may be used for garnish if desired.)

LUNCH 13

(SUMMER)

Hot consommé with slice of lemon
Cold curried shrimp with cold rice and chutney *
Romaine and lettuce salad
Wined watermelon, hollowed out and filled with summer fruit

The cold curried shrimp are a nice surprise; the cold rice must be fluffy; the heat comes from the seasoning. Watermelon served this way is a

(203)

perfect cooler on a summer day.

An Alsatian wine would go well with the shrimp.

COLD CURRIED SHRIMP WITH COLD RICE AND CHUTNEY
(Serves 8)

3 lbs. shrimp
1 lb. long-grain rice
4 medium-sized apples
2 large onions
6 stalks celery
¼ lb. butter
4 tablespoons flour
4 tablespoons curry powder
4 cups chicken broth, heated
½ cup light cream
1 jar chutney

Boil 3 lbs. shrimp, shell and devein. Refrigerate until ready to serve. Cook 1 lb. long-grain rice, following directions on box, and cool.

Peel, core and cut up 4 medium-sized apples. Peel and chop 2 large onions. String, wash and chop 6 stalks of celery. Cook apples, onions and celery together in 6 tablespoons butter until they are soft and lightly brown (10 to 15 minutes). Add 2 additional tablespoons butter and 4 tablespoons flour mixed with 4 tablespoons curry powder. Stir and add 4 cups of clear hot chicken broth and simmer for an additional 30 minutes, stirring occasionally. Cool. Run through blender, then chill. Add ½ cup light cream and stir well. Pile shrimp in center of large, chilled serving platter, and surround with cold rice. Pour part of sauce over shrimp and serve the rest in sauce boat. Accompany this with chutney.

LUNCH 14

(SUMMER)

Jellied borscht with sour cream
Cucumbers with shad roe *
Green salad
Iced Brie *
Strawberries with orange juice

Serving strawberries with orange juice is an Italian trick we like—especially if the strawberries are the tiny *fraises des bois*. The Brie should be brought right from the refrigerator to the table.

A Chilean Riesling would be my choice for wine to go happily with the cucumbers and the Brie.

CUCUMBERS WITH SHAD ROE
(*Serves 8*)

Cucumbers

10 6″ to 8″ cucumbers
3 7¾-oz. cans shad roe, or 3 pairs fresh shad roe
1 tablespoon Worcestershire Sauce
Salt, pepper to taste
Juice of 1½ lemons
2 tablespoons parsley, chopped

Peel 10 6″ to 8″ cucumbers. Carefully scoop out all the seeds; set aside. If you are using fresh shad roe, cook it first. If not, drain contents of 3 cans of shad roe; remove membrane enclosing the roe and place roe in small bowl. Break up gently with fork and season with 1 tablespoon Worcestershire Sauce, salt and pepper and the juice of 1½ lemons. Stuff the cucumbers with roe, leaving about ¼″ at both ends unstuffed. Place the cucumbers on the rack of a large fish boiler over about 1½ quarts of boiling water. Cover and steam the cucumbers until fork can easily be inserted (about 30 minutes). Place cucumbers on a hot platter and sprinkle with two tablespoons chopped parsley. Serve with hollandaise sauce made according to your own favorite recipe or as follows:

Hollandaise Sauce

Juice of ½ lemon
4 tablespoons vinegar
Pinch of salt
⅛ teaspoon white pepper
4 egg yolks
2½ bars butter
Pinch of cayenne

Squeeze and strain the juice of ½ lemon; set aside. Put 4 tablespoons vinegar in top part of a double boiler over direct low heat with a pinch of salt and about ⅛ teaspoon white pepper. Reduce the vinegar by simmering until only 2 teaspoons of it are left. Add 2 tablespoons cold water and 4 egg yolks slightly beaten. Beat well with wire whisk and add ½ bar butter cut in small pieces.

Place the pan over boiling water, on low flame, and be sure that the bottom part of the top pan does not actually touch the water. Beat constantly with wire whisk until the mixture has thickened. At this point remove pan from heat and add 2 bars butter little by little, beating constantly with whisk. When all the butter has been added, stir in the juice of ½ lemon, season with a pinch of cayenne, and more salt and pepper if desired. Serve in warm, not hot, sauce boat, with the stuffed cucumbers.

ICED BRIE

(*Serves 8*)

1 8-oz. box Brie cheese
6 tablespoons dry white wine
¾ cup heavy cream
¼ teaspoon salt
Pinch of cayenne
3 tablespoons white bread crumbs
¼ cup Parmesan cheese, freshly grated

Let 8 oz. of Brie stand at room temperature until it is soft. Force Brie through fine sieve, using wooden spoon. (Skin may be left on if cheese is not too ripe.) Gradually add 6 tablespoons dry white wine and ¾ cup of heavy cream until mixture is almost liquid and smooth; add ¼ teaspoon salt, a pinch cayenne and 3 tablespoons white bread crumbs. (To make crumbs, heat stale bread in 450° F. oven for 4 to 5 minutes, but do not brown; crumble well.) Pour mixture into ice tray 10″ x 4″ x 1½″. Place in freezing compartment until set firm (about 2 hours). Cut into 1½″ squares, sprinkle with ¼ cup freshly grated Parmesan cheese and transfer to chilled serving plate. Serve while still very cold as an accompaniment to the salad.

LUNCH 15

(SUMMER)

Jellied turtle soup
Zucchini stuffed with lobster, artichoke hearts and raw
mushrooms, green mayonnaise *
Trifle *

The zucchini is a marvelous dish—a different combination of four favorite flavors; the zucchini is poached in wine first. And trifle is one of the few truly English specialties I find delicious.

A Montrachet would be superb with the zucchini.

STUFFED ZUCCHINI

(*Serves 8*)

4 to 5 6″ zucchini
4 cups clear chicken broth

3 cups dry white wine
12 peppercorns
1½ teaspoons salt
1 bay leaf
4 small ripe tomatoes
¾ lb. lobster meat
¼ lb. small fresh mushrooms
1 7¾-oz. can artichoke hearts
2 cups mayonnaise
¼ teaspoon green vegetable coloring
4 hard-boiled eggs
2 tablespoons chervil or parsley, chopped

Scrub 4 to 5 6″ zucchini and split in half lengthwise. Remove seeds and part of the pulp, making them hollow; do not peel. Place in pan and pour over them 4 cups clear chicken broth and 3 cups dry white wine. Sprinkle with 12 peppercorns and 1½ teaspoons salt. Add 1 bay leaf and 2 sliced ripe tomatoes. Bring to a boil and poach until tender but not too soft (about ½ hour). Cool in broth, remove and drain. Place on large serving platter. Mix together in a bowl ¾ lb. lobster meat, cut into bite-sized pieces and ¼ lb. fresh mushrooms, washed, stemmed, peeled if necessary and sliced fine. Drain a 7¾-oz. can of artichoke hearts and quarter them. Add these to the lobster and mushrooms. Color 2 cups of mayonnaise by stirring in ¼ teaspoon green vegetable coloring until completely blended. Use mayonnaise to bind lobster, artichoke hearts and mushrooms. Fill the zucchini boats and garnish with quarters of peeled ripe tomatoes and hard-boiled eggs. Sprinkle with chopped chervil or parsley and serve well chilled.

TRIFLE

(*Serves 8*)

1½ quarts custard sauce (double recipe for *Gâteau Mousse* sauce, Informal Dinner 4)
9 ripe peaches
9 ripe plums
¾ lb. ripe black cherries
2 dozen stale ladyfingers (or equivalent slices of stale sponge cake)
¾ cup dry sherry (12 tablespoons)
2 dozen almond macaroons, crumbled

Make and chill 1½ quarts custard sauce. Two hours before serving, peel and slice 9 ripe peaches and 9 ripe plums and pit ¾ lb. ripe black cherries. Mix the three fruits together. Split 2 dozen ladyfingers and place half of them on the bottom of a deep oval 3-quart serving dish. Sprinkle with 3 tablespoons dry sherry. Cover with half the fruit, sprinkle with 3 more tablespoons sherry. Add the remainder of the lady fingers, sprinkle again with 3 tablespoons sherry, and top with balance of fruit and another 3 tablespoons sherry. Pour custard sauce over all and chill. Just before serving, sprinkle 2 dozen crumbled macaroons over top.

LUNCH 16

(SUMMER)

Summer soup *
Salmon mousse, curried mayonnaise
Cold leeks, vinaigrette sauce
Creamed lime ice *

Made with lots and lots of shrimp, this soup, accompanied by a salad and bread, can serve as the mainstay of a light lunch on a day when you're too busy to make the mousse. The recipe for the mousse is the same as the one given for Formal Dinner 2, with salmon substituted for the sole. The lime ice is as delectable as it is easy to prepare.

Dry white Chianti would be pleasant to serve with the main course.

SUMMER SOUP
(Serves 8)

1½ lbs. shrimp
1 medium-sized cucumber
1½ tablespoons fresh dill (or ¾ tablespoon dried dill weed)
1½ teaspoons salt
1½ teaspoons granulated sugar
2¼ teaspoons prepared mustard
1½ quarts buttermilk

Cook 1½ lbs. fresh shrimp, remove shells, devein and cut into small bits. Peel and dice a medium-sized cucumber. Cut fine 1½ tablespoons fresh dill (or ¾ tablespoon dried dill weed). Mix together 1½ teaspoons salt, 1½ teaspoons granulated sugar and 2¼ teaspoons prepared mustard. Stir this into 1½ quarts buttermilk. Add the shrimp, cucumbers and dill. Chill thoroughly before serving in chilled bouillon cups.

CREAMED LIME ICE
(Serves 8)

4 egg yolks
1 cup granulated sugar

Juice of 4 limes
Grated rinds of 4 limes
4 egg whites
1 pint cream, whipped
2 teaspoons powdered cinnamon
2 cups graham cracker crumbs

Beat 4 egg yolks and 1 cup of sugar together until pale yellow. Cook in a double boiler for 3 minutes, beating constantly. Add juice and grated rinds of 4 limes and allow to cool. Beat 4 egg whites stiff, add to first mixture and fold in 1 pint whipped cream. Mix 2 teaspoons cinnamon with 2 cups graham cracker crumbs. Line a shallow 2-quart mold with waxed paper and spread half the cracker crumbs on bottom of mold. Fill mold with the lime mixture. Spread remaining half of graham cracker crumbs on top. Put mold in freezing compartment of refrigerator for about 3 hours. When ready to serve, unmold on a cold platter.

LUNCH 17

(FALL)

Hot beef consommé
Lobster with special sauce
Green salad
Fall fruits　　Cheese

The recipe for the lobster is given for Formal Dinner 3. Serve popovers for a change; they're very little trouble and so spectacular.

Add one of the Alsatian white wines.

LUNCH 18

(FALL)

Clam chowder Ely *
Beet salad
French bread
German apple pancakes *

A warming meal, this time starring New England's favorite soup as we have often enjoyed it at Jean and Ted Ely's.

Beer seems right to me for this lunch.

CLAM CHOWDER ELY

(*Serves 8*)

1 quart steamer clams
4 thin slices salt pork, cut in cubes (about 2 oz.)
1 large yellow onion
4 tablespoons butter
2 tablespoons flour
5 cups milk, scalded
Salt, white pepper to taste

Scrub 1 quart steamer clams thoroughly, and wash them well in cold water several times. Look them over carefully, discarding any doubtful or broken ones. Wash again in cold water. Place in a big kettle and add 1¼ cups cold water. Place over moderate heat until the water comes to a boil (about 5 minutes). Cover, lower heat and steam for about 3 minutes longer. Remove clams, discard any that do not open, and strain liquid through several thicknesses of cheesecloth wrung out in cold water. Measure and reserve the juice, of which there should be at least a cup. As soon as the clams are cool enough to handle, open them and remove the meat. At one end you will find the black snout, which must be pulled back and off and with which will come a thin grayish strip known as the rim. Next snip off and discard the tough end of snout and the black part of stomach. Grind the remaining part of clams through meat grinder, using the coarse blade. Set aside. Now cut 4 thin slices (about 2 oz.) of lean salt pork into tiny cubes and peel and chop fine 1 large yellow onion. Fry the pork bits stirring constantly over low heat for about 5 minutes, then add the onion and continue cooking, stirring constantly with wooden spoon, until onions and pork are a light brown (about 5 minutes longer). Add the strained clam juice and simmer 5 minutes. Add the chopped clams and allow to come to a boil. Remove from heat and set aside while you make a very thin cream sauce. Blend 2 tablespoons flour into 4 tablespoons melted butter without browning for 2 minutes, then gradually add 5 cups scalded milk. When sauce is smooth and thickened, add the clams, onion and salt pork mixture and its juice. Season to taste with salt and a dash of white pepper. Serve hot with heated hardtack crackers.

GERMAN APPLE PANCAKES

(*Serves 8*)

8 apples
1 bar and 2 tablespoons butter
1⅛ cups light rum
4 eggs
¾ cup flour
2 teaspoons granulated sugar

1 teaspoon salt
¼ teaspoon nutmeg
1 cup heavy cream
¾ cup confectioners' sugar mixed with 2 teaspoons cinnamon
Preheat oven to 400° F.

Peel, quarter, core and slice 8 apples. Place in baking dish, dot with 4 tablespoons butter and pour over all ⅜ cup light rum. Bake until soft, basting occasionally (about 20 minutes). Remove from oven and set aside.

Beat 4 eggs, then gradually beat in ¾ cup flour sifted with 2 teaspoons granulated sugar, 1 teaspoon salt and ¼ teaspoon nutmeg. Stir in 1 cup heavy cream slowly. Divide batter in three parts, cooking each third in 2 tablespoons butter on large, heavy iron skillet, turning only once and cooking over moderate heat for 7 minutes in all. Spread ⅓ of the apples over each pancake, sprinkle with one half the cinnamon-and-sugar mixture. Roll up and place the three pancakes in large baking dish. Sprinkle with balance of cinnamon sugar. Cut each pancake in three portions, heat ¾ cup rum and pour over all, ignite and serve flaming.

LUNCH 19

(WINTER)

Tomato clam broth *
Shrimp in dill sauce *
Boiled potato balls   Puréed spinach
Stewed strawberries and rhubarb

Don't spare the dill—fresh if possible.
Verdicchio is especially nice with the shrimp.

TOMATO CLAM BROTH
(*Serves 8*)

2 1-pint-2-oz. cans tomato juice
2 8-oz. bottles clam broth (2 cups)
¾ cup heavy cream, lightly whipped

Mix together contents of 2 1-pint-2-oz. cans tomato juice with 2 bottles (2 cups) clam broth. Heat to boiling point. Pour into serving cups and serve very hot with a little lightly whipped cream on top of each cup.

SHRIMP IN DILL SAUCE
(*Serves 8*)

4 tablespoons butter
2 tablespoons shallots, chopped

3 lbs. shrimp, cooked, shelled and deveined
1½ cups dry white wine
3 cups medium white sauce
2 tablespoons fresh dill, chopped, or 1 tablespoon dried
　dill weed

Melt 4 tablespoons butter in a saucepan, add 2 tablespoons of chopped shallots, 3 lbs. cooked, shelled and deveined shrimp and 1½ cups of dry white wine. Simmer 5 minutes. Add 3 cups medium white sauce (see below) and 2 tablespoons chopped fresh dill (or 1 tablespoon of dried dill weed) and simmer for another 5 minutes, stirring with wooden spoon. Serve immediately.

Medium White Sauce

6 tablespoons butter
6 tablespoons flour
3 cups scalded milk
1 teaspoon salt
¼ teaspoon white pepper

Melt 6 tablespoons butter in top part of double boiler over direct low heat. Stir in 6 tablespoons flour. Cook 2 or 3 minutes, stirring constantly with wooden spoon, and gradually add 3 cups scalded milk. Season with 1 teaspoon salt and ¼ teaspoon white pepper. Place over boiling water and continue cooking for 5 or 10 minutes longer.

Brunches　　　　Elaborate drinks aren't called for at brunches. I like to offer orange juice, seasoned tomato juice, Bull-Shots (vodka and beef bouillon on the rocks) and Bloody Marys. To accompany the meal, serve coffee, coffee and more coffee.

BRUNCH 1

Smoked salmon with pumpernickel
Herring in sour cream
Chopped chicken livers
Sliced tomatoes and onions in a dressing made of dill,
oil and vinegar
Assorted cheese　　Crackers
Bagels　　Cream cheese　　Assorted jams
Scrambled eggs
Schnecken　　Brownies

This brunch is one of Linda's specialties. It is a menu calculated to delight guests who love nothing better than sampling lots of very good things to eat.

BRUNCH 2

Mackerel in white wine sauce
Quiche Lorraine
French bread
Sliced tomatoes and cucumbers
Fruit compote
Cookies

The *quiche* is hot, substantial and couldn't be more appropriate (see Lunch 11 for the recipe). A sprinkling of basil is nice on the tomatoes and cucumbers.

BRUNCH 3

Scrambled eggs with tomatoes
Green salad
Creamed finnan haddie
Crisp rolls
Apple sauce and gingerbread

Scramble the eggs in a chafing dish at the table. The finnan haddie should be served on toast.

BRUNCH 4

Crab omelets *
Sliced cucumbers in sour cream
French bread
Griddle cakes with maple syrup

This is a nice combination of international foods and different textures.

CRAB OMELETS
(*Serves 8*)

8 egg yolks
8 egg whites

1 lb. crabmeat
1 medium-sized green pepper
1 large onion
½ teaspoon salt, pepper
Pinch of thyme
3 tablespoons butter, melted
⅓ teaspoon baking powder
Additional butter
3 tablespoons parsley, chopped
Preheat oven to 350° F.

Pick over 1 lb. crabmeat, removing all cartilage. Wash, quarter and remove seeds and stem from one medium-sized green pepper and chop fine. Peel and chop fine one large onion. Beat 8 egg yolks until light and season with ½ teaspoon salt, a dash of pepper, and a pinch of thyme. Add crabmeat, onion and green pepper and 3 tablespoons melted butter. Add ⅓ teaspoon baking powder and mix well. Beat 8 egg whites until stiff and fold into mixture. Heat a large heavy frying pan and melt in it a little butter. When sizzling hot, drop batter by heaping tablespoonfuls onto the pan, making not more than 6 small rounds at a time. Cook over moderate heat until brown on one side, or for about 45 seconds, turn and cook until brown on the other side. Place on heated serving platter and keep warm in oven while you fry the rest of the batter, making about 24 small omelets. Sprinkle with chopped parsley and serve.

BRUNCH 5

Curried eggs with rice and chutney
Romaine and hearts of palm salad
Assorted toast
Swedish pancakes with lingonberries *

The imported lingonberries can be bought in jars and are worth looking for—they make these Scandinavian pancakes really special.

SWEDISH PANCAKES WITH LINGONBERRIES
(*Serves 8*)

1 cup unsifted flour
2 tablespoons granulated sugar
¼ teaspoon salt
3 eggs
3 cups milk
¼ lb. sweet butter, clarified
1 14¾-oz. jar sweetened lingonberries
1½ cups heavy cream, whipped

Sift 1 cup unsifted flour with 2 tablespoons granulated sugar and ¼ teaspoon salt; set aside. Beat 3 eggs in bowl with rotary beater and stir in 1 cup milk. Add about ¼ of the flour-and-sugar mixture. Stir with spoon, and gradually add remainder of flour mixture and 2 additional cups milk. Strain through sieve. Let rest at room temperature for 2 hours.

Preheat oven to 250° F.

Heat Swedish pancake pan and brush surface with hot clarified butter. Wipe clean with paper toweling. Reheat clarified butter; when the pan is smoking hot, coat again with butter. Fill hollows with about 1 tablespoon of batter which must be stirred well before using. Cook until well done before turning over with small spatula to brown the other side. Place finished pancakes temporarily on buttered cookie sheet in warm, but not hot, oven until all are baked, rebuttering the pan each time a batch is made. Arrange on hot serving platter and serve accompanied by a bowl of sweetened lingonberries and some whipped cream.

BRUNCH 6

Cheese blintzes *
Green salad
Baked apples with cream
Small Danish pastries

If you use the frozen blintzes and buy the pastries, this can be an almost don't-do-it-yourself type brunch.

CHEESE BLINTZES

(*Serves 8*)

Pancakes

4 eggs
2 cups milk
1½ cups unsifted flour
2 tablespoons baking powder
¼ teaspoon salt
8 tablespoons butter, cut into 16 parts

Butter 2 rectangular baking dishes, each 11½″ x 7½″ x 2″. Beat 4 eggs lightly and beat in 2 cups milk. Add 1½ cups flour sifted with 2 tablespoons baking powder and ¼ teaspoon salt. Beat with rotary beater just long enough to make a smooth mixture. Heat an 8″ frying pan, add ½ tablespoon butter, and when sizzling hot, pour in ¼ cup of the batter, tilting pan to coat bottom. Cook over moderate heat until pancake is brown on bottom (about 1½ minutes). Flip over with spatula and cook the other side about 1 minute longer. Turn out on dish towel and continue process until you have made 16 pancakes, using all the batter.

Filling

2 eggs
2 lbs. Ricotta cheese
4 tablespoons butter, melted
½ teaspoon salt
Dash of pepper
⅔ cup superfine powdered sugar
2 tablespoons cinnamon
6 cups sour cream
Preheat oven to 350° F.

Beat 2 eggs, stir in 2 lbs. Ricotta cheese, 4 tablespoons melted butter, ½ teaspoon salt and a dash of freshly ground pepper. When well mixed, divide into 16 parts, placing some of the mixture off-center on each blintz. Roll up neatly, and place in buttered baking dish.

Mix together ⅔ cup superfine powdered sugar with 2 tablespoons cinnamon and sprinkle over all the blintzes. Cover each baking dish with 3 cups sour cream spread evenly. Bake 30 minutes in preheated 350° F. oven, and serve at once.

BRUNCH 7

Smoked sturgeon
Omelets fines herbes
Rye toast
Salad Niçoise
Palacsintas *

Here's your chance to star: make the omelets to order at the dining-room table. The *Palacsintas* were originally made for us by Jenny Szabo, our Hungarian caretaker, and they are very good indeed.

PALACSINTAS
(Hungarian Pancakes)
(*Serves 8*)

Pancakes

4 large eggs
¼ teaspoon salt

1½ tablespoons granulated sugar
1½ cups club soda
1½ cups flour
1 bar and 1 tablespoon butter, clarified

Filling

¾ lb. dried apricots
3 tablespoons butter, clarified
¾ cup granulated sugar
¼ cup heavy cream
Preheat oven to 400° F.

Clarify 1 bar and 4 tablespoons butter. Keep warm over hot water.

For filling, wash ¾ lb. dried apricots, cover with 4½ cups of cold water and cook gently for 1 hour. Add ¾ cup granulated sugar and continue cooking until mixture thickens (about 30 minutes longer). Purée apricots and stir in 3 tablespoons clarified butter. Keep warm over hot water.

For pancakes, break 4 large eggs into an electric blender, add ¼ teaspoon salt, 1½ tablespoons of granulated sugar, 1½ cups club soda, 1½ cups flour, and 3 tablespoons clarified butter. Blend for a second or two, or until smooth and free from lumps.

Butter a casserole dish. Heat a small frying pan or pancake skillet and when it is hot, brush it lightly with clarified butter. Pour 2 tablespoons batter onto center of pan and fry the pancakes on both sides very quickly. Repeat until all the batter is used, keeping the finished cakes warm. Place one at a time, brownest side down, on a plate and place about 2 tablespoons of the apricot purée on each pancake. Roll up and place in buttered casserole. Repeat with all 24. If you pour a very little cream over the cakes as you make them and keep them covered in the oven, they can be kept warm for about an hour before serving.

BRUNCH 8

Curried crab meat
Green noodles with truffles *
Beet salad
Baked apples and cream
Schnecken

The green noodles with truffles delight the eye and taste wonderful besides.

GREEN NOODLES WITH TRUFFLES
(*Serves 8*)

1 cup Parmesan cheese, grated
6 truffles (1 2-oz. can)

2 tablespoons salt
2 12-oz. packages green noodles
6 tablespoons butter
1½ cups heavy cream, warmed
Black pepper

Grate 1 cup Parmesan cheese; set aside. Peel six truffles and slice very fine; set aside. Heat at least 6 quarts of water in a large deep pot and when it boils, add 2 tablespoons salt, then gradually add 2 12-oz. packages green noodles. Cook until just tender (about 6 minutes). Drain noodles in collander over hot water. When ready to serve, remove to heated serving bowl, add 6 table-spoons butter and 1½ cups warmed cream. Toss noodles lightly with two forks. Add the cup of grated Parmesan cheese and mix well. Scatter sliced truffles throughout and serve sprinkled with freshly ground black pepper.

Sunday
Suppers

SUPPER 1

Sherried black bean soup
Cold lobster, sauce verte *
Avocado salad
Assorted fruit with Kirsch

Serve the soup from a lovely large tureen. The *sauce verte* is delicious with cold beef or veal, too. Then stand back and admire the colors of this menu, please!

I would enjoy an Alsatian white wine with this supper.

SAUCE VERTE
(*Serves 8*)

2 10-oz. packages fresh spinach
1 bunch watercress
16 oz. mayonnaise
Juice of 1 lemon
2 tablespoons fresh dill, chopped
2 tablespoons fresh chives, chopped
2 tablespoons fresh tarragon leaves, chopped
2 tablespoons fresh chervil, chopped

Wash 2 10-oz. packages of fresh spinach and remove all the stems. Wash 1 bunch watercress and remove all the stems. Place together in wooden chopping bowl and chop. Place part of this mixture in an electric blender along with some of the mayonnaise, and reduce to a purée. Repeat process until all is well blended. Place in bowl with the remainder of mayonnaise and mix well. Fold in the strained juice of 1 lemon and 2 tablespoons each of chopped dill, chives, tarragon leaves and chervil. (If dried herbs are used, cut amounts in half.) Chill and serve in glass bowl with cold veal, beef, fish or shellfish, such as lobster, shrimp or crabmeat.

SUPPER 2

Split pea soup with sausage
Cold roast duck   Pink applesauce
Potato salad *
Pineapple water ice with crème de menthe

Be sure the duck's skin is very crisp. These Sunday night suppers should be very easy to prepare—as easy as duck soup, which, incidentally, is very, very good; so is turkey soup.

A rich red Burgundy seems ideal for this one.

POTATO SALAD

(*Serves 8*)

2 lbs. small red potatoes
2 teaspoons sugar
1 teaspoon salt
½ teaspoon dry mustard
4 teaspoons pickled horseradish
4 tablespoons vinegar
2 cups sour cream
Freshly ground black pepper
2 tablespoons fresh dill, finely chopped, or chives

Wash and boil 2 lbs. small red potatoes in their skins, until they can be pierced with a long pronged fork (about 25 minutes). Drain and rinse in cold water and peel while still warm. Slice into a salad bowl. Mix together 2 teaspoons sugar, 1 teaspoon salt, ½ teaspoon dry mustard, 4 teaspoons pickled horseradish and 4 tablespoons vinegar; stir into 2 cups sour cream. Pour over the potatoes, turning slices gently until all are coated with sauce. Grind black pepper over all, sprinkle with 2 tablespoons of fresh dill or chives, chill and serve.

SUPPER 3

Mushroom-and-barley soup
Chicken in tarragon jelly *
Artichokes vinaigrette
Fresh pineapple and strawberries with rum

The soup is made with mutton stock and dried mushrooms.
A Montrachet would be lovely.

CHICKEN IN TARRAGON JELLY

(Serves 8)

2 3½- to 4-lb. roasting chickens
Salt to taste
Dash of pepper
6 sprigs fresh tarragon or 2 teaspoons dried tarragon
1½ bars butter
4 envelopes plain gelatin
8 cups clear chicken broth (5 12½-oz. cans)
5 tablespoons brandy
8 to 10 truffles
24 additional tarragon leaves
Preheat oven to 450° F.

Wipe 2 3½- to 4-lb. chickens with damp cloth and sprinkle cavities with salt and a dash of pepper. Insert in each 3 sprigs fresh tarragon or substitute 1 teaspoon dried tarragon. Spread a little butter over bottom of roasting pan and spread the rest of 1½ bars butter over the birds. Place in preheated 450° F. oven and roast, basting occasionally until chicken is lightly browned, then reduce heat to 400° F. and continue cooking birds until done (about 1¾ hours). Cool and then chill the birds in refrigerator.

Soften 4 envelopes plain gelatin in 2 cups clear chicken broth. Heat 6 cups broth and stir in the soaked gelatin. Place over low heat and stir until liquid is clear and gelatin is thoroughly dissolved. Add 5 tablespoons brandy and strain through several thicknesses of cheesecloth wrung out in cold water. Pour a ⅛″ layer of jelly onto large deep oval serving platter and chill until set. Carve the cold chicken, discarding skin, and arrange dark meat first on top of gelatin, then place the thin slices of white meat on top. Peel and chop 8 to 10 truffles and sprinkle them over the chicken. Chill 15 minutes.

In the meantime stir the remainder of the gelatin over ice until it is syrupy and spoon a little over the chicken. Chill again, and repeat process until almost all the gelatin has been used. Place 24 fresh tarragon leaves in a strainer and plunge them first into boiling, then quickly into ice water. Dry on dish towel and arrange on the aspic before it sets completely. Chill thoroughly but remove platter from the refrigerator 15 minutes before serving, so that dish will not be too cold.

SUPPER 4

Onion soup au gratin
Paella *
Lettuce and avocado salad
Raspberry water ice
Madeleines *

Of all the *paellas*, this is one of my favorites; it was invented by my sister-in-law Wilhelmina. You can add or subtract fish or seafood to make it your own.

Serve Soave with this supper.

PAELLA
(*Serves 8*)

2 green peppers
2 tomatoes
10 chicken breasts, boned (halved breasts of 5 chickens)
¾ lb. fresh halibut
¼ lb. salt pork, cubed
4 cups chicken broth
1 lb. long-grain rice
1 large onion
3 shallots
4 tablespoons olive oil
1 teaspoon salt, pepper
1½ teaspoons saffron
1 tablespoon parsley, chopped
1 2-oz. can pimentos

Place 2 whole green peppers one at a time on large pronged fork and hold over heat until blisters form all over. (This facilitates removal of thin outer skin.) Peel, split in two, remove seeds and cut in small squares. Plunge two ripe tomatoes in boiling water for a second or two, remove skins, cut in half, scoop out seeds and cut in squares. Cut 10 boned chicken breasts into pieces. Simmer chicken, ¾ lb. fresh halibut and ¼ lb. cubed salt pork in 4 cups of chicken broth for 15 minutes. Remove fish and break into small squares; discard skin and bones. Set fish aside.

Place 1 lb. uncooked long-grain rice in fine sieve and shake but do not mash. Peel and chop 1 large onion and 3 shallots. Heat 4 tablespoons olive oil in large deep casserole and lightly brown the onions and shallots in it. Add the rice and stir with wooden spoon until rice begins to brown (about 10 minutes). Add the prepared green peppers and tomatoes. Season with 1 teaspoon salt and a dash of freshly ground pepper and sprinkle with 1½ teaspoons saffron crumbled to a powder. Cover with the partially cooked pieces of chicken and all but 1 cup of the chicken broth from which you have strained out the salt pork. Bring gently to simmering point on very low heat. Cover tightly and cook for 30 to 35 minutes. Shake casserole occasionally but do not stir. Add remaining cup of broth as needed to prevent drying out or scorching. Five minutes before serving, add the cubes of fish. Garnish with chopped parsley and strips of pimento and serve.

MADELEINES

(*About 36 cakes*)

1 lb. butter, clarified
4 eggs
1½ cups granulated sugar
1 teaspoon grated lemon rind
1 teaspoon light rum
1 teaspoon vanilla
2 cups unsifted flour
Confectioners' sugar
     Preheat oven to 450° F.

To make the batter, place in the top part of large double boiler 4 unbeaten eggs and add 1½ cups granulated sugar. Place over small quantity of boiling water and beat with electric or rotary beater until the mixture is light, creamy and lukewarm. Remove from heat and continue beating until mixture is very thick and has cooled (about 6 minutes). Add gradually 1½ cups clarified butter, still beating with electric beater and leaving about ¼ cup of clarified butter for buttering molds.

Add 1 teaspoon grated lemon rind, 1 teaspoon light rum and 1 teaspoon vanilla. Stir with wire whisk and gradually fold in 2 cups unsifted flour. Paint the madeleine molds with a pastry brush dipped into the reserved clarified butter and fill the molds almost level full. Bake in preheated 450° F. oven until a light golden brown (8 to 9 minutes). Remove immediately from tins and place on cookie racks to cool. Repeat process until all are baked. When madeleines are cold, dust with confectioners' sugar and serve.

Large Buffets   With all these large buffets, I think it is pleasant to offer both red and white wines.

BUFFET 1

*Platter of Nova Scotia smoked salmon with capers, lemon,
thinly sliced pumpernickel
Bowl of spaghetti with choice of sauces
Breasts of chicken tarragon in wine aspic
Bowl of seasoned steak tartare with rye bread
Cold Holland ham
Lettuce and tomato salad, basil-flavored dressing
Assorted cheese   Crackers
Ginger and pineapple trifle **

Be sure to set out pepper mills near the salmon. Offer at least two sauces for the spaghetti; one might be a white clam sauce and the other, a tomato-meat sauce with grated Parmesan cheese. Serve some chopped onion with the steak tartare for people who talk to themselves. The trifle recipe comes from Australia via Dorothy Hammerstein.

You might offer both Italian Soave and Lancers Crackling wine.

GINGER AND PINEAPPLE TRIFLE
(Serves 8)

1 small ripe pineapple
1 cup and 4 tablespoons granulated sugar
2 oz. almonds, blanched and slivered (about 48)
1 cup candied or preserved ginger
2 cups milk
4 egg yolks
½ teaspoon powdered ginger
9 slices stale sponge cake
1 cup dry sherry
1 cup heavy cream

Quarter, peel, core, and shred fine 1 small ripe pineapple. Cover with 1 cup water, bring to a boil, skim and cook 10 minutes. Add 1 cup granulated sugar and cook 5 minutes more. Remove from heat and cool. Finely cut 1 cup candied or preserved ginger. Heat 2 cups milk in the top part of double boiler over boiling water. Stir in 4 tablespoons granulated sugar. Beat the yolks of 4 eggs and add to them gradually part of the hot milk. Blend, stirring constantly, with the remainder of the milk and cook until mixture coats the spoon (3 to 4 minutes). Flavor with ½ teaspoon powdered ginger and cool. When ready to assemble the trifle, cut stale sponge cake into 9 pieces 2″ x 2½″ x 1″ thick, then split the slices in two, making 18 pieces. Cover the bottom of a rectangular dish (approximately 11″ x 7″ x 2½″) with half the sliced cake. Drain and save the syrup from the cooked pineapple and spread the pineapple over the cake. Sprinkle the prepared ginger over the pineapple and cover with remaining pieces of cake. Add 1 cup dry sherry to pineapple syrup, pour over the whole and wait until liquid is fully absorbed by the cake. Pour the cool custard over all, cover with waxed paper and refrigerate until ready to serve. Whip 1 cup heavy cream until almost stiff and spread over the custard-covered cake. Sprinkle the slivered almonds over all and serve.

BUFFET 2

Tomato aspic ring with lump crabmeat mixed with curried
mayonnaise
Stuffed cabbage *

Cold roast beef
Cold roast turkey
Crisp dinner rolls and croissants, butter
Spinach and bacon salad
Assorted cheese   Crackers
Macédoine of fruit flavored with light rum
Small cakes

The stuffed cabbage recipe is Hungarian, contributed by Pearl Magyar. A good, full-bodied red wine would be very nice with this menu—also a white Chianti. Perhaps some guests would enjoy beer with their buffet.

STUFFED CABBAGE

(Serves 8)

2 medium-sized heads young cabbage
3¼ teaspoons salt
1½ lbs. lean pork (cut from bone of 8 pork chops)
¼ lb. lamb (cut from bone of 3 lamb chops)
½ lb. top round of beef
1 cup long-grain rice
1 lb. sauerkraut (4 cups)
1 medium-sized onion, peeled and finely chopped
1 sliver of garlic
2 strips bacon
¼ teaspoon paprika
¼ teaspoon pepper
1 egg, beaten
1 10½-oz. can condensed tomato soup
1 pork chop (excess fat cut away)
1 tablespoon parsley, chopped
Sour cream (optional)

Remove and discard outer leaves from 2 medium-sized heads of young cabbage. Cut down into root ends and remove cores. Have ready a 6-quart kettle of boiling water seasoned with 3 teaspoons salt, and place the cabbage heads into the water. Cook for 6 to 7 minutes, or until leaves start to fall apart. Remove from water and separate the leaves, one by one, placing them to drain on a large cloth. Choose the 16 best leaves. If the centers of the cabbage are not quite cooked through, replace in boiling water to continue cooking a few minutes longer. When cooked drain and chop cabbage centers coarsely.

With a sharp knife cut meat from 8 pork chops. Do the same with 3 lamb chops. Add to this ½ lb. of top round of beef. Run the three meats through meat grinder, using coarse blade. Place in bowl and refrigerate while you cook 1 cup long-grain rice. Wash the rice thoroughly and cook 6 minutes in large amount of actively boiling salted water. Drain and allow cold water to run over it. Wash 4 cups sauerkraut in cold water, drain and pat dry on paper towel.

Fry 2 strips of bacon in small frying pan and when crisp, remove bacon and sauté the chopped onions and a sliver of garlic in the remaining fat until they are a pale golden brown. Add this to the rice. Combine with the meats and season with ¼ teaspoon salt, ¼ teaspoon paprika and freshly ground pepper. Bind together with 1 beaten egg.

Distribute the stuffing equally onto the 16 whole cabbage leaves. Fold the two sides of leaves over the meat and, starting with core end, roll up neatly into little packages, placing them smooth sides up on the cloth.

Pour a 10½-oz. can condensed tomato soup into a 6-quart casserole. Add an equal amount of water. Add half the sauerkraut and half the chopped cabbage, and place on this bed half the stuffed rolls. Top with a pork chop. Cover with remaining sauerkraut and cabbage and top with remaining stuffed rolls. Pour 1 cup water over all. Place on low flame and bring gently to a simmering point. Cover tightly and cook slowly for about 1½ hours counting from the time it starts to simmer. Watch carefully to avoid scorching on bottom and if necessary add a little water as needed. Sprinkle with parsley and serve very hot. Sour cream may be added just before serving.

BUFFET 3

Cold salmon mousse with lobster and sauce verte
Cold smoked turkey
Beef Stroganoff with rice
Cold Polish ham
Crisp French bread and salty rye
Raw mushroom and lettuce salad
Assorted cheese   Crackers
Apple tart and cherry tart

The salmon mousse looks its most attractive in a fish-shaped mold; the recipe is the same as that for the fish mousse given in Formal Dinner 2; for the sauce, see Supper 1. The Beef Stroganoff is my own variation (see Informal Dinner 16). Offer a choice of red or white Burgundy.

CHAPTER

8

Parlor Games and Other Diversions

F O R theatre people, the late 1920's were New York's golden age. Television didn't exist, and radio was too young to offer the stage much competition. Hollywood was a separate world a whole continent away, and Roman movie making was unheard of. New York was the center where everything happened and everyone was.

True, hit shows didn't run as long as they do today; but then, they didn't have to. They cost so little to bring in that a six months' run always meant profits. Of the sixty-odd theatres open and running on Broadway, fifteen or sixteen housed musicals. Revues like the *Follies* and the *Vanities* and the *Scandals*—all of which came out in yearly editions—presented what would, today, be considered an incredible number of tremendously talented people. And after work they all relaxed, entertaining each other at parties.

The parties were of two kinds, mainly. There were the Mayfair subscription dances for which theatre people gathered in the Crystal Room of the old Ritz-Carlton every Saturday night. And there were giant private galas, where the guest list was made up of show people, who came because they had a wonderful time, and café society, who came because they loved meeting the show people. At parties given by Jules Glaenzer of Cartier's, nothing but champagne was served, and entertainment was seldom formally scheduled. As you walked in the door, it was marvelous, but

(226)

scarcely remarkable, to discover Noël Coward and George Gershwin playing two pianos or to be treated to a *Charlot's Revue* turn by Gertrude Lawrence or a *Follies* bit from Fanny Brice or a couple of songs by Chevalier. Edgar Bergen and Victor Borge and many others who later became big stars on radio and television got their first hearings at parties where Cole Porter and Bea Lillie and Jack Buchanan and half a hundred others were not only guests but entertainers. There weren't any microphones; in those days, singers and actors were trained to project, and audiences made a real effort to listen. And no one went on because he or she was forced; all of them were simply so young and bursting with talent that no earthly power could have kept them from performing.

Costume Parties

Elsa Maxwell's parties were huge and elaborate and always had a theme. Today costume parties have a faintly forced New Year's Eve air to me, but we all loved Elsa's. We took great pains with our get-ups and always had make-up men put on the finishing touches. I still have a picture taken at one of Elsa's "Come as Somebody Else" parties in 1929, just after Dick and I announced our engagement. In it, Jules Glaenzer, George Gershwin, Justine Johnson and Dick look startlingly like the four Marx Brothers. Jules was Chico; George, a remarkable Groucho; Dick was Zeppo; and—with the wig and horn she borrowed from Harpo—you'd certainly never guess that Justine was one of the world's most beautiful women.

My theory is that women's costumes should be authentic, but like any party dress, they should also be becoming and comfortable to live in all evening. I learned my lesson at a Hollywood party the year the movie *Maedchen in Uniform* was such a hit. Dressing as its star, Dorothea Wieck, I wore a dreary gray-flannel outfit with a high hot collar, a tie and black Mary Janes. I pulled my hair back under a wig, and the make-up man thinned my lips. I certainly looked like Dorothea, but it just wasn't a costume calculated for fun and good times, and I spent the evening feeling overheated and underpretty. Dick, meanwhile, was the envy of every man present; to become a Paul Muni (as seen in *I Was a Fugitive from a Chain Gang*), he had simply let his beard grow for three days and put on a striped convict's suit as easy and loose as pajamas.

Show-Business Parties

That kind of party would be impossible today. Show business is fragmented. Movies are made in Hong Kong and Africa and Rome. Television is as much at home in Los Angeles as in New York. And performers shift from TV to films to Broadway as casually as they jet around the world. There is no single show-business capital. And splendid star-spangled private parties like Jules' and Elsa's are a thing of the past.

The parties where theatre people still invariably perform for each other's amusement are company parties, a very special, very intimate kind of celebration. There are the parties that celebrate anniversaries or a show's hundredth performance. They're fun because they give people who see each other working night after night a chance to relax together. Where morale may have worn thin, such parties smooth and restore it.

I like the second kind even better. They take place on the road some time before the show is due to move into New York. Everyone has been under tremendous pressure. There has hardly been a night without a change in this cross or that line or that second-act chorus. Everyone is worried about the show and how he will do. Then comes the party, and it is great because everyone really needs a chance to have some fun.

The ingredients are simple. You need lots and lots of food and something to drink. (Contrary to legend, actors and singers and dancers don't drink much; but they can and do out-eat any crowd in the world.) And you need a piano. At this point the company takes over and provides its own entertainment. There's singing, and if the show is one of Dick's, he usually plays the piano. One time he and Oscar got into dresses and did an Ado Annie-and-Laurie take-off on *Oklahoma!* that almost broke up the party. Many times talented kids in the cast try something they don't get to do in the show: a dancer gets out his guitar and does folk songs; a girl singer does a comedy bit. Since everyone writes his own material, the jokes are inside-inside. And there's a wonderful family sort of closeness that you just can't help but love.

Opening-
Night Parties
Opening nights are very, very different. There's a touch of hysteria mixed with every kind of emotion you can name—love, envy, jealousy, good will, hope. Emotions are rubbed raw. And though you'd probably see a better show any other night of the run, if it's a friend's opening, you go. If you don't, your absence is read as a snub unless you have a first-class alibi.

When the show is Dick's, we sit in the very last row. Dick joins me during the overture, but at intermission and just before the last curtain we make a break for it. I always wear a gray dress—one I've worn before. (It's not that I'm superstitious, but I just have a feeling that buying something dazzling especially for the occasion is asking for trouble; and I *know* that gray is good luck.) If I'm feeling very brave, I linger in the lobby during intermission and put out my antennae. You know you won't hear much on a first night; still, you're sensitive to the slightest inflection. There are people who single out one thing and say, "Aren't the costumes beautiful?" and "How about that number!" and "*I* liked it," all of which translate as "The show is a dog." You recognize all these variations on the death motif—just as on *very* rare evenings the opening is electric, and you're absolutely certain (almost) that you have a hit.

Those huge glamorous opening night parties everybody pictures happen only when you're really sure of your show. *Oklahoma!*, based on a play that failed, was written after Oscar had had a resounding series of flops and the word was out that Dick couldn't work with anyone but Larry Hart. After nearly dying of economic anemia (no money), *Oklahoma!* snuck into town. There were actually some empty seats on the opening night. On the other hand, everyone felt *South Pacific* would be tremendous, and we planned a wonderful party at the St. Regis with pink tablecloths and champagne and music and—when the papers *did* arrive and they liked it, hundreds of elegant people devoured *The New York Times* by romantic candlelight. It was a rare and wonderful evening.

Even when we're absolutely certain, we insulate ourselves before putting in an appearance at the big party. For *South Pacific's* opening night my diary says, "To Sardi's with girls and Hammersteins; then on to St. Regis." When you feel things are very iffy, the family—your own and your show family—gathers at some restaurant to wait the wait together. Big party, little party, sure party, worried party, your personal opening-night menu, if it is your husband's show, is a little cold chicken and coffee; the butterflies take up so much room you can't swallow anything else. And as you choke it down, you pray and try to smile and talk and wish the night were ordinary again.

Away from the theatre most show people, like the rest of the world, prefer entertainment in the form of conversation. Today when lives are so pressured, I think good talk is the pleasantest possible form of party amusement. I have never particularly enjoyed the Hollywood kind of thing where a screen drops out of the ceiling and a movie—any movie—inevitably follows dinner. It is uncomfortable to begin with; you never know which of the guests are related to the producer, the director, the camera man or the prop girl. And I miss the reactions of a normal theatre audience around me. It has always seemed to me that this gilt-edged kind of home movie reflects the hostess's fear that her guests have nothing to say to each other. Actually, the reverse is often true. Your fellow guests seem so interesting, you'd like to get to know them better; but there's never any chance.

Small parties seldom need any formalized entertainment plans. Larger groups—a buffet supper for thirty people, for example—often do, simply because, if not carefully watched, they tend to develop the same conver-

Special
Parties

sational ills that crop up at too-long cocktail parties. Sometimes a once-in-a-lifetime kind of gimmick can be both theme and amusement for an evening. I remember one marvelous night Gilbert and Polly Kahn and Elly and Randy Guggenheimer gave an Oriental "do." They made reservations at a Chinatown restaurant, loaded thirty of us on a bus and gave us cocktails on the way downtown (few Chinese restaurants in Chinatown have liquor licenses). Dinner was a banquet, the kind of delicious meal you have to order days in advance. The whole night was like a big exotic picnic.

On Dick's fiftieth birthday, the Hammersteins chartered one of those yachts that circle Manhattan and took a great party of us cruising up the Hudson. We danced and sang and ate wonderful food, and on the way we put in at 138th Street, where a whole choir of "Siamese" children from *The King and I* serenaded Dick and helped us demolish a giant birthday cake. Even the fact that a sudden thunderstorm rained out the scheduled fireworks couldn't dampen our spirits. It was one of the happiest evenings we've ever spent.

Surprise
Parties
Admittedly, both these were elaborate productions. Surprise parties, which fall into the gimmick category, may be simple or expensively complex. Everyone in our family has had at least one surprise birthday party, yet no two have been alike. Most of them we have loved. But a very few occasions have been more shock than surprise. Once, years ago, unaware that Dick—in cahoots with my mother—was planning a surprise party for me, I fired the cook the day before my birthday. The new cook arrived and was asked by Dick to produce a buffet for forty the same evening. Unable to believe I hadn't known all about it, she left in a home-cooked huff the next morning.

On the other hand, I think one of the best times I've ever had was at a surprise party for me on which Mary and Linda collaborated. It was a games night, and the guest list consisted of fifteen people, every one of whom was as passionate about parlor games as I. In honor of the evening Phyllis Cerf and Madeline Sherwood constructed a fabulous "birthday cake," really a grown-up Jack Horner pie, full of gag gifts; the tiny "Gauguin" Ginger Rogers painted for me still sits on my desk in the country.

Without doubt, the most successful surprise party I've ever engineered was an all-day picnic at Rockmeadow on another of Dick's birthdays. To start things off, the whole cast of *South Pacific*, led by Mary Martin, formed a motorcade a mile or so away. Honking horns and ringing bells, they all drove up the driveway, to Dick's utter and genuine surprise. All day long we swam and loafed and ate and rowed and played softball; we even square-danced that night. The weather was fine and we all had a marvelous time.

While it's not half so important where men are concerned, I think a woman ought to be given an inkling that something nice is going to happen. A subtle hint gives her a chance to get a little dressed up. The total effect of fifty friends catching you in last year's bathrobe is really more trauma than thrill. (I remember that on the night of the Great Cook Catastrophe I was wearing the drabbest dress I owned.) To me, the greatest thing about any surprise party is that, as guest of honor, I get to enjoy the fun with none of the bother. And since it's a party of people I love, I like to look my best for them.

A large party can be enhanced by professional entertainment. Perhaps it's a matter of music—a piano, a small combination or simply recordings playing softly on the hi-fi. Though it may sound strange, we ourselves never have "background" music. There's a double reason for it: first, Dick finds it literally impossible to concentrate on anything else when music is being played; and second, he feels that any music worth playing is also worth listening to. However, we have a number of friends who use "distant" music quite pleasantly.

Professional Entertainment

Sometimes when we have guests, Dick plays the piano after dinner; sometimes he doesn't. And often friends like Johnny Green or Dick Lewine take over. Between them, I think, they know every show tune written since *The Ziegfeld Follies of 1066*. In addition, both are blessed with what I call "terminal facility"—which is to say, they know when to stop. A sixth sense that should be born into all amateur and professional entertainers, it's a must for party performers; otherwise, guests can be "musicked to death" before the evening is over. Whenever you ask friends to entertain, you should be reasonably sure your piano is as perfectly tuned as it can be. An off-key instrument is crippling to a musician.

A three- or four-piece combination does nicely for informal dancing. At cocktail parties, one man who sings and plays piano is enough. If you want him to seem like more, investigate a new electronic gadget that provides enough "rhythm section" to make a single piano sound like a whole orchestra.

Ideally, anyone who plays at your party should be someone you've heard before. But whether the band is made up of friends or strangers, you should confer on timing and repertoire before guests arrive. Few groups play a tango every set unless you ask in advance.

My feelings about strolling players are distinctly mixed. I've heard wonderful trios who go from table to table improvising lyrics about guests; and when they are truly clever, they are very amusing. However, when such wandering souls thrust themselves upon defenseless guests and demand requests for favorite numbers, I want to be miles away. You just can't win. It is considered churlish to say you have no favorite; and if you do come up with a title, you must register rapt attention until the last note wheezes away (the villain in most such crimes is armed with an accordion). On the whole, I'm much happier when the music is anchored; that way guests who have requests can take them to the leader and every one else can enjoy the festivities in peace.

Not all professional party entertainment is musical. I remember one remarkable mind-reading man who, after riffling through the pages at a fast clip could quote specific lines from any book chosen by a guest. And there are experts who expose gambling tricks and "show" you how card-sharps operate. Magicians can be fascinating; but they have to be really skillful to perform at close living-room range.

A number of hostesses we know hire palm readers to amuse their guests. This sort of entertainment fascinates me, but it worries me too. Although most men are strong-minded enough to shrug the whole business off, I know quite a few women who, like me, tend to forget the good and remember the bad. And, foolish as we may feel, for us a predicted fight or accident can sometimes turn a gay party gloomy.

Card Games

Often among old friends a long-established bridge rivalry is accorded a reverence akin to that inspired by Baseball and Mother. I think formal card games like bridge and canasta are fine when the prestated purpose of the evening is to gather a group who like to play either. However, I don't think it can ever be taken for granted that everyone does. And only an unthinking or desperate hostess automatically sets up card tables and drives her guests to them without first investigating their preferences in the matter.

Although Dick doesn't like gambling much, I enjoy it in small flings. Jimmy Durante taught me to play poker and Jean Harlow, to shoot craps. Besides, the family tours that introduced me to the Louvre and the Pitti Palace also gave me my first peek inside Europe's casinos. Still, we never have gambling at our parties—that is, the variety you'd find at a casino. The mere fact that the bank has an edge rules out home roulette. More important, among friends in your own house, it is impossible to set betting limits, and this almost always leads to unhappiness. To take one example, poker is no fun unless the stakes are high enough so that losing hurts a little. The longer the game goes on, the greater the chance that someone will be a big loser. Naturally he'd like to recoup, and whichever of his friends has won most wants to give him the opportunity. Gradually the amounts involved get larger. And without anyone's really knowing how it happened, suddenly losses are being reckoned, not in units of one or ten, but in hundreds, which is more than anybody can afford.

Next to conversation, I really like parlor games best. And although Dick's attitude can be more accurately described as tolerant than enthusiastic, some of our wittiest friends like them as much as I do. John and Barbara Hersey like question-and-answer games. Phyllis and Bennett Cerf are big pencil-and-paper game people. Johnny Green is a great parlor gamesman. Cleveland Amory loves The Game, all word games and chess. (The only outdoor sport he really enjoys is an occasional open-air match at the chess tables in Central Park.) His wife, Martha, once made a game of a bread-and-butter note by writing it on heavy paper which she cut into intricate pieces to make a jigsaw puzzle. Leonard Bernstein and Stephen Sondheim are addicted to puzzles—preferably the impossible kind that almost no one else can solve. Our daughter Mary will take endless trouble in planning party games, and they turn out brilliantly. All her friends are game-mad—so much so that they invest vast stores of energy and effort in plotting Treasure and Scavenger Hunts and Murder situations. Our daughter Linda's crowd would rather spend an evening bouncing on beds of nails than "waste" it swapping Passwords or Twenty Questions.

Parlor Games

Pro- and anti-game sentiment is often expressed in terms as strong as those used to describe feelings about cats. In practice, you often find guests' feelings about games are neither as strong nor as irreversible as they think. Obviously you can't bludgeon people into having fun with games. But while it is ideal to start with a group of ready-made enthusiasts, it is frequently possible to convert a self-proclaimed non-gamester if you can only tempt him to play along for a while.

Behind every case of true game-love lies the discovery of skill. The games you like best are the ones you play best. That is why the most successful selections for any given evening are those everyone present can be expected to be reasonably good at. Obscure games are no fun; while providing two or three guests with a dazzling chance to show off specialized knowledge, they bore everyone else so thoroughly that sooner or later impatience leads to rebellion and the premature end of the evening. Mean games—the ones based on pseudo-psychology that leads to too-personal remarks and often downright defamation—are even worse. And games that show people up as clumsy or badly informed end by making everyone uncomfortable—hardly the aim of a party. Gimmick games of the sort that demand pre-party conspiracy are all right in their way, but since they depend on a single trick, they can't be counted on to supply a whole evening's entertainment.

Good party games come in a choice of sizes. Some are fine for big parties; from ten to thirty can play. Others work best for groups of ten or twelve or of four or six or eight. Properly set up, a good game can bring a party to life more quickly and more pleasantly than anything else I know. But they must be used sparingly, like seasoning. One or at most two good ones are enough to fill any evening. And sensing when to stop if the game has no end built in is easily as important as knowing how to get things off to a lively start.

The ultimate success of any party game depends on two elements: first, a core of players enthusiastic enough to draw shy souls into the group and keep things moving; second, adequate preparations on the part of the hostess. Setting the stage may involve nothing more taxing than having enough pads and pencils on hand, but it could also mean an hour or two spent locating the very best places to "hide" twenty smallish objects in plain sight.

The delightful thing about really good games is that they are never the same from one playing to the next. The Game in its pantomime version as it is most often played and The Game as we played it with drawings at Neysa McMein's are two distinctly different pastimes. And Botticelli as played by college professors is not Botticelli as theatre people or sportswriters play it. The best choice for any particular party will always depend on the night and the guests you've invited. Here are ten games our friends and relations seem to enjoy especially.

For large parties:

Games for
Big Parties

THE GAME had its start in old-fashioned charades. It reached great popular heights several years ago, then dropped out of sight for a while. We think it is such good fun that it's due for a revival.

Props and Preparations: Lists of eight to ten familiar phrases or quotations to be acted out by teams of players.

Object: For each team to guess, as quickly as possible, all the phrases on the list with the aid of players' pantomime.

The Play: Divide guests into two teams; send teams into separate rooms. The nonplayer who compiled the list sets up headquarters halfway between the two. He starts the game by giving the first phrase on the list to one player from each team; each player returns to his respective team and pantomimes the phrase for his team. When a team has guessed a phrase correctly, the player who actually solved it runs to the list keeper for a new assignment which he, in turn, acts out. (Addicts have evolved elaborate systems of hand signals which vary from group to group. A few basic ones are very useful, but they should be understood and agreed upon before the play starts.) The play is repeated like a relay race until one team completes the list. This is the way we like best to play.

There are other variations. In one of them, each team makes out a phrase list for the other. Subject limits (book titles, quotations, slogans, and so on) are set; foreign words may or may not be allowed; a made-up string of words is never permitted. Otherwise, anything goes, and putting together the most difficult list becomes part of the competition. Teams remain in the same room and act out phrases in turn. Records of total elapsed guessing times are kept; when both teams have gone through their lists, the one with the lower time score wins. Advocates of this system like it because everyone at the party, including the hostess, gets to play; and all the fun is shared by all. To me, the disadvantage of this version lies in the fact that one list may turn out to be much more difficult than the other— even too difficult to be fun.

A third version—one we like a lot—was invented by Neysa McMein. In it, the "acting" player tries to get his phrase across by making drawings instead of miming the words. Talking is forbidden; and, paradoxically, the least artistic are usually the best players; true artists tend to become involved in creation and forget about time; also their drawings are often so complete that details cloud the whole and cause confusion.

THE PORTFOLIO GAME was also Neysa McMein's invention—or at least we first played it at her apartment. It requires a great deal of preparation on the hostess's part. But guests seem to have such tremendous fun playing it that I've always felt it was worth every bit of the effort. Besides, once made, the portfolios can be used again and again for different groups of guests. When you've really finished with a set, you can lend or give it to a friend with a different circle of acquaintances or one in another city.

Props and Preparations: You need ten to fifteen manila folders, each marked with a different letter of the alphabet and an individual heading ("Who Are They?," "Who Painted These?," "What Do They Advertise?" and so on) inside; mounted within each folder are eight to ten numbered cut-out pictures. (In all, there should be about one hundred to identify.) You'll also need a pad and pencil for every pair of guests; or, if you have time, prepare sheets with spaces for answers for each team. To make folders, collect pictures from several months' discarded newspapers and magazines; then divide them according to subject and select the best ten or twelve in each group. Pictures should be large enough to be clear, but not so big that they take up the whole folder. Mount those selected for each category in a separate folder and give each picture within each category a number. Mark the folders with letters outside and appropriate question-headings inside. To make the game more challenging, you might select details (a pillar from the Lincoln Monument rather than the whole building, a hand from a famous painting, an eye from a famous face) or use an unusual view (we've puzzled lots of people with a back shot of John L. Lewis and a baby picture of Marilyn Monroe). Simply using obscure people or places to make things difficult spoils the fun. Category possibilities are endless: harbors, flowers, trademarks, dogs, cities and so on.

The Object: To identify correctly each picture in every folder in circulation.

The Play: Pair off players around the room (no fair husbands with wives) and distribute the folders. Each pair then works together to identify the folder's contents. When they've finished with one folder, or at a given signal, they pass it along and start on a new portfolio. The order doesn't matter as long as everyone sees every folder. To pick the winning team, score one point for each correct answer.

Once you've got the hang of it, you may want to try your hand at a children's version or add extra folders to challenge grown-up specialists in sports or art or theatre.

HIDING THINGS IN PLAIN SIGHT is a children's game, really, but in this version we've found it makes a hit at grown-up parties, too.

Props and Preparation: You'll need twenty small objects to be "hidden," plus a copy of the list and a sharp pencil for each guest. If you can set aside a room that will be out of bounds to guests until the game begins, "hide" your twenty objects in advance. The rule is that players must be able to see each thing on the list without moving or touching anything in the room. The more skilled you are at camouflage, the more exciting the game. To give you a start, how about a gold ring on a lamp finial, an aspirin in the center of a white flower, a stamp pasted on the label of a bottle, a cigarette on a white window sill, a rubber band around a door knob, eyeglasses in a crystal vase? If you can't manage to put one room off limits until game time, have the twenty objects ready and a place for each decided on in advance; then while your guests are at dinner, it's a very few minutes' work to set everything out.

The Object: For guests to locate all twenty hidden items in the shortest possible time.

The Play: Distribute lists and turn players loose in the room. The winner is the first player to spot all twenty objects; he sings out and then must point them out to all his fellow searchers.

You've no idea how this game sharpens your powers of observation. I'll never forget one night when we played it at a beach house in California. Imagine my triumph when, in the first two minutes of searching, I discovered a tennis shoe squeezed in between two novels on a book shelf. And imagine my let-down when, after an item-by-item examination of the official list, it became crystal clear that there was no tennis shoe on it.

CREATION is a game we played at Tobé Davis' parties, and even the men seemed to get a kick out of it. Actually more a contest than a game, its competition may reveal hidden, even hilarious, talents.

Props and Preparations: Tobé used two huge bins: one containing lengths of every possible kind of fabric; the other, feathers, ribbons, fake jewels, braid—every sort of trimming material imaginable. Pins and scissors are also provided. There should be enough raw material to allow each guest some choice. Once these are assembled, decide on prize categories (The Most Sporting, The Most Grotesque, The Handsomest, the Best Suited for Skin Diving and so on), and wrap the appropriate number of awards.

The Object: To drape, pin and otherwise put together a dress, coat, hat or what-have-you. (You decide which.)

The Play: Again, guests pair off. This time one is artist, the other, model. Give all creators fifteen or twenty minutes' working time, then judge the results. Two small-scale seasonal variations—both forms of individual competition: Easter Egg Decorating and Christmas Ornament Making. Collages or *découpage* might be fun, too.

PASSWORD, the game they now play on television, is just as much fun played live in your own living room. We actually helped audition it one summer evening when the Bennett Cerfs and the Mark Goodsons came to dinner at Rockmeadow, and we've loved it ever since.

The Object: For one player on each of two competing pairs to communicate as quickly as possible a word (the Password) to the second player by means of one-word clues.

The Play: Before the party, make a list of words (not proper names or foreign words), then write each word on three separate cards. Pair guests into teams of two. Choose two teams to start the game, and let them toss to see who plays first. Give a Password card to one member of each team. Circulate the third card among the guests so they can share the fun. The play starts when the Team A player holding the Password gives his partner a one-word clue; within fifteen seconds the guessing partner must come up with a word he hopes might be the right one. If it isn't, the play is repeated by Team B. (Actually the guessing player on Team B has two clues to work with because he has heard the first round.) Play alternates until the word has been guessed.

The clues may be synonyms, opposites, homonyms or even rhymes. For example, if the password were "Desk," the play might go like this:

Team A Clue: "Office."
Team A Guess: "Secretary."
Team B Clue: "Pupil."
Team B Guess: "Teacher."
Team A Clue: "Table."
Team A Guess: "Desk."

The winning team is then challenged by another pair of players.

Games for Medium-Sized Groups

Question-and-answer games are good for medium-sized groups—any number up to twelve. What's more, if you've asked lively guests, all the preparation is done.

IMPROBABLE CONVERSATIONS is a game we first played on a summer week end at Rockmeadow. Because it offers lots of dramatic scope, theatre people seem to like it especially; so do punsters.

The Object: To recognize both members of a conversational team whose actual meeting might be described as highly unlikely. Such improbable pairs might include Napoleon and Zsa Zsa Gabor, Queen Victoria and Mickey Spillane, General De Gaulle and Cleopatra.

The Play: Two players who are "it" leave the room to decide on their identities. When they return, they hold a brief conversation within which are woven clues to their names. (*Jimmy Hoffa* to *Joan of Arc:* "How do you feel about steak (stake)?" *Joan:* "I don't like it hot, but you'd better move on; I think I see a Bobby.") As the audience gets ideas, individuals ask leading questions designed to confirm the questioner's suspicions about either character without tipping off anyone else. (To *Joan:* "Weren't you awfully burned up at one point?") Each installment goes on until both conversationalists are identified; then the two players who have guessed correctly assume two new identities, and the play starts over again.

It should be made clear at the outset that men may be taking women's roles and vice versa; characters may be real or fictional or both—but you should settle on which in advance. Again, obscurity dulls the point; so rule out such unsung heros as Mesopotamian mystics and thirteenth-century bike racers.

ESSENCES, also known as "Associations," is a highly imaginative guessing game.

The Object: To identify a well-known figure from clues consisting of the things (songs, clothes, colors, places, etc.) players associate with the unknown's character.

The Play: The person who is "it" leaves the room while the remaining guests choose a character, living or dead, real or fictional—it may or may not be stated which. The "it" player returns to the room and questions the others about the things they associate with the mystery character. The responses reveal the things the answerers are reminded of by the chosen man—not his personal likes or tastes. Say, for example, the man in question is Chairman Khrushchev. The questions and answers might run something like this:

Q. What color does he or she remind you of?
A. Red.
Q. What article of clothing?
A. A shoe.
Q. What animal?
A. A bear in a China shop.

There is no single right or wrong response. If, for instance, the answerer is thinking of Russian winters, he might reply "a fur hat" instead of "a shoe." Sometimes to get a cross section of associations, the same question is asked of more than one player. When the correct character is guessed, another player leaves the room, and the play begins again.

BOTTICELLI, also called BIOGRAPHY, is another guess-who game.
The Object: To identify the mystery character.

The Play: One player chooses to "be" a real or fictional, living or dead celebrity. He gives his guessing companion the last initial of his assumed name. That letter acts as both hint and limitation on the questions and answers that follow.

To demonstrate, let's say the "it" player decides to be Winston Churchill. He announces that his initial is "C." The first questioner might then ask, "Are you a famous French author?" The "it" player searches his mind for French authors and replies, "No, I am not Camus." Or "No, I am not Cocteau." Next question: "Are you a famous actress?" Answer: "No, I am not Katharine Cornell." If the questioner can think of another "C" actress, he may repeat the question. If he gets a response, the queries continue. However, if the questioner succeeds in stumping the player, he must give the name of the person he had in mind—Mrs. Patrick Campbell, perhaps, or Claudette Colbert—and may ask one direct question like "Are you a man?" or "Are you living?" or "Are you American?" Some people rule that the yes-or-no answer given in such circumstances limits the play that follows— that once it is known that the character is a man, all subsequent questions and answers must be about men. But we've found such limitations slow the game too much. The player who finally identifies Sir Winston picks a new personality, gives his or her initial, and the game goes on from there.

ADVERBS, sometimes called "In the Manner of," is a pantomime game that can be great fun without props or previous preparation.

The Object: For one player to guess the key adverb or adverbial phrase by analyzing the actions of the others.

The Play: The player who is "it" leaves the room while the rest decide on one word that describes a way of acting. "Mysteriously," "miserably," "hysterically" or "like a fox" might all be possibilities. When "it" returns, he asks individuals to act in the chosen manner—to walk, to smile, to lie down and so on. He keeps handing out such acting assignments until he guesses the word from his fellow players' pantomime.

Hunting Games

SCAVENGER AND TREASURE HUNTS are beloved of all our daughter Mary's friends. Partly for fear guests might wander off into the night never to be heard of again, I've never given either. But if you have an energetic young group to work with, you might like to give one a try. Both require considerable pre-game work on the part of the host or hostess.

For a Scavenger Hunt guests are paired or divided into groups of three or four. Each team is given a copy of a list of ten to fifteen obscure items to be collected within a given period of time—usually about three hours. The items on the list should be difficult, not impossible to obtain.

For the most part they should be small, portable and self-authenticating (an autographed lipstick print from a Copa girl, a Tuborg beer coaster, a picture of President McKinley). And their capture should not involve risk of life or limb or arrest. The game ends when one team assembles all the items called for or, if no group is entirely successful, at a deadline hour when the team that has bagged the greatest number of items wins.

Treasure Hunts have many variations. One of the most intriguing I've ever heard of followed a plot worked out by Stephen Sondheim who, when he's not writing music or lyrics, loves to dash off conundrum-like clues. He began with a party of twenty-one people and divided it into seven groups of three; he took particular care to see that each team was made up of people who were relative strangers to each other. Before the party each guest received an envelope in the mail; in it were the name of a meeting place (the top of the Empire State Building was one), a password ("*Mea culpa*") and one section of a clue sheet which had been torn into three pieces. The player was to arrive at the spot at the given hour, identify two strangers by using the password and match his piece of paper with the other two. The complete sheet gave six clues which, taken in order, led to the elements of a telephone number; you phoned the number to discover the exact location of the treasure. One clue led to Trader Vic's, where a man with a sandwich board lettered "BU" was strolling in front of the entrance; another ("The fountain owned by Henry and Jane's cousin Sol") led to the Fonda del Sol restaurant, where an "8" was taped to the side of the fountain. Similar hints spelled out the remaining digits. The search area was limited (Thirty-fourth to Fifty-ninth Streets, Broadway to the East River); and each group was given an "emergency" phone number which could be called once each half hour for a broader hint about any one destination. Practice proved all this to be not nearly as impossibly complicated as it sounds. Planned with the thought that it would take three hours to follow up all the clues, the night's course was completed in a brisk forty-five minutes by a team led by Mike Nichols.

CASTING THE RUNES, inspired by Druids who allegedly circulated curses on little scraps of wood, is another Sondheim invention. The only prop needed is a small object like a child's sock or a mitten which can be easily concealed. A dried apricot works well because it sticks obligingly to the bottom of trays and glasses. This is the "rune," and the aim of the game is to avoid being stuck with it at the zero hour. The game consists of passing the "rune" from guest to guest. The catch is that it must be so concealed or disguised that the player accepts it willingly; if he sees it, he is permitted to refuse. The "rune" might be passed in the pages of a magazine or folded in a napkin or stuck to the bottom of a tray. The party goes on with talk or other games, and often the recipient is unaware that the "rune" is in his possession. So to keep the game going, after ten minutes, the player who passed it says to his victim, "You know, you have the rune." If the victim has passed it on, well and good. If not, he is spurred to action. The player left holding the "rune" at deadline hour must act out a forfeit decided on in advance.

Pencil-and-Paper Games

I love pencil-and-paper games, especially on rainy days. But, like Jotto and Crosswords, almost all the ones I know are designed to be played by no more than two people. I know only one that is fun for small parties. The game we know as *Guggenheim* and others call "Categories" is ideal for five or six people. On unlined paper, each guest rules off a square five spaces wide by five spaces deep, each space big enough to write a word in; the hostess can speed up the start by making blank sets in advance. The group then decides on five categories of things—for example, cars, crackers, tooth-pastes, rivers and authors—and writes them in a column to the left of the square, one category opposite each row of spaces. Then someone suggests a word of five nonrepeating letters, and that is written across the top of the square with one letter directly above each column of spaces. At the word "Go," each player tries to fill in his chart with proper names. If the word chosen were "BLOCK," he might write "Buick" or "Bentley" in the "Car" space under "B"; "Lincoln" under "L"; "Oldsmobile" under "O"; and so on across and down the square until every space is filled. After five or ten minutes, time is called. In scoring, one point is awarded for each word that appears on three or more papers, three points for each word that appears only twice, and five points for each one that appears only once.

Prizes

My favorite solution to the problem of prizes for grown-ups is wine. Whether it's a half bottle of rosé or a magnum of champagne wrapped in colored tissue, it has an air of gaiety and celebration about it. Best of all, it's something both men and women like.

Children's Parties

The entertainment at children's parties has to be tailored to size. Too much party, too many games are lost on the very small. While I'm all in favor of birthdays, I think parties of their contemporaries are wasted on the majority of one- and two-year-olds. (If parents enjoy inviting friends in for the celebration, fine. But for most babies like my grandson Matthew, the party's chief excitement lies in attacking the cake with both hands at once.) Even at three many toddlers feel amply celebrated when given a cake with candles, presents and extra helpings of special attention from their immediate families. For very little children very simple parties are best; an hour's play with two or three young guests plus an hour to deal with the ice cream and cake is about as much as preschoolers and their parents can honestly enjoy. For five-year-olds, the time should be short, the group should be small, and games, if you feel they're needed at all, should move quickly; children this age have no special gift for waiting their turns patiently.

Grade-school children can handle a bit more sophistication. The games they like best are reassuringly like the ones we played at their age: Three-Legged Races, Potato Races and Musical Chairs still produce high-level excitement. To vary the Musical Chair theme, try standing the players in a circle and having them pass a balloon while the band, or record, plays on; eliminate the player caught holding the balloon each time you stop the music.

One word of warning in the old-fashioned game department: indoor Hide and Seek is never a good idea. We let it happen once on Mary's birthday, and the repairs and restoration to draperies, bath tubs, shower curtains and closets took weeks.

Pin-the-Tail-on games remain the same in principle, though from time to time present heroes like Yogi Bear or Mickey Mouse substitute for the stoic old donkey. From about eight on, most children love Penny Hunts (coins, shiny and new from the bank, make lots less mess than jelly beans or peanuts); children this age have also acquired enough patience to enjoy following through on a Treasure Hunt (begin with as many strong, colored threads as there are guests; wind them around chairs, table legs, door knobs and such, and finish with a prize at the end of each line). Bobbing for apples around Hallowe'en and egg hunts at Eastertime are still sure-fire if you have enough eggproof or waterproof play space around your house or apartment. Incidentally, if you do live in an apartment, it's good community relations to warn neighbors who might be disturbed by the pounding of little feet that you are having a party and to let them know the approximate hour at which peace will be restored.

Ten- to twelve-year-olds like spelling bees and a spelling game we used to play that went like this: divide twelve guests into two teams of six; supply each team with a box containing identical sets of the individual letters e,t,a,o,i,n,s,h,r,d,l,u, blocked out on big pieces of cardboard. Make a list of six-letter words using these letters; no one letter should appear twice in the same word. (Twenty possibilities: drains, trades, tuners, hotels, strain, radios, stored, dilute, strand, thread, radish, return, tailor, detail, shared, retain, salute, rushed, toiler, tinsel.) When the word is called, the players on both teams take the required letters from the boxes (each player holds one letter). The teams line up to spell the word and the fastest wins the point.

As added attractions, clowns score an unqualified hit with any group of five- to eight-year-olds. So do ponies at outdoor parties. In some cities you can even hire a clown or a magician as master of ceremonies to take over and run the whole two- or three-hour shebang. But I recommend reserving such heavy ammunition for birthday number eight, nine or ten, when guests are inclined to be more demanding and your store of ideas is more likely to be depleted. Older children will also sit still for 16-millimeter films (although television cartoons set a fairly high standard to match), for Punch and Judy shows and trained dogs; but on the whole, I think most children like doing better than watching.

After they have achieved a degree of civilization, children are thrilled by trips to the circus or a very special play or movie. For such excursions, transportation by miniature bus, borrowed or rented for the afternoon, is ideal and lots easier to cope with than a swarm of taxis or cars. For minimum wear on mothers, I strongly suggest lunch first when everyone is fresh and happy and delivery to home immediately after the show—before tired tempers have a chance to display themselves.

Children's Prizes and Favors

Prizes and favors should be nonmessy and sturdy enough to reach home in one piece. Fancy hats and things that suggest costumes are very successful: a cowboy hat plus holsters, a fairy crown and wand, a witch's hat and broom or a space helmet with matching ray gun. Being all for simplicity where such items are concerned, I consider the ten-cent store a gold mine. Among its appealing treasures: miniature flashlights, paint sets, blunt-nosed scissors, crayons (all flavors), fabulous "jewels" for girls and "loot bags" in which to carry them all away.

Children are enchanted with souvenir snapshots, the kind developed on the spot and showing each guest in his party hat. To make them very special, you might build or borrow a prop cut-out, like those used by boardwalk photographers, with holes for subjects' faces.

Children's Refreshments

Creamed chicken and pebbly peas are as passé for children as they are for grown-ups. At parties children should be treated to food they really like: hot dogs, hamburgers, sandwiches, any kind of picnic food, mountains of ice cream in any old shape rather than dainty rose molds and, of course, The Cake. Avoid knives and forks entirely if you can. Not only will less cutting assistance be needed, but your silver will be preserved. I remember an impromptu "fencing" exhibition at Mary's ninth birthday party that forced me to have the blades replaced in every one of my knives. One final homey note from Linda: it's a good idea to inspect all napkins after the party. At teeth-straightening age, there's almost always one frantic phone call in search of braces or a retainer the child "thinks he left at your house."

Our daughter Mary has given wonderful parties for children (she has four to celebrate for). Once she offered a sort of sandwich smorgasbord with all the ingredients—bologna, sliced turkey, jellies, cheeses, tomatoes, lettuce, pickles, mayonnaise, mustard, ketchup, relish, butter and several kinds of bread. In spite of the fact that I'd banished peanut butter from our house, Mary included that, too; she assures me children love the way it sticks to the roofs of their mouths. Each guest stacked his own sandwich (no cooking for Mother); completed works were identified by name pennants on sticks, and a prize was awarded for the most impressive creation.

For my oldest granddaughter, Nina, Mary actually produced an indoor picnic. She rented one of those bright-green fake grass carpets, and it became both stage set and protection for her own rug. Each child was given a brand new lunch box filled with sandwiches, deviled eggs, pickles and candies; cake and ice-cream sticks came along later. And guests were permitted to consume all these delicacies while sprawled on the dining-room "lawn." (The lunch boxes were take-home presents, but to avoid aged remnants of the meal turning up later, a home search was suggested to mothers.)

Teen-Age Parties

The "serve them what they like" rule holds true for guests of all ages. When Mary and Linda reached high school, we established a family custom. On Fridays, when classes were over at one o'clock, lunch became a kind of weekly party. I suggested it as a first lesson in grown-up entertaining; they went along because they found it was fun. Usually there were six or eight girls and a buffet: perhaps spaghetti and meatballs with a salad and lots of brownies, fruit and Cokes. Steak sandwiches were another favorite. Plans were anything but elaborate. In fact, those lunches were a clear demonstration of a basic menu truth: young appetites are much better served with simple meals—sometimes in astounding amounts—than with tidbits of gourmet food, however rich and intriguing.

Teen-age requirements for evening parties are almost as uncomplicated. For dancing, there should be hi-fi or a good record player, records and floor space. For refreshments, set out soft drinks, milk, sandwiches, cake or cookies, potato chips and maybe some ice cream (order only enough of each to fill a *small* bottomless pit). To insure complete success, you need only add minimum adult presence and no advice whatever.

For our girls, college vacations meant luncheons and cocktail parties or dinner parties before the big formal holiday dances. For the first time there was champagne before and during the meal. Then Dick and I would watch a little wistfully as they hurried off on the arms of boys whose new dinner clothes, new dignity and slightly self-conscious pipe-puffing had earned them the title "young men."

No two parties were ever alike. But then, they never are. They change with time and place and people. Mary's daughter Kimmy has confided that, as of yesterday, her set considers home movies "very good, but Musical Chairs are a bore." Next week they may take up potato racing or chess. There's no telling. For the party you're planning to have this Saturday, Guggenheim may be all wrong. Next month you might try it and end with a version twice as exciting as ours. For that is how games—and parties—are. And that is how they should be. That is what makes them fun.

CHAPTER

9

House Guests

FOR years I used to lie awake at night dreaming of the house we would one day build on a hilltop in Connecticut. My architectural designs began with a living-dining room—huge yet perfectly proportioned. Except for a one-room glass-walled second floor with a magnificent 360-degree view, the house was to be laid out on a single level. And although its lines were to be eloquently contemporary, my decorating scheme included antiques that lent just the right touches of warmth. It was going to be the most flawlessly beautiful house in the world. And since actual building will never prove otherwise, to me it always will be.

Every day of my life I am surer that people have only partial control when it comes to choosing the houses they learn to live in and love. Rockmeadow's only resemblance to the house I dreamed about is that it is in Connecticut. Built in the early 1930's, its style is shingled Colonial. It sits on level ground well back from the road, and it is three stories high (since there are no front windows on the third floor, it looks two-storied from the front). At first glance its insides seemed so chopped up that we almost didn't buy it. The pantry was tiny and had a ridiculous little breakfast room attached. By throwing the living room and dining room together we could easily capture the majesty of a home bowling alley with a two-step drop in the middle. But we fell in love with the apple trees and the winding drive before we set eyes on the house. And we ended by falling in love with the whole place, problems and all.

To be fair, Rockmeadow had its redeeming features. For one thing, it had all the room we needed for ourselves, the girls and guests; yet from the outside it looked small and inviting. What's more, it was possible to add all the things it lacked: the gardens it didn't have plus an extra bathroom and an up-to-date kitchen. And doing away with the breakfast room left me with a fine big pantry.

Now, fifteen years later, it is a house that both Dick and I love dearly: Dick for its cheerfulness and its comfortable, sunny colors; I, because it is visually pleasing in a way that to me is always exciting. It has hardly changed in appearance since the very beginning, and yet I have never been able to take it for granted. I admit that, in spite of the fact that I love it, there are times when it seems overwhelmingly troublesome. Still, when, after seeing it for the first time, someone says, as Diahann Carroll did one summer afternoon, "I like it—it looks just like you," I feel both delighted and amply rewarded.

Rockmeadow pleases us both because all of it is livable. There isn't a corner of it that is stiff or unused. We love its informality. We like being able to have lunch on the terrace when the weather is fine, and we like the taste of steaks charcoal-broiled outdoors. The living room is in the true sense a living room. The dining room is the kind of room in which men look and feel right in sports shirts on a warm August day. And with a winter fire, the library is one of the most hospitable rooms I know. It is a house where friends seem to feel very much at home. And since we can't conceive of a country house without guests, this pleases us most of all.

We seldom have overnight guests in our city apartment. The rare exceptions are very dear friends from Britain who are so close that we consider them our English children. And once in a great while we do have out-of-town visitors who are so completely at home in New York that most of their days and evenings are taken up with friends and plans of their own. When friends new to New York stay with us, I love to do the museums and sights and theatres with them. But in the rush of city winters, obligations pile up. Too often command lunches, meetings and business necessities force us to abandon guests to *Cue* and their own devices. In the end we hardly see them, which defeats the idea of having house guests in the first place.

In summer all that changes. Around the end of May we move to Rockmeadow. From then until mid-September, although we still spend three days a week in the city, the country is home, and house guests are the order and pleasure of week ends.

Tastes in relaxation vary tremendously. Some people love week ends of lunches, cocktail parties and dinner dances. We know golfers who are unhappy spending more than a day where there is no course within driving range and racing fans who feel that a track-less resort is a trackless wilderness. In our part of the country there are a great many clubs—yacht clubs, beach clubs, hunt clubs, golf and country clubs. Many of our neighbors who could afford servants don't have them; instead, they limit their home entertaining to cocktail parties that caterers handle easily and well. The rest of the time they entertain by inviting their guests to join them for golf and tennis and swimming, for lunch or dinner or a summer evening dance at the club.

The Tempo of Week Ends

Our week ends, on the other hand, are spent around our own house. We often go out for one week-end meal. The rest of the time variety and change of pace come from people coming to us for swimming, for croquet, for the afternoon, for dinner or for lunch. Except for mealtimes, which do have to be set, people do pretty much as they like. They swim or laze by the pool. They do needlepoint or crossword puzzles or talk or read or sky-gaze. We have vast numbers of friends who are champion long-range sitters and one who considers the edge of our pool the perfect place to catch up on his yoga exercises. Nothing could be less formal or more relaxed. It's an atmosphere we cherish and which Dick, especially, thrives in. Still, the very peace that charms us would, I know, be acute torture to many of the theatre people we love best in the world. But perhaps because today lives seem increasingly frantic, we also know lots of others who treasure do-nothing week ends as we do.

It's an elementary fact of week-ending that the most satisfactory guests are those who enjoy the kind of life you like—be it clubby or sporty, elaborate or informal. Basically, for example, the happiest house guests from everyone's point of view are those whose time habits are reasonably like your own. If they are late sleepers and you get up with the sun, one man's lunch becomes another man's breakfast and the twain don't meet all day long. I remember years ago being the only early-rising guest at a big house party out on Long Island. As the day got older and I got lonelier, it was the butler who came to my rescue; it turned out he played croquet.

Choosing House Guests

Everyone accepts the fact that an unconventional guest can sometimes mean complications for a conventional household. But, honestly, it works both ways. Margaret and Herbert Swope were two of the most hospitable people I've ever met in my life. They had an enormous house with marvelously comfortable rooms—beautiful linens, dozens of pillows, everything you could possibly want or need. Yet being a guest there took some getting used to. Herbert, having worked on morning papers all his life, was used to being up all night. So they had two shifts of servants to cope with things. And just as nobody rose before one P.M., nobody (only sissies) went to bed before four in the morning. It always took at least a day's period of adjustment to break me of my midnight bedtime (jeers), eight-o'clock rising (me and the ghosts), one o'clock lunch (for others, breakfast—real lunch was at three-thirty) and evening starvation until dinner was served at ten.

I don't for a minute mean we never sleep late or that we creep off to bed at dusk (I suppose midnight or half past is about average on country week ends). But I'm somewhat chagrined to realize it is getting difficult for me to prop my eyes open until three or four in the morning even when I know that's when the party will hit its gayest stride. And I admit I do find it a bit difficult to make the household run smoothly around a guest who is, quite literally, incapable of putting in an appearance until four in the afternoon any day of his stay.

We also have a few friends who frankly can't stand week-ending. Dick's father was one of them. He loved to come out to see us for the day, but at night he wanted to be back in his own bed, surrounded by his own comforts.

In the end, I think, it comes down to this: there are always more people you'd like to invite than there are week ends and beds; so you have to choose. Because our week ends are inclined to be quiet, we seldom have overnight guests who crave constant excitement and action. Faced with decisions to make, you pick people you like, people who wear well (not all wonderful dinner guests are great week-enders) and people you can make entirely comfortable.

Naturally you don't ask five people if you have only enough beds for four. But physically speaking, comfort goes a bit further than that. While one couple might be perfectly happy sharing a bathroom with the children, another would be miserable. Some people sleep like babies wherever they are, and others would never close their eyes if their bedroom weren't isolated enough to protect them from the gentlest household noises. Everyone invited should be able to live happily in the space and place provided. And my own feeling is that that should be a pleasant room with all possible comforts, including a measure of privacy.

Now that the girls have homes of their own, Rockmeadow has three guest bedrooms. Theoretically, we could invite six people every single summer week end. While we know couples like the Harrimans and the Cerfs who give wonderful big house parties with what seems to be no effort, two or three guests seem the right number for us. I'm afraid I tend to worry when the house count gets larger. Or else I get so taken up with logistic detail that there's no time left to enjoy the guests themselves.

　　I think making people feel at home begins with invitations. The more *Invitations* guests know about plans for the week end ahead, the better prepared and the more relaxed they can be. We're delighted to have people come Friday afternoon ("any time before dinner—cocktails at seven, we'll be eating at seven-thirty") and stay through until Monday morning if they can. But not all households are scheduled that way. There are Friday-to-Sunday week ends and Saturday-Sunday week ends, and guests should know just which sort they're embarking on the moment they're invited. We know one couple who expect everyone to leave Sunday afternoon before supper. But they never actually say so. You may discover it by finding that the beds in your room have been stripped. If not, the hostess may hint, "Would you mind making a phone call for me when you get back to town this evening?" Or the host says, rather pointedly, "We find Sunday traffic lightest in the early afternoon." The message gets across, but it would be so much more considerate to be definite at the time of the invitation.

　　A few days before the week end itself I phone guests to let them *Clothes* know just what we'll be doing and, incidentally, what kind of clothes— formal or informal—are involved. Men are satisfied with a simple statement: sports shirt, sports coat or suit (ours isn't a life that requires summer dinner clothes often). With women the shades of formality are subtler, so a brief description of what I'm planning to wear is usually the quickest cue. It might be long pants if we're all invited to an informal dinner or a summer evening dress if it's to be a really big party. I remind guests about the pool, and if there are any other sports possibilities (golf at a club or tennis at a friend's house, for instance), I mention them, too. Without such advance warning, people have no choice but to pack all sort of unnecessary clothes "just in case" or risk arriving without some essential.

　　There's no doubt that smooth transportation helps start a week end *Transportation* off well. Train service to our part of the world is an uncertain business at best; so if our going and coming schedules coincide, we often ask guests to drive out with us on Friday afternoon and in again on Monday. Otherwise they usually drive themselves. Like many of our neighbors, we've had maps printed to guide people through Connecticut's maze of highways. These cards show the area within a few miles of Rockmeadow in considerable detail. We've marked the easiest approaches from Westchester and New England as well as the road from New York. Mileages between landmarks are given for the benefit of others who, like me, find themselves nonplussed when they read "Stay on Route 109 until you come to the red barn across from the gas station" without being given the faintest clue as to whether the barn is five blocks or five miles down the road.

Arrivals   We know that after a hot summer drive a cool drink is very, very welcome. So it is the first thing we offer our guests when they arrive. While we're fixing it, we show them where the makings are kept and let them know we hope they'll feel free from then on to speak up or mix something for themselves whenever they like.

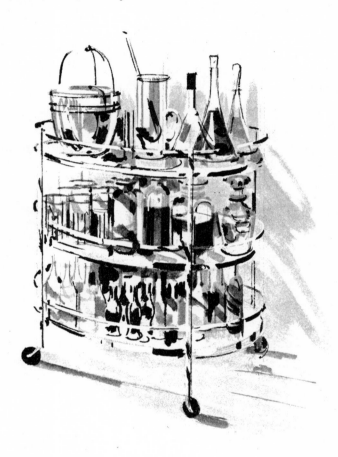

Making house guests feel at home is a curious thing. A good friend of ours used to be so casual about her welcome that you sometimes wondered whether she was actually glad you had come. On the other hand, an oversolicitous hostess—one who flies about with perpetual offers of pillows and lap robes and glasses of warm milk—not only puts a tremendous strain on her own poor nerves, she exhausts the people she's trying so hard to pamper. The ideal relationship is one in which both hostess and guests can feel at ease. The hostess says, in effect, "Please let me know if there is anything you'd like" and says it so convincingly that whether it's a book or a blanket, a safety pin, a sandwich or a cup of afternoon tea, her guests never feel hesitant about asking.

Because a good hostess must always anticipate her guests' needs, I think she should sleep in her own guest room at least once a year, unless she has a visiting mother like mine was or a daughter like Linda who, as a practicing perfectionist, is careful to point out any shortcomings. It's the only foolproof system for making sure the reading lamp is good and in the right place, doors don't rattle, window shades do keep out the sun and screens keep out the bugs.

It is also one sure way of discovering how comfortable the guest beds really are. I say "beds" rather than "bed" because I think twin beds are the most considerate choice for a guest room. It always seems easier for double-bed people to split up than it is for people accustomed to sleeping separately to get any kind of rest when they're forced to share a bed. If the room is large enough, I like having a chaise longue, too, for reading or napping or simply relaxing. It should be endowed with a nice lightweight throw at one end and at the other a large down-filled pillow; I like the big square ones rather than those slippery little things that never seem to stay where they're put.

The table next to the chaise may be relatively small, but big enough for books and a lamp—unless a floor lamp provides good light for reading. However, the perfect night table, to me, is a large, sure-footed specimen with drawers. On top there should be room for a lamp (if there is no wall fixture), a book, an ashtray, cigarettes, a clock with an alarm and a reasonably subdued tick, a Thermos jug and glasses, plus a bit of extra space for shifting these items around and adding one or two more. For example, whether I'm at home or away, I like having a radio to bring me up to date on news and weather (men guests use it for ball games). And at night when the beds are turned down, I have fruit—with some napkins and plates—put in the bedrooms.

Though people often bring books of their own to read, I think every guest room should have its own book shelf. Books add color and personality to a room. And even guests who arrive with their own reading matter love to browse and sample. Six-hundred-page novels and philosophical tomes are too weighty for week-end consumption, but light novels, essay and short-story anthologies, humor and mysteries go very well indeed. To keep the selection lively, I make regular additions and subtractions.

Most confirmed bedtime readers find sleep impossible before they've ticked off the night's chapter. Their desperate need is a strong light properly focused—which is to say, aimed at the book, not diffused into the

whole room or aimed at the eyes of the person in the next bed. I'm especially conscious of bedside lights, not only because I read myself to sleep, but also because our old friend, the literary agent Mark Hanna, once confessed to us that he tucked a hundred-watt bulb into his suitcase whenever he packed in an effort to stave off what he called "bedside blindness."

Night-table drawers provide space for things that are nice to have but not in constant use: a box of cleansing tissues, a pad and pencil, a flashlight. At Rockmeadow, we keep a flashlight and candles in every room because from time to time a violent summer storm cuts off our electric power. A flashlight is ideal any time you need to see but don't want to disturb a roommate, whenever you suddenly have to search for a robe, a bathroom or a blanket in the middle of the night.

Two thoughtful bits of equipment: a sewing kit and writing things— pen, pencils, stationery and assorted stamps—which, though they're needed only very occasionally, are awfully nice to find waiting in a bedroom drawer. And one last addition: flowers in the bedroom; probably they do more than anything else to make a room say welcome.

Though it's rarely done, I still think having a maid unpack for guests, press what needs pressing and hang things away comes under the heading of pleasant pampering. But I know people—Madeline Sherwood, for example—who'd much rather empty their own cases. And however much they appreciate having big bags taken care of, women never want their cosmetic cases unpacked.

Maid Service

There is such a thing as too much service. The British and French feel pressing is much more important than laundering, and I remember spending a visit hiding slips and nightgowns from a Gallic maid so anxious to please that every time I'd set a piece of lingerie aside to wash, she'd ferret it out, iron it, and put it back in the clean pile.

I feel quite strongly that guest-room drawers and closets should be left free for guests' clothes. It's so much pleasanter to be able to unpack all your things and store luggage and racks away than to be forced to rummage through suitcases all week end long. I don't mean to sound unrealistic, and I know I'm very fortunate in the amount of closet space we have, but there is something unwelcoming about opening a door only to discover that the closet inside is so full of retired ski equipment, sun lamps and old evening dresses that there is no place to hang the things you've brought. When a guest closet must be used for family storage, this clutter should be kept to a minimum and so organized in boxes and hanger-bags that it leaves as many cubic feet free as possible. For appearance's sake, you might curtain off the family section and leave an open space for guests' belongings. In the remaining space there should be a full supply of hangers: heavy-shouldered ones for coats and men's jackets; lightweight ones for dresses and blouses; and, most important of all, enough trouser and skirt hangers to accommodate all possible guest requirements. It is also thoughtful to provide an iron and board in a closet convenient to the guest room.

Guest Closets

In town or in the country I keep extra blankets stored in every room —usually in the closet—and I'm careful to point it out to guests first thing. There is no more forlorn feeling than the realization that you're doomed to shiver away the rest of the night because you've no notion of where to start looking for the blanket that would make life warm again.

Guest Bathrooms

Another spot that is likely to be inhospitably crowded is the medicine cabinet. When a guest shares a family bathroom, a certain amount of clutter is, of course, necessary and understandable. Even so, some small place should be set aside for guest toothbrushes and razors. A bathroom used solely by guests should be reserved for them alone and should contain only things placed there for their convenience. I love choosing cologne and bath oil or foam bath for guest bathrooms mostly because I enjoy sampling them in other people's homes so much. On a less frivolous level, I always see that there are stocks of aspirin, bicarbonate of soda, mouth wash, emery boards and an orange stick. For minor first-aid operations and cosmetic repairs, I add strip bandages, an antiseptic, cotton and extra tissues. And I keep toothbrushes, toothpaste, combs, a razor or two, blades and shaving cream in reserve in case they've been forgotten. Whenever I can, I buy all these in the small ten-cent-store sizes just because I think it is nicer for each guest to start out with a toothpaste tube of his own.

There should, of course, be extra face cloths and towels within obvious reach (I know some people love those tremendous bath sheets; I don't —they always seem to trip me up). In the bathroom, where spills don't matter and hot water and supplies are close at hand, there should be a well-lit mirror suitably placed for making up as well as for shaving. An electric hair dryer is useful; I keep one on the guest floor or in the pool dressing rooms, depending on the time of year. Of course, every bathroom should have its own wastebasket, an item which, for some inexplicable reason, people tend to forget. And, now that every woman (almost) wears nylon underthings she rinses out herself, bathroom supplies should include soap flakes or a detergent and plastic hooks and hangers as well as some place to hang them. In our bathrooms there are clothes hampers which guests hardly ever use—probably because they are afraid they'll forget and leave something behind; for years I've yearned for some kind of presentable paper laundry bags—sort of a dressed-up version of the kind hotels often supply—which guests could use, roll up and take home.

Household Eccentricities

I do think you ought to be as objective as possible and warn guests about any lovable eccentricities to which your house is subject. I'll never forget one unbelievably wintry week end we spent at Goldenhurst, Noël Coward's old house in Kent. Wearing a suede suit and sweater with a fur-coat outside and two martinis inside, I was still completely congealed. The only place I was comfortable was in bed with a hot-water bottle; and only the steam rising from the tub warmed things up enough so that Dick could shave. There was, as Noël had promised, central heating—that is, a furnace in the middle of the cellar; but communication between it and any resident radiator was utterly nonexistent.

Because so many people we know are hypersensitive to bedroom heat and cold, we have air conditioners in all the guest rooms and, for winter use, a thermostat in the guest room we use most often. On occasion, the furnace sets up a thumping and gurgling which, try as we may, we can't seem to diagnose. Rather than have people lost in the dark or think the *Queen Mary* is battering her way out of the basement, we always try to forewarn and hope to be fore-armed against similar lapses of pump and pipe when we're guests.

On most summer week ends, Friday is a quiet night. It's a chance for guests to settle in and for all of us to relax and talk and catch up. So we rarely ask outside guests to come in for the evening. We usually go to bed early, leaving the activity, such as it may be, for Saturday and Sunday.

Week-End Plans and Entertainment

Even when attacked by acute starvation, guests are often shy about suggesting food themselves. I remember one long-ago house party. Our hostess became ill and, though all of us had been struck ravenous just at bedtime, no one wanted to make trouble for the rest of the household. Four of us climbing the stairs to bed came upon two cardboardy sandwiches left curling on a forgotten tray in the hall. We fell on them as though they were fresh caviar. We divided them meticulously, impartially —we'd have used calipers if there had been any within reach. So I always suggest something to eat just before we say good night.

When hosts are late sleepers, I think they should give guests a basic breakfast briefing before turning in for the night. I love to visit friends of ours, the Elys, who don't keep hours that are in the least bit strange, but who do keep the small guest-house refrigerator stocked with all sorts of good things so I can cook breakfast for Dick and me whenever we happen to wake.

At home or in the country Dick and I, both early risers, have breakfast trays in our rooms. So at night just before everyone drifts off upstairs I usually ask guests whether they prefer breakfast trays brought up or if they would rather come downstairs. (Generally, women like trays; men would rather come down.) Then I leave a note for the cook as to just who'd like to have what where. For people who want trays upstairs I actually make out menus. Guests who are coming down simply ask for what they'd like. I think it simplifies things to have trays set up so that guests can carry them wherever they like.

My pet morning extravagance is separate newspapers for everybody in the house. Especially on Sunday morning, it's tantalizing to have to wait until the one and only *Times* journeys from host to guest to guest and finally arrives in your lap folded, unfolded, refolded and possibly (horror of horrors) with the crossword puzzle done.

On Saturday people may be expected for a swim or a drink and lunch. And we usually plan to have friends join us either for dinner Saturday night or—if we've been invited out that evening—for Sunday lunch or dinner instead.

Having friends call if they happen to be in the neighborhood is delightful; it's fun to be able to say, as we can ninety per cent of the time, "Can't you come by for a drink or stop for a swim?" But I have honestly never felt that "dropping in" on anyone—including your very own daughters—totally unannounced is excusable. Not calling can cause inconvenience whether the conflict is with an impending dinner or only with a backlog of letters. It is especially distressing when the sudden guest is someone you'd love to see and when as little as half an hour's postponement might have made a real visit possible. It is so easy to pick up a phone and call now that telephone booths have sprung up at almost every intersection, even in the wilds of Connecticut.

Going out for one week-end meal is pleasant. It gives our cook time to breathe, and it gives guests a change of scene. But for the most part, I think asking people in is much pleasanter for house guests than being carted to and fro over the countryside. Unless you are a really unrelenting extrovert, finding yourself in one strange place after another is more exhausting than exhilarating.

I don't mean that we never let people off the reservation. We always make sure there is time and a car available for guests who might like to call on friends or relatives who live near by. Guests who are new to our part of the world enjoy going for drives—especially if it's spring and the Greenfield Hill dogwood, which is big and old and beautiful, is in bloom. Southport harbor looks like a New England picture post card, and the village itself is full of lovely old houses. There must be hundreds of antique shops scattered over Fairfield County. Some are very good, some not so. I love trying to keep up with which are which. So if it's an antiquing expedition—whether it's a search for something very special or just a general browsing trip—I do the guiding. Otherwise Dick takes over, giving me a chance to run an errand or to catch up with a chore or possibly to close my eyes and do nothing at all for half an hour.

Dick is an easy host because he so thoroughly enjoys having people he likes around him. But these days many men do more driving or guiding or just taking over while wives are busy elsewhere simply because they've discovered they enjoy the role of host.

Some men make marvelous outdoor cooks, and outdoor cooking, now that it has matured past the hot-dog-and-hamburger stage, is a most enjoyable way of eliminating labor and strain for week-end hostesses who don't have regular help. For that matter, do-it-yourself breakfasts—the kind for which you set the table the night before and leave all the ingredients waiting in the refrigerator—have the same effect. So do soup-and-sandwich lunches (the soup is set out in a tureen on a warmer; the sandwich makings are put on platters, and dessert is something uncomplicated like a tart or fruit and cookies). All such informal plans—thanks to the help of freezers, electric warmers and old-fashioned friends like the lazy susan—leave the hostess free to concentrate on locating someone to help with the morning

Simplifying Meals

(259)

housework or dishwashing and other unloved time-consuming chores.

Rainy Days   Knowing how people look forward to swimming and tanning and tennis, I feel terribly apologetic when it rains. Thank goodness, a two-day downpour is rare. And we have stacks of games and cards and books and records to call on in bad weather. (I love pencil-and-paper word games, whether it's wet or fine.) Actually, shut-in days have their own cozy kind of charm. They give me and needlepointing guests like Betty Furness a chance to catch up on current projects. Madeline Sherwood can turn out some pretty remarkable Double-Crostics (gifts for friends) on a soggy Sunday. And though rain halts the action on the croquet lawn and forces Harlan Thompson to postpone his *bocci* game, only a deluge stays Edna Ferber from her appointed afternoon walk.

Whatever the weather, whatever the plans, guests should never feel herded or hemmed in. When hostesses feel compelled to stage constant active entertainment and guests feel obliged to sit still for incessant "amusement," everyone feels the strain. Somewhere in the day there should always be time for guests to go off by themselves, take a walk, read a book, explore the garden or plainly and simply do nothing. I've found that establishing the fact that I have chores to take care of relaxes things considerably. When it comes right down to it, guests can do a good deal to put hosts and hostesses at ease. When you know your guests are enjoying themselves, you can't help but relax, too. That's why, in a way, I'm complimented when a guest who is tired says, "Do you mind, I think I'd like to turn in

early." For, much as we'll miss his company, I know he feels at home, and that makes me feel happy too.

Guests have their own responsibilities, of course: to be adaptable about fitting in with group plans that have been made; to be prompt for meals; to keep reasonable track of their things (relaying small packages after departed guests can be an awful nuisance). *Guests' Responsibilities*

Our house doesn't happen to be a place where people feel impelled to pitch in and make beds or set tables. Still, there are sometimes flowers to be picked and occasional village errands. In homes where there is no full-time help, there are all sorts of possibilities: rooms and baths to be picked up (that's taken for granted these days), mail to be called for, trains to be met, children to be diverted, bars to be tended. I think it's nice for house guests to feel like co-hosts when other people come by for a drink or a meal. Again, it's evidence they feel at ease and at home. In the end, guests have two obligations: they should be quick to offer aid and, I think, just as quick to understand and accept "no" for an answer when assistance is not needed.

As I have said, I know how fortunate I am to have Inez and Elna to help me. It is not only help in the mechanical sense of cooking and cleaning and fixing flowers; it is help from people who share our pride in Rockmeadow and who are in a very real sense hosts along with us. Because the people who work for us feel this way, no guest's request for a cup of tea or for pressing a dress evokes scowls or black looks, and our guests, I think, are made to feel especially at home.

But no matter how large and skillful the staff, it can't do its work alone. I remember the era of the Splendid Houseparty, which will always be epitomized for me by our visits to Margaret Emerson. Her "camp," Sagamore, in the Adirondacks, was a fabulous establishment, where no expense was spared yet nothing was done for show alone. The paths were garnet gravel—but only because it provided the best possible drainage after a mountain rain. Guests came from Broadway and Honolulu and Europe. Whatever you happened to feel like doing—bridge or backgammon or croquet or bowling—you could always find the necessary equipment and someone interesting to play it with you. We never dressed for dinner, but we dined on grouse and filet mignon and baby lobster flown in from the best market in New York.

But luxury was not what made this a wonderful place to be. Margaret was a hostess in the grand manner who never, never let it get away from her. In spite of Sagamore's scope, everything was run so personally and so beautifully that you always knew she had chosen the book on your night table and that the bedside clock worked because she'd checked it herself. She ordered every meal, superintended every detail.

It was that kind of personal concern, not her wealth, that made her a great hostess. Money alone does not insure a guest's comfort. For example, I seriously consider packing chocolate bars whenever we visit another enormously rich woman who, because she has no interest in food herself, gives so little thought to meals that she almost literally starves her guests.

In the end, I suppose, as in everything from shopping to safe driving, being a good hostess or a guest is a matter of good manners, which is to say, considerate relationships between people. Courtesy—one of those old-fashioned words with a kind of stuffy connotation—makes life a great deal richer every time it is used.

Our country week ends give us time to get to know people we've met and liked on repeated brief occasions in the city; the unhurried atmosphere is like that in which you got acquainted on shipboard in the old days. These things make all the work and all the planning worthwhile. Besides, after all, some of our best friends are house guests.

POSTSCRIPT

Things in the World Outside

N O matter how dedicated or absorbed she may be, her home alone is not enough to satisfy any woman completely. She needs some outside interest, some time away from togetherness. Far from stealing time from her husband and children, she owes it to them to break with routine household tasks occasionally, to give herself a view of things beyond her own walls. Far more important than making her a more stimulating dinner-party companion, widened horizons make her more interesting everyday company for her family. She gains inner pleasure and gratification, of course. But she also broadens her friendships, escapes the tyranny of her own problems and comes back with fresh vitality to share with her family.

I am not taking time for granted. Arranging to be away from home is often difficult, especially when children are small and when home is a place in the country with no baby-sitting service, expensive or otherwise, just around the corner. There are limits to the amount of paid outside help a young household can afford. On the other hand, there are highly successful baby-sitting pools in which couples who sit for each other pay, or are paid, in point credits and no money changes hands. Less formally, it is often possible for two wives in the same neighborhood to take care of each other's children a few hours each week, so that each gets some time off.

What I am saying is this: though getting away may take some doing, the satisfaction makes the effort worthwhile.

Almost every woman I know gives time to some interest outside her home. Ellin Berlin and Dorothy Fields work hard and effectively for the Girl Scouts. So does Allene Talmey of *Vogue*. Anna Crouse does a wonderful job for The Manhattanville Community Center. Friends in the theatre volunteer time and guidance to young people in public schools and colleges who are aspiring designers, dancers, musicians and actors; my "civilian" friends (as Mike Todd would have called them) work tirelessly for dozens of good causes.

Mary Warburg gives great energy and enthusiasm to the Institute of International Education. So does Beth Moore, whose other activities—as a member of the Board of the China Institute of America, for example—reflect her love for the Orient, where she was born. Jean Kintner, wife of NBC's president, helps arrange touring shows as a member of the Junior Council of the Museum of Modern Art; she is active for Wiltwyck School, too. My sister-in-law Sue Rodgers contributes time and ideas to the City of New York as an assistant to the Commissioner of Public Events. Jean Stralem works for the Lighthouse and the George Junior Republic; Margery Loengard is on the boards of the Public Education Association and the United Negro College Fund. My cousin Norma Stonehill is a school volunteer; she teaches English to Puerto Rican children. Zim Van Raalte, my closest friend, works as a volunteer in the public relations office of Lenox Hill Hospital.

More important than any money they may contribute is the fact that these women give of themselves. It is an attitude that often startles Europeans who, for hundreds of years, have lent patronage in name and in money but have left the actual administration and day-to-day workings of their favorite worthy causes to others. Since World War II this situation has changed somewhat, particularly in England; but people are still a shade astonished to see an American woman write out a check and then pitch in and work behind a desk or ring doorbells or organize a benefit as well.

In Europe contributing to charity has always been to some extent the responsibility and the privilege of the privileged. In the United States everyone helps. Money is terribly important, but so are hands and minds. Realizing that a donation of time can free an organization's funds for other purposes, people who can't give dollars give hours instead. A secretary may spend a night a week as a hospital volunteer; a high-school teacher, as a counsellor at a girls' club; a housewife, as a home nursing instructor. Through a wonderfully and practically compassionate organization called Cancer Care, a maid who once worked for us and is now retired gives a day each week as a helper in a home where the mother is ill and the family can't afford paid help.

The method doesn't matter. What does matter is satisfying the need we all have to do something for people outside our immediate families.

It was not until we moved to Connecticut during the war that I did my first real volunteer work. Before that we had been living in California, and to a born New Yorker this always feels like a temporary arrangement even though it goes on for years. Then we came back to the East, and I started Repairs, Inc. My life as the woman who ran Repairs, Inc., was a beautifully organized thing: there was Dick, the children, the house, the business and no time for anything else. People understood that I couldn't volunteer.

Then came the war, and we bought a house in Fairfield and moved there with the three children—Mary, Linda and Zoë, our "adopted" English daughter. With the house more or less under control and the girls in school, I presented myself at the Red Cross. I have time, I told them—what do you need?

They needed first-aid instructors, and there my troubles began. On the first night of the "crash" course for instructors, I broke my leg; so I finished the two weeks' tour on crutches. I felt my coverage of the fracture section gained from depth of personal feeling. Actually I liked teaching the course, and I think I did a good job. From time to time theatrical background turned out to be a great help—as it did the night I staged a mock incendiary bombing. At a pre-arranged time, and with the principal's permission, the "bomb" exploded, and my cast of "victims" obligingly distributed themselves around the courtyard of the school in which the course was being held. My class rushed to the scene and fell apart. When the tumult and the shouting died, there was only one question: "What did you do right?" The answer was practically nothing—in the name of mercy, they had done almost everything but apply neck tourniquets to stop bleeding from head wounds. But if my "bomb" served no other purpose, it did demonstrate how far we had to go, and the class from then on was a good deal livelier.

It was wartime, and the hospitals were desperately in need of help. And yet, though I know many glamorous women—Mrs. William Rhinelander Stewart is one of them—who became gifted and efficient nurses' aides, nursing, along with fund raising, is one kind of volunteer work at which I knew I would be miserable. But because the need was acute, I began steeling myself to become a nurses' aide.

The patients and I were reprieved by a telephone call from Clifton Fadiman. He asked me to head a committee of the Writers' War Board to provide dramatic material—skits, sketches, blackouts, monologues and short plays—to be performed by men in the armed forces. Whether a piece was an original or, as most of them were, a cut version of an existing work, it meant making use of my contacts with writers in the entertainment field. And they always came through. As a matter of fact, never during World War II nor in all the years since have I called in vain upon friends— writers for material, performers for appearances at benefits. The knowledge that in giving their time, they are not only giving of themselves, but quite literally giving of their capital always makes me very humble about asking for their help. It also makes me proud to be related by marriage to the people of the entertainment industry.

My work at the Writers' War Board was one of those perfect niches. It was a job I enjoyed, and part of the reason I did it so happily was that it seemed so tailor-made for me. Just as the personal touch is the quality I most admire in entertaining and decorating, the personal approach to serving the community is, to me, most important. It is not frivolous to ask yourself whether or not you will enjoy a certain job before you agree to do it. For the things you enjoy doing are usually the things you do well.

Some people work best in large, well-organized groups and are happiest when their tasks are spelled out for them. Others need to assume responsibility; they love the freedom of approaching a problem creatively. Some people are best suited to "inside" jobs, while others are at their best dealing directly with people. Perhaps you need to give of yourself to people you know personally, in a very personal way—by taking children off a harassed neighbor's hands for a few hours, by cooking and freezing meals for a friend who is ill, by visiting someone who is lonely, by writing letters or shopping for someone in the hospital.

There are all sorts of organizations that need volunteer help—the big highly organized national institution, the local community project, the neighborhood group—and there is a great variety of work to be done within each. When you hear the word "charity" or "volunteer," the first things that come to mind are routine fund raising and canvassing. Yet in any large organization like the Heart Fund or the Girl Scouts, hundreds of different jobs need to be done—everything from typing to public relations, from coffee making to bookkeeping. I worked for the Red Cross for twenty years: in the first-aid program, in the blood program and in the Junior Red Cross. And I never once rang a doorbell.

You may find an organization that needs exactly the kind of work you are best equipped to offer. Or you may have to create a place for yourself. Don't assume that because the job that appeals to you doesn't exist, it isn't needed. It may simply be that no one has recognized the need. If your special gift is needlework, the fact that neither the Red Cross nor the Community Chest needs seamstresses does not mean that you can't contribute by sewing. Perhaps the hospital needs curtains or the church has no tablecloths or a neighborhood girls' club needs a sewing teacher. At New York's Memorial Hospital, where many patients are alone, far from family and home, our friend Donald Hirst developed an entirely new and much-needed volunteer service. He began on his own by supplying the personal nonmedical services—letter writing, shopping, even finding housing for out-patients—that Memorial's nurses and staff were too busy to give. Now a whole volunteer section is devoted to this work. So don't give up until you have really examined all the possibilities.

Some of the most satisfying moments I've known have come about through volunteer work. By the time the war and the Writers' War Board ended, I was conditioned. I had to be doing something I really cared about. I decided there was nothing more important than education, yet I couldn't join the United Parents' Association because we had no children in public schools. It was then I discovered the Public Education Association, a private organization chartered to act as a sort of watchdog of the New York City public schools. With the permission of the Board of Education, PEA inspects schools and reports on physical conditions, curricula, classroom atmosphere, attitudes, crowding—any noteworthy conditions it finds. Working as a pair, Frederica Barach and I became volunteer inspectors and, like a couple of nuns, we toured and reported, toured and reported. Near the end of the 1940's, all of us at the PEA put our hearts and minds into a publicity campaign to alert the public to what PEA felt were alarming existing conditions. But no one wanted to hear about them, much less do anything. For eleven years it was frustrating, but, at the same time, fascinating work. And it taught me a great deal.

Some time later I found, to my delight, that my voice and diction were suitable for recording textbooks for the blind. (It is interesting that actors' and actresses' aren't always: a voice that is too rich or too charged with emotion may be too distracting for a textbook, and an actor's habit of adding emphasis can sometimes give material a meaning its author never intended.) I used to read philosophy and history to a tape recorder in a soundproof booth—no fund raising, no asking performers to work benefits. After years of big organizations and committees, I loved the solitude of it. And the fact that a real person was waiting for each completed chapter gave me a wonderful feeling of doing something direct and meaningful.

On another occasion, I was asked to help redesign some merchandise sold at the Elder Craftsmen's Shop. The store's stock included knitted things, children's clothing, hooked rugs and a great many gift items all made by people over sixty-five and sold for their benefit. Feeling that I was able to make suggestions for restyling some of the merchandise (like removing the clipper ships from the rugs) and adding some new useful items (such as a typewriter cover of appliqued felt like one Phyllis Cerf had) was both satisfying and fun.

While a member of the Board of Trustees of the Federation of Jewish Philanthropies, I persuaded them to vary their approach to fund raising by trying the special benefit that is so glamorous that people are delighted to part with vast sums of money. With the help of top-flight volunteer talent—Mary Martin and Edward R. Murrow for starters—we gave a $100-a-plate luncheon which netted over $200,000 and was the beginning of the Federation's present performing-arts series.

No two of these jobs were alike, and I think that is important: I think there comes a time to change. I know that after a certain period—and I don't necessarily mean months or even a few years—I often get to feeling a bit stale. And I think when you lose enthusiasm, you lose an important part of your value to an organization. It is not merely the work you do for them, it is the fact that enthusiasm leads you to talk about it, to make the cause known to other people and even to involve them in it.

I have always been interested in politics, yet, like many women, I have done very little about it. We have on occasion given parties to introduce friends to a candidate about whom we felt strongly, but the candidate was there to do the work and to speak for himself. We have purposely kept our political roles small and anonymous because we have always felt it is wrong to lend our names to any party unless we are prepared to work seriously. This is a matter in which I think prominent figures have a special responsibility: because their names are inordinately influential, they should be particularly careful. They have every right to their own opinions, but a performer celebrated for his acting isn't necessarily qualified to give political advice to the public.

I think many interested women are hesitant about the field of politics because they do not know where to start. If you are new to a community or if you simply want to gain an over-all impartial picture of the political structure of the city in which you live, there is no better starting place than the League of Women Voters. Their sole aim is to get people—both male and female—to exercise their franchise in an informed and intelligent way. Working with them familiarizes you with key figures, shows you where power groups exist, may give you a clear idea of where as a partisan worker you can be most effective for your candidate and your party.

Whether the field is politics or volunteer work or business, a woman has something special to contribute. She is apt to be more flexible and adaptable than a man. She feels less need to save face for face-saving's sake. She is perhaps less direct than a man, she is often able to accomplish things with charm where directness would produce only head-on collision. Her point of view is not the same as a man's, and for that very reason it is important and valid that she offer it.

One of the most remarkable women I know, Mrs. Randolph Guggenheimer, is serving now as the first and only woman member of the New York City Planning Commission, a board of seven. She is also President of the National Committee for Day Care of Children. These very important posts have been earned after years of dedicated, intelligent, constructive and creative work on behalf of the community; and yet she has always remained very much a woman. She is the devoted wife of an extremely successful lawyer, who has always come first in her thinking. She is the mother of two enormously likable and attractive young lawyers, and, she has three grandchildren. She is also an excellent cook, and she has the time and capacity for friendship. She doesn't demand special treatment as a woman, but she has remained special.

Up to this point I have been talking of part-time volunteer work. And for many women who can afford to contribute time without pay, it is enough. Others, especially women who have worked in business before they were married, find a special kind of satisfaction in being paid for the work they do. What about careers for women with children?

So much has been written recently about married women and their problems, prime among them that American women are confused about their identity. In the 1930's and 1940's, women felt that freedom to compete in the world of men was all-important. With the end of the war came a change: suddenly women were told their rewards should come from their homes and their families. Authoritative books and magazines drummed this new message home all through the 1950's.

Since World War II women have been having more and more children. Unfortunately they have also had less and less help. And many bright, capable—even gifted—women have suddenly found themselves utterly committed to endless household routine. They become starved for adult companionship, privacy and a few hours in which to do what they want to do.

I don't think there has ever been a time in any culture when women have been expected to work at being mothers twenty-four hours a day. And I don't think they should be expected to now. There are a great many women with whom marriage and children come first, but who because of their intellectual capacities, talents or training, want a career too.

I think they can have it, but I think they must be willing to subordinate the career part of their lives to their husbands and children. As long as they bear the children, women have a built-in roadblock. For, no matter how well they organize their lives, they still must stay home when a child gets sick or the nurse walks out. They must be able to lay aside their work in times of emergency, and therefore I don't think they can ever give to a career the kind of single-minded drive that is needed to reach the top.

I am not talking about the dedicated career woman, the woman who prefers not to marry. Nor am I thinking of the woman who must work to pay the grocery bill. The girl who wants a career first and foremost should go after it, but she should not try to fit a husband and children into her spare time. It won't work. Being allowed to concentrate all her energy on a career is simply not possible for a woman who is also a wife and a mother. And without that concentration, she cannot reach the professional heights.

Having made such a four-square statement, I must immediately admit there are exceptions. I am reminded first of a husband-and-wife partnership: Madame Curie not only achieved professional greatness, but was also happily married and the mother of two children.

Millicent McIntosh is a brilliant present-day exception to all the rules. Married to a distinguished pediatrician, she not only achieved outstanding success in her years as Headmistress of the Brearley School, but brought up five remarkable children at the same time. She went on to become the first President of Barnard College, where she set a glowing example of what women of great intellectual capacity can accomplish.

Mrs. McIntosh is an exceptional woman, but she would be the first to point out that her circumstances were somewhat exceptional, too. Since her husband was a professor of pediatrics, they both had uninterrupted months of summer vacation to devote to each other and to their family. Often they would all pile into a station wagon and head for the West Coast, taking with them a college girl whose chief qualification was that she could read aloud to the children in a moving car. And every seventh year they would have coinciding sabbaticals.

Mrs. McIntosh believes firmly that married women can make important contributions to a college faculty. Their points of view are better rounded than those of instructors who know only the academic life. And they provide an example for students of a way in which they might later make use of their own education. Realizing that few married women with children can manage full-scale careers like hers, she made a point of encouraging qualified women to return to teaching at Barnard on a part-time basis. I think this kind of solution is both constructive and sound because it permits a woman to put her husband's and her children's needs first.

As a group, I think women lack the male urge to create works that earn world acclaim because they are biologically creative. The happiest women I know have always been those who put a happy marriage and good relations with their children ahead of their careers. They love and respect their husbands and feel that a man should be truly the head of his family. Because they know that in most successful relationships the man is the initiator, they do not try to compete with men on a man's level.

Militantly aggressive females bewilder me. I don't know why any woman wants to be a man's equal when she can be a woman's equal. I don't consider myself a man's inferior or superior—just different.

Women's lives are fragmented because from the very beginning they have shown talent for juggling many widely varied activities. In the ordinary course of events a woman is expected to function in many roles: to be amateur dietician, chauffeur, committee chairman, budget director, laundress, conversationalist—all in rapid succession. It is a peculiarly feminine gift and a woman's responsibility to regulate the emphasis given to each of these elements and in doing so to keep the balance in her family's life. Whether it is an amateur interest or a professional career, a golf championship or a job as a fashion consultant, anything that disturbs this delicate mechanism is a potential source of trouble.

During child-bearing years and while her children are young, I think a woman must find ways of fitting her work in as best she can. Surely she cannot be expected to stop thinking for fifteen years and suddenly, at the end of that time, take up her intellectual life where she dropped it. It is essential that each of us work out her own compromise.

Sometimes a part-time career comes looking for you; the trick is to recognize it. It has happened to me on several occasions. During the war I found myself cleaning the bathrooms and wondering why there wasn't a pleasanter, more efficient method of cleaning toilet bowls. I hated those nasty brushes. The problem nagged at me until I thought of designing a disposable pad which fit on a plastic handle. Timidly I approached Lawrence Langner, who, in addition to being one of the heads of New York's Theatre Guild, was senior partner in one of the city's largest patent law firms. To my astonishment he obtained a patent complete with ribbons and seal in my name. Then, after five long years of trying to sell it, the gadget known as Jonny Mop was launched. For the twelve remaining years of the original patent, it earned a respectable royalty for me.

In the days when I was making a lot of dresses, I was often infuriated by the flimsy paper of which most patterns are made; so I set out to find a substitute. I discovered it in a nonwoven Pellon-like cotton which is as soft as fabric but, unlike muslin, which is woven, does not stretch. A large pattern company bought the idea and produced a basic pattern in which permanent alterations can be stitched rather than pinned; and the pattern itself can be used over and over.

I have taken out other patents and worked on other ideas with varying degrees of success. In every case the first step has been my refusal to be satisfied with existing methods. Unwilling to settle for the bathroom brush or the tissue pattern, I was prodded into coming up with better solutions. Once a need is recognized, it is almost always possible to fill it. The essential thing is to free your mind to see where needs exist. And this is true not only of inventions, but also in the world of business and volunteer work.

Each of us faces her own set of limitations. Dick does his writing at home rather than follow the kind of regular schedule that takes most men to their offices between nine and five. The household has to be organized so that he can work when he wants to. Fortunately his habits are wonderfully untemperamental; inspiration doesn't strike him in the middle of the night. Very often his work takes him out of town, and he likes me to go along. So I have never felt free to accept a job in which I had to guarantee my presence at any definite or regular time.

Yet it has always been possible for me to find time for some of the things I have wanted to do. The key word in that sentence is "some." There have occasionally been interests I would have liked to pursue that would have interfered with Dick's needs or the children's. Those I have had to put out of my head. But there were always workable substitutions. My point is that it is possible to compromise successfully.

My objection to the theories expounded by so many current writers on women's problems is the black/white either/or choice they offer. Have a career, they say, and let someone else bring up your children, or forget the career and be happy washing diapers. I think there is something in between. Recognizing that it is not in the cards for her to be the top in business or art or science and have enough time and energy to devote to a fulfilling marriage, a woman's particular talent makes her capable of blending inside and outside interests to create her own uniquely satisfying world. The secret is compromise, and placing the emphasis on her marriage, her family and home.

It can lead to the very deepest kind of happiness. I know that it has for me.

INDEX

AID. *See* American Institute of Interior Designers

Allen, Adrianne, 43

Alliance Française, 99

"America at Home" (United States Travel Service program), 99

American Federation of Arts, 84

American Institute of Interior Designers (AID), 19

American Scandinavian Foundation, 99

Amory, Cleveland, 233

Amory, Martha (Mrs. Cleveland), 233

Archipenko, Alexander, 3

Arts Club (of Chicago), 87

Auctions, art, 91–92

Auw, Frederick von, 7

Balanchine, George, 102

Barach, Frederica, 267

Bergen, Edgar, 227

Berlin, Ellin, 263

Bernheim, Elly, 69

Bernheim, Leonard, 69

Bernstein, Leonard, 233

Borge, Victor, 227

Brice, Fanny, 227

Brooks, Frances (Mrs. Harold), 32–33

Brooks, Harold, 32–33

Brown, Cassie (Mrs. John Mason), 112

Brown, John Mason, 112

Buchanan, Jack, 227

Carlisle, Kitty, 40, 107

Carroll, Diahann, 248

Cerf, Bennett, 232, 238

Cerf, Phyllis (Mrs. Bennett), 71, 230, 232, 238, 268

Chapman, Mrs. Gilbert, 87

Château Ausone (vineyard), 137

Château Haut-Brion (vineyard), 137

Château Lafite (vineyard), 137

Château Lascombes (vineyard), 137

Château Latour (vineyard), 137

Château Margaux (vineyard), 137

Château Mouton-Rothschild (vineyard), 137

Chevalier, Maurice, 227

Cleveland Museum of Art, 87

Colbert, Claudette, 112

Colin, Georgia (Mrs. Ralph), 115, 162

Colin, Ralph, 115, 162

Comden, Betty, 103

Cornell, Katharine, 96

Cott, Sue, 15, 57

Cotten, Joseph, 102

Coward, Noël, 73, 227, 256–57

Crichton, Judy, 72

Crocheting, 72

Crouse, Anna (Mrs. Russel), 263–64

Cullman, Howard, 5, 72

Cullman, Peggy (Mrs. Howard), 5, 72

Dale, Chester, 87

Darrow, Middy (Mrs. Whitney), 126–28

(275)

Index

Darrow, Whitney, 127
Davis, Tobé, 237
Decorating:
  with antiques, 3, 13, 63 ff; *see also* furniture
  for atmosphere, 7, 9, 15–16
  bathrooms, 22, 41
    fixtures, 41
  bedrooms, 36–37, 39–40, 57
    men's, 37–38
  budgeting, 7, 10–11, 13, 15, 18, 20–21, 56, 65
  children's rooms, 43–45
  clutter, use of, 32, 36
  colors, 9, 12, 14, 23, 26, 30, 32, 37–38, 39, 41, 43, 47, 50, 51 ff
  company living rooms, 32
  dens, 27
  dining areas, 7, 13, 14, 36
  dining rooms, 33–35, 48
  draperies, 14, 58–59
  dressing rooms, 41
  drawing rooms. *See* company living rooms
  entrance halls, 23–24, 50, 70
  fabrics, 12, 47, 51 ff, 60 ff
  floors, 8, 12, 14, 24, 41, 50, 60, 61
    painted, 61
    See also rugs
  furniture, 8–9, 12, 23, 35–36, 37, 38–39, 44–45, 46, 51 ff
    antique, 10, 36, 37, 53, 64
    Biedermeier, 66
    Chippendale, 65, 68
    Eighteenth Century English, 13, 37
    Empire, 13, 66
    Flemish, 14
    French provincial, 70
    Georgian, 66
    Louis XV, 3, 24, 53, 62, 64, 65
    Oriental, 68
    Queen Anne, 14, 65
    Regency, 13, 24, 66
    Venetian, 36
    Victorian, 10, 53
    William and Mary, 14

Decorating (*continued*)
  hand-me-downs, 7, 14–15
  heavy effects, 3
  high fashion, 10
  and home building, planning for, 10–11, 13–14, 247 ff
  individuality, 3 ff, 23, 39–55
  kitchens, 27–31, 49
    appliances, 30
  lamps and lighting, 10, 17, 22, 37, 50, 62 ff
    built-in, 49 ff
  living rooms, 32, 36
  paintings, 9–10, 12, 13, 15, 39, 50, 86 ff
  pantries, 31–32
  patterns and prints, 9–10, 26, 52
  and planning, basic, 46–68 *passim*
  professional help, 17–23, 56
  and repairs, 4 ff. *See also* Repairs, Inc.
  rugs, 14, 60–61
    figured, 61
    hooked, 70, 75
    imported, 61
    needlepoint, 61, 70, 74
    painted, 61
  sculpture, 13
  spatial relations, 51, 59
  storage spaces, 41, 43, 48–49
  upholstery, 52–53
  for variety, 53 ff, 83 ff
  walls, 8, 9, 12, 24, 33, 43, 48–49, 50, 51, 56, 58
    wallpaper, 62
  windows, 56–57
  and wiring, 49 ff
Design Center for Interiors (New York City), 19
Dinner at Eight (play), 97
Durante, Jimmy, 232

Eldridge, Florence (Mrs. Fredric March), 133
Ely, Jean (Mrs. Ted), 209, 257
Ely, Ted, 209, 257

(276)

Emerson, Margaret, 261
Entertaining:
  brunches, 142, 212–18
  buffets, 107–8, 121, 133, 138,
    141–42, 222–25, 229
  business, 100–1
  centerpieces. *See* table decorations
  children's parties, 242 ff
  cocktail parties, 108–9, 231, 249
  crystal, 118–19, 135
  formal dinners, 121, 133, 135,
    144–51
  and gambling, 100
  games, 233–46 *passim*
    Adverbs, 240
    Botticelli (Biography), 234,
      239–40
    Casting the Runes, 241–42
    for children's parties, 242 ff
    Creation, 237
    Essences (Associations), 239
    Game, The, 234–35
    Guggenheim (Categories), 242
    Hiding Things in Plain Sight,
      236–37
    Improbable Conversations, 238–
      39
    Password, 237–38
    Portfolio Game, 235–36
    Scavenger and Treasure Hunts,
      240–41
  holiday parties, 100, 102–3
  house guests, 247–62 *passim*
  informal dinners, 132, 133, 136,
    141–42, 151–86
  introductions, 112–13
  invitations, 95, 100, 108–9
  luncheons, 107, 186–212
  musicians, hired, 231–32
  opening night parties, 229
  performers, hired, 232
  in restaurants, 101–2
  seating guests, 113
  service equipment, 123–24
  serving problems, 120 ff, 141
  stocking a bar, 110
  suppers, 218–22

Entertaining (*continued*)
  table decoration, 114 ff
  ventilation, room, 112
  week end parties. *See* house guests
Erskine, Marisa, 129

Fadiman, Clifton, 265
Ferber, Edna, 6, 76, 97, 102, 125,
  260
Fields, Dorothy, 69, 263
Flower arranging, 78 ff
Flower Drum Song (musical comedy), 71
Fontanne, Lynn, 73
Food:
  American, 128, 129, 132
  beef, 129, 132, 137, 141, 148,
    157–58, 160–61, 177–78,
    179, 183, 196–97, 224, 225
    consommé, 165, 193, 209
    pot roast, 167
    short loins, 132, 148
  beer, 138, 167, 200
  bread, 140–41, 142, 209, 213,
    214, 216, 222, 224, 225
  brunches, 142, 212–18
  buffets, 133, 138, 141–42, 222–
    25
  canapés, 132, 142–43
  casseroles, 132, 133, 138, 179–80
  cheese, 140, 142, 144, 146, 148,
    149, 151, 157, 160, 167, 173,
    200, 202, 212, 215–16, 224,
    225
  Chinese, 128
  color and texture, balancing, 131,
    134, 141, 144 ff
  Danish, 128, 129, 132
  desserts, 127, 128, 129, 130, 131,
    132, 134–35, 142–225 *passim*
    See also Recipes
  first courses, 133–34, 141, 144 ff
  formal dinners, 133, 135, 144–51
  French, 128, 129, 141
  German, 128, 129
  ham, 132, 136, 200, 222, 225

Food (*continued*)

　　prosciutto, 151, 162, 167, 174, 181–83, 186, 192–93

　Hungarian, 130, 224–25

　Indian, 129

　informal dinners, 132, 133, 136, 141–42, 151–86

　Italian, 128, 129, 138, 141

　lamb, 130, 132–33, 168, 184–86, 191

　lunches, 186–212

　main courses, 132, 141–42, 144 ff

　meat courses, planning, 132

　menu planning, 131 ff, 144 ff

　menus and recipes. *See* Menus, Recipes

　Mexican, 127

　pastas, 141, 169, 217–18, 222

　Polish, 132

　port, 132, 165–66

　poultry and game, 131, 133, 141, 144, 147–48, 149, 154, 162–64, 168, 170–71, 173–74, 179–80, 198, 212, 219–20, 221–22, 224, 225

　roasts, 131, 132, 138–39, 140, 167, 224

　salads, 127, 129, 132, 140–225 *passim. See also* Recipes

　sauces, 129, 131, 133, 134, 146–47, 148, 159, 164, 169, 177–78, 181–83, 200–1, 205–6, 208, 212, 218–19, 225

　Scandinavian, 128

　seafood and fish, 129, 131, 133–34, 136, 141–225 *passim. See also* Recipes

　soups, 127, 131, 133, 135, 154–225 *passim. See also* Recipes

　Spanish, 221–22

　stews, 132, 133

　suppers, 218–22

　veal, 130, 131, 132, 141, 154–55, 156–57, 169–70, 171, 193–94

　vegetables, 131–32, 134, 138–225 *passim. See also* Recipes

　Viennese, 128

　wines, 133, 135 ff

　　Asti Spumante, 138

　　Bordeaux (Claret), 137, 149, 159, 170

　　　white:

　　　　Château d'Yquem (sauterne), 138

　　Burgundy, 137, 138, 148, 150, 157, 159, 167, 219, 225

　　　Beaujolais, 137, 178

　　　white:

　　　　Chablis, 138

　　　　Châteauneuf du Pape, 138

　　　　Montrachet, 138, 206, 219

　　　　Pouilly-Fuissé, 138

　　Champagnes

　　　Bollinger, 138

　　　Mumms, 138

　　　Piper-Heidseick, 138

　　Chianti, 137, 184, 208

　　Chilean Riesling, 138

　　Gewürz-Traminer, 138

　　Lachryma Christi, 138

　　Neuchâtel, 138, 202

　　Riesling, 138

　　Rosés

　　　Anjou, 138, 197

　　　Portuguese (Lancer's Crackling), 138, 191

　　　Tavel, 138, 197

Furness, Betty, 102, 260

Gallico, Paul, 96

Games. *See under* Entertaining

Gershwin, George, 227

Gibson, Mrs. Charles Dana, 55

Glaenzer, Jules, 226, 227

Godowsky, Leopold, 35

Goodson, Mark, 238

Gozzi, Countess Elsie Lee, 96

Grande Chaumière (Paris), 3

Grant, Jane, 96

Green, Johnny, 102, 231, 233

Guggenheimer, Randolph, 230

Guggenheimer, Mrs. Randolph, 269

Halliday, Mary (Mrs. Richard). *See* Martin, Mary

Halliday, Richard, 15, 55, 69–70, 110

Hammerstein, Dorothy (Mrs. Oscar), 13, 36–37, 70, 72, 84, 131, 230

Hammerstein, Oscar, II, 13, 27, 39, 131, 228, 230

Hanna, Leonard, 87

Harlow, Jean, 232

Harriman, Averell, 50, 96

Hart, Kitty (Mrs. Moss). *See* Carlisle, Kitty

Hart, Lorenz, 84, 229

Hart, Moss, 40

Haupt, Enid, 87

Hayes, Helen, 4

Hayward, Pam, 116

Hayward, Slim. *See* Keith, Mrs. Kenneth

Hecht, Ben, 22

Heetman, Paul, 81

Hersey, Barbara (Mrs. John), 82, 233

Hersey, John, 82, 233

Hilson, Mildred, 115

Hirst, Donald, 267

Hobbies and projects, 69–92 *passim*, 263 ff

Hoffman, Paul, 98

Holm, Celeste, 73

Hornblow, Arthur, 32

Hornblow, Leonora (Mrs. Arthur), 32

Hughes, Larry, 104

Hughes, Rose (Mrs. Larry), 104

I Was a Fugitive from a Chain Gang (film), 227

Johanson, Inez, 120

Johnson, Justine, 227

Kahn, Gilbert, 230

Kahn, Polly (Mrs. Gilbert), 230

Kaufman, George S., 97

Kaye, Danny, 77, 104

Kaye, Sylvia (Mrs. Danny), 77

Keith, Mrs. Kenneth, 86

Kent, Duke of, 126

King and I, The (musical comedy), 230

Kintner, Jean (Mrs. Robert), 264

Knitting, 72, 75–76

Knopf, Alice, 30

Langner, Lawrence, 271

Lasker, Mary, 55

Lawrence, Gertrude, 227

Lewine, Kimmy, 71

Lewine, Mary (Mrs. Richard), 71

Lewine, Richard, 71, 231

Lillie, Beatrice, 96, 227

Lindsay, Dorothy (Mrs. Howard), 69, 103

Lindsay, Howard, 69, 103

Lodge, Henry Cabot, 98

Loengard, Margery, 264

Loening, Grover, 35–36

Logan, Joshua, 9–10, 55, 102

Logan, Nedda (Mrs. Joshua), 9–10, 55, 102

Low, Barbara (Mrs. Ted), 63

Low, Ted, 63

Lunt, Alfred, 73

Lunt, Lynn (Mrs. Alfred). *See* Fontanne, Lynn

McIntosh, Millicent, 270

McMein, Neysa, 96, 234, 235

Maedchen in Uniform (film), 227

Magyar, Pearl, 224

Mamoulian, Azadia (Mrs. Rouben), 71

Mamoulian, Rouben, 71

March, Florence (Mrs. Fredric). *See* Eldridge, Florence

March, Fredric, 133

Marcus, Betty, 129

Martin, Mary, 15, 55, 69–71, 110–11, 230, 268

Marx Brothers, 227

Index

Massey, Anna, 43
Massey, Daniel, 43
Massey, Raymond, 43
Maxwell, Elsa, 227
Melnick, Danny, 130
Melnick, Linda (Mrs. Daniel). *See* Rodgers, Linda
Menus:
    brunches, 212–18
    buffets, 222–25
    formal dinners, 144–51
    informal dinners, 151–86
    lunches, 186–212
    suppers, 218–22
Merman, Ethel, 102
Metropolitan Museum of Art (New York City), 4
Moore, Beth, 264
Muinonen, Elna, 120
Muni, Paul, 227
Murrow, Edward R., 268
Museum of Modern Art (New York City), 90, 264

National Society of Interior Designers (NSID), 19
Needlepoint, 72
Neuberger, Roy, 84
Newman, Alfred, 96
New York Times, The, 229, 258
Nichols, Mike, 241
NSID. *See* National Society of Interior Designers

Oklahoma! (musical comedy), 228–29
Orry-Kelly, 71

Paintings, collecting, 9–10, 12, 13, 15, 39, 50, 86 ff
Porcelains, 84–86
Porter, Cole, 227
Prager, Georgann (Mrs. Stanley), 72, 104–6, 165
Prager, Stanley, 104

Preminger, Hope (Mrs. Otto), 9–10
Preminger, Otto, 9–10
Pressman, Mrs. Joel. *See* Colbert, Claudette

Recipes:
  Cheese
    Cheese blintzes, 215–16
    Iced Brie, 206
    Quiche Lorraine, 201–2
  Desserts
    Apples maison, 190
    Black-and-white soufflé, 160–62
    Brandy snaps, 183–84
    Chocolate cake Aix en Provence, 197
      bittersweet icing, 197–98
    Chocolate roll, 151, 153–54
    Cour à la Crème, 199
      for nondieters, 199–200
    Creamed lime ice, 208–9
    Crème brûlée with crushed strawberries, 144, 145–46
    Crêpes Normandie, 177, 178
    Crêpes with orange sauce, 172
    Fraises Romanoff, 191–92
    Gâteau mousse, 157, 158
      chocolate Bavarian cream filling, 158
      custard sauce, 159
    German apple pancake, 210–11
    Ginger and pineapple trifle, 222–23
    Ginger roll, 165–67
    Hot fruit, custard sauce, 162, 164
      cold custard sauce, 164
    Ice cream bombe, 174–75
    Madeleines, 222
    Miniature jelly rolls, 168–69
    Oeufs à la neige, 186–87
    Oranges in red wine, 149
    Palacsintas, 216–17
    Palets de dames, 195
    Peaches in red wine, 151
    Pears in red wine, 202

Recipes (*continued*)

    Pots de crème chocolat, 173–74

    Sour cherry tart, 175, 176–77

    Stewed nectarines with Sabayon sauce, 200–1

    Strawberry tartlets, 179, 180–81

    Swedish pancakes with lingonberries, 214–15

    Trifle, 207–8

  Fish and Seafood

    Cold curried shrimp with cold rice and chutney, 203–4

    Cold filet of sole mousse with lobster sauce, 146–47

    Cold lobster, sauce verte, 218–19

    Crabmeat quiche, 187–89

    Crab omelets, 213–14

    Crêpes filled with crabmeat and mushrooms in cheese sauce, 149–51

    Cucumbers with shad roe, 204–5

    Hollandaise sauce, 205–6

    Filet of sole with shrimp and wine sauce, 175–76

    Lobster with special sauce, 148-49

    Paella, 221–22

    Shrimp in dill sauce, 211–12

    Tomato clam broth, 211

    Zucchini stuffed with lobster, artichoke hearts and raw mushrooms, green mayonnaise, 206–7

  Meats

    Beef stew with onions and mushrooms, 157–58

    Beef Stroganoff, 178–79

    Beef tenderloin sauté, 160–61

    Boeuf en gelée, 196–97

    Broiled filet mignon with tarragon sauce, 177–78

    Chicken vealburgers, 170–71

    Ham with Madeira sauce, 181–83

Recipes (*continued*)

    Lamb in pastry, 185–86

    Poached eggs in jelly with ham, 192–93

    Pork rolls, 165–66

    Paupiettes de veau, 154–55

    Veal in lemon butter, 156–57

    Veal rolls, 169–70

    Vitello tonnato, 193–94

  Pasta

    Green noodles with truffles, 217–18

  Poultry

    Breast of chicken on tongue with tarragon sauce, 147–48

    Breasts of chicken in wine surrounded by artichoke bottoms with squash, 162–64

    Chicken and turtle soup with sherry, 168

    Chicken casserole, 179–80

    Chicken-caviar soup, 198

    Chicken gumbo soup with crabmeat, 154

    Chicken in tarragon jelly, 219–20

    Chicken vealburgers, 170–71

    Chicken with tarragon sauce, 173–74

    Danish chicken with rice, 151–53

    Paella, 221–22

  Soups

    Beet and buttermilk soup, 192

    Billi-bi, 181–82

    Boula soup, 162–63

    Chicken-caviar soup, 198

    Chicken gumbo soup with crabmeat, 154

    Clam chowder Ely, 209–10

    Clam vichyssoise, 160

    Cold wine soup, 170–71

    Consommé with beaten egg, 187–88

    Cressonnière soup, 189–90

    Greek egg-lemon soup, 184–85

Index

Recipes (*continued*)
    Red caviar soup, 186–87
    Senegalese soup, 203
    Sorrel soup, 191
    Summer soup, 208
    Tomato clam broth, 211
  Vegetables
    Potato pancakes, 167
    Potato salad, 219
    Purée of peas, 155
    Stuffed cabbage, 223–25
    Zucchini stuffed with lobster, artichhoke hearts and raw mushrooms, green mayonnaise, 206–7
Repairs, Inc., 4–8, 36, 46, 55–56, 60, 72, 82, 265
Restoring. *See* Repairs, Inc.
Robinson, Edward G., 87
Rockmeadow (Rodgers' Connecticut home), 4, 8–9, 31–32, 36, 38, 54, 70 ff, 84, 88, 238, 247 ff
Rodgers, Linda (Mrs. Daniel Melnick), 43, 102, 212, 230, 233, 245, 254, 265
Rodgers, Mary (Mrs. Henry Guettel), 4, 43, 102, 122, 230, 233, 243, 245, 246, 265
Rodgers, Richard, 4, 6, 9, 11, 12, 21, 28, 38–39, 48–49, 53, 70 ff, 84, 88, 90, 104, 124, 130, 227 ff, 248 ff, 265, 272
Rodgers, Sue, 129, 264
Rogers, Ginger, 230
Rome, Florence (Mrs. Harold), 33–35, 133
Rome, Harold, 33–35, 133
Roosevelt, Franklin Delano, 104
Roosevelt, Mrs. Theodore, Jr., 5
Ross, Harold, 96

Saarinen, Aline, 15
Saarinen, Eero, 15
Sail Away (musical comedy), 73
Schary, Dore, 33, 129
Schwartz, Arthur, 103

Sewing, 73 ff
Sherwood, Madeline (Mrs. Robert), 71, 230, 255, 260
Sherwood, Robert, 71
Shore, Dinah, 104
Sinatra, Frank, 73
Sondheim, Stephen, 81, 233
South Pacific (musical comedy), 229, 230
Stanish, Rudolph, 107
Stewart, Mrs. William Rhinelander, 265
Stonehill, Norma, 264
Stralem, Jean, 264
Swope, Herbert, 249–50
Swope, Margaret (Mrs. Herbert), 249

Talmey, Allene, 263
Taylor, Suzanne, 76
Thompson, Harlan, 260
Todd, Mike, 264

United Nations (New York City), 98 ff, 107
United Nations Hospitality Committee, 99
United States Travel Service, 99

Van Raalte, Zim, 264
Vitsaxis, Mrs. Basile, 184
Vogue magazine, 263
Volunteer assistance and organizations, 263 ff

Warburg, Mary, 264
Wells, George, 70–71
Whitney, Betsy (Mrs. John Hay), 70
Whitney, John Hay, 70
Wieck, Dorothea, 227
Windsor, Duke and Duchess of, 119
Wines. *See under* Food
Wolfe, Elsie de, 15
Woollcott, Alexander, 96

DOROTHY RODGERS

Dorothy Rodgers was born in New York City in 1909 and has lived there most of her life. She attended Wellesley College and then studied in Europe. She has traveled a great deal, both in this country and abroad, and has lived in California and London. For many years Mrs. Rodgers worked as an interior designer in her own firm, called Repairs, Inc. During the war years she worked at the Writers' War Board and after the war at the Public Education Association, the Red Cross and the Federation of Jewish Philanthropies. She is also a part-time inventor and holds several patents. She is married to Richard Rodgers, the composer, and has two daughters, Mary and Linda, and several grandchildren. She lives in New York City and in Southport, Connecticut.